the life of an unknown

European Perspectives

EUROPEAN PERSPECTIVES

A Series in Social Thought and Cultural Criticism

Lawrence D. Kritzman, Editor

European Perspectives presents outstanding books by leading European thinkers.
With both classic and contemporary works, the series aims to shape the major intellectual
controversies of our day and to facilitate the tasks of historical understanding.

For a complete list of books in the series, see pages 271–272.

the life of an unknown

*The Rediscovered World of a Clog Maker
in Nineteenth-Century France*

alain corbin

Translated by Arthur Goldhammer

COLUMBIA UNIVERSITY PRESS   NEW YORK

COLUMBIA UNIVERSITY PRESS
Publishers Since 1893
New York
Chichester, West Sussex

Columbia University Press wishes to express its appreciation for
assistance given by the government of France through the Ministère de la
Culture in the preparation of this translation

Library of Congress Cataloging-in-Publication Data
Corbin, Alain.
[Monde retrouvé de Louis-François Pinagot. English]
The life of an unknown : the rediscovered world of a clog maker in nineteenth-century
France / Alain Corbin ; translated by Arthur Goldhammer.
p. cm. — (European perspectives)
Includes bibliographical references and index.
ISBN 0-231-11840-6 (cloth) — ISBN 0-231-11841-4 (paper)
1. Pinagot, Louis-François, 1798–1876. 2. Woodworkers—France—Origny-le-Butin
Region—Biography. 3. Country life—France—Origny-le-Butin Region—History—19th
century. 4. Origny-le-Butin Region (France)—History. I. Title. II. Series.
DC801.05968 C6713 2001
944'.23—dc21
[B]
00-069403

Casebound editions of Columbia University Press books are printed on permanent and durable
acid-free paper.
Printed in the United States of America
c 10 9 8 7 6 5 4 3 2 1
p 10 9 8 7 6 5 4 3 2 1

CONTENTS

investigating the torpor of an ordinary existence

Louis-François Pinagot did in fact exist. His birth and death certificates prove it. He was born on 2 Messidor, Year VI (June 20, 1798) "on the stroke of three in the afternoon." He died at home on January 31, 1876. After that, he sank into total oblivion. He never spoke out on behalf of his fellow man. It probably never occurred to him to do such a thing; his being illiterate made it less likely that it would. He was not involved in any important affair. His name appears on no surviving court document. He was never placed under surveillance by the authorities. No ethnographer observed his manner of speech or work. In short, he was exactly the man I was looking for.

My purpose was to stand the methods of nineteenth-century social history on their head. Social history, not just of elites but of "the people," is based on the study of a very small sample, of people whose fates were exceptional.[1] These were people who, by the mere fact of taking up their pens, excluded themselves from the milieus they described. Their purpose was to bear witness or to put themselves forward as examples. On the basis of their writings we have been treated to any number of studies of "working-class language," "women's language," and the "literature of the excluded." Since the late 1960s publishers have delighted in publishing such works. Rarely has anyone paused to ask what the members of that collective entity known as "the people"—an entity that struggled throughout the century to emerge— might have thought of these militant witnesses.

To be sure, a fortuitous event might now and then cast a brief and lurid light on the myriads of the disappeared. An anonymous individual might become the subject of a detailed investigation in the wake of a catastrophe, a riot, or a crime. But such cases were exceptional, products of a paroxysm offering momentary access to an underlying reality without telling us much about the torpor of ordinary existences.

My purpose here is first to collect traces of Louis-François Pinagot's life and then to assemble them into a picture. None of these traces is the product of a desire to construct a destiny for Pinagot or even to suggest that he was a person capable of having one. My task is like piecing together a puzzle. Along the way I will have occasion to write about people who have been swallowed up by history, erased by the passage of time, but my purpose is not to "bear witness." In meditating upon disappearance, I hope to reconstitute the existence of a person whose memory has been abolished, a man to whom I have no emotional ties, with whom I share no *a priori* faith or mission or commitment. I want to re-create him, to give him a second chance—in the short run a reasonably substantial chance—to become part of the memory of his century.

On a global time scale such a project must seem ridiculous. No resurrection can be anything other than a prelude to ultimate erasure. Conversely, every disappearance presupposes a spectator. As much as the ineluctability of death, it is this certainty of vanishing without a trace that accounts for the persistence over the millennia of our sense of the vanity of all things. It was this certainty that gave rise to the idea of the Last Judgment as a vast historical canvas in which every person's past would be recapitulated in its entirety. Nevertheless, what moves us most profoundly is not the fact that virtually all the denizens of the prehistoric and historic past have vanished without a trace but that such has also been the fate of people relatively close to us in time. What is troubling is that even those so near to us have vanished, and for that reason I have chosen to write about a person who only recently departed from human memory, along with everyone whose life he touched.

Louis-François Pinagot probably gave some thought to leaving a trace of his existence after him. He may have earnestly wished to leave a mark, might even have taken active steps to secure his memory. He might have trained an animal, planted and cared for a tree, built a house, dug a garden, fashioned a tool, passed on a technique, set an example, or posed for a photograph. In the memory of those who knew him, something about him might briefly have outlived him: the sound of his voice, a certain way of conversing in the evening, a claim to fame of some sort, or, at the very least, a reputation. Such survivals are a matter of scale, of breadth of the temporal horizon. In any case, none of these things has endured. If we wish to come closer to this Jean Valjean who never stole a loaf of bread, we must penetrate the silence and the void that surround him.

It was necessary to choose at random one of a myriad of identical social atoms. There was no other way to honor with remembrance a unique individual from an undifferentiated mass. Anyone whose fate was unusual in any way, who left an unusual record of any kind, had to be eliminated. Anyone who had not been totally forgotten, even by his descendants, had to be ruled out. It was essential to choose a person about whom the only documentary record would consist of materials not brought to light by a specific interest in *that* individual.

Using these materials, I planned next to ascertain whatever definite, verifiable information I could find. I would then set these bare facts in context by describing as fully as possible everything that constituted the daily life of the person I had chosen. I would provide the reader with enough information to re-create for himself or herself the possible and the probable. I would sketch a virtual history of the landscape, the entourage, and the ambiance. I would speculate about hypothetical emotions and fragments of dialogue. I would try to imagine the social hierarchy as seen from below, try to grasp the way in which memory is structured. Of course, we will never know the moral qualities of the individual in question. How keen a worker was he? How intensely sensual a man? How ardent was his desire for women? How did he conceive of this world and the other? We will never know as much about him as we know about the miller Menocchio or the murderer Pierre Rivière.[2]

Strange as it may seem, this book is not really an exercise in microhistory, nor should it be seen as an instance of the kind of study that Lucien Febvre used to propose, a sort of geological cross section of the depths of society. We will not learn any of the things that would be important to know if our goal were to write a history of the individual subject. But we will at least be attempting, in a small way, to repair the neglect of historians for all those things that are irrevocably relegated to oblivion. Modestly, we hope to reverse the work of the bulldozers that have lately been digging up our rural cemeteries.

Fragments of a journal kept in the early days of my research:

May 2, 1995, 2 P.M. The moment of choice has arrived. Feeling emotion in anticipation of my first meeting with a stranger whose company I will be probably be keeping for several years, a stranger who could never have conceived of such a meeting and for whom I feel no special affection or empathy. I think of the dead waiting to be chosen. Would they find the idea outrageous? What right do I have to pose as a minor miracle-worker pretending to restore life to a person who might not wish to be disturbed—in the unlikely event that the afterlife exists?

The men and women of the milieu and generation to which my still unchosen subject belonged were generally quite hostile toward anyone who put on airs or aspired to leave some trace of his or her existence. In the country, gravestones that called attention to themselves were often targets of such hostility, which would no doubt also have been directed at any form of autobiographical writing. Hence what I intend to do is not without insolence.

The first day of this delicate quest marks a new departure in historical inquiry. I am probably the first historian ever to plan to devote years to the resurrection of an individual about whom I still know nothing. In a few minutes I will be the only person who knows anything about him, the only person with any chance whatsoever of coming to know him as an individual. At this moment he has in fact vanished from the collective memory forever; he is not and cannot be remembered as an individual human being.

In fact, it is quite risky even to speak of individuality in this context. There is no evidence that the person I am about to choose ever looked upon his own life as constituting a destiny. It is unlikely that he did. He may have had only the vaguest memory of the episodes of his own existence. He may have possessed no sense of chronology whatsoever. Yet in his life I am going to identify sequences of events, arrange them in order, impose on them a direction—with caution, to be sure. Hence there may well be something wrong with the story I tell, because it will not have the form of a narrative about someone who lacks self-awareness, who forgets his own story.

3 P.M. I have chosen the archives of the Orne, my native region, partly for reasons of convenience but partly, too, to minimize the difficulties and facilitate a comprehensive view despite the temporal distance between historian and subject. I close my eyes and select at random a volume from the inventory of the municipal archives. The volume on which my hand happens to fall is the one for the commune of Origny-le-Butin, a nondescript locality, a tiny cell in the vast tissue of French communes. Its name does not figure in the "subject catalog" of the archival register or in the inventory of Series M, that treasure trove of the social historian. [Later I was to discover that it does not appear in the catalogs of the Bibliothèque Nationale or the index to the *Bibliographie annuelle de l'histoire de France* either.] This absence of visibility is confirmed by a perusal of the summaries of a variety of surveys. Like so many other tiny communes, Origny-le-Butin has vanished from memory in the same way as its individual inhabitants. I therefore find myself confronting a riddle within a conundrum.

Next I open the decennial tables of vital statistics from the late eighteenth century and choose two names at random. In alphabetical order they are Jean Courapied and Louis-François Pinagot. At this point I am obliged to intervene: Jean Courapied died young. To choose him would spoil the fun. That leaves Pinagot. I remember that the German writer Ernst Jünger once apostrophized an insect he came upon in the course of a collecting expedition: "So there you are!"

May 7, 1995. Thanks to the experience acquired over forty years of work in departmental archives, the puzzle has come together rapidly. After two days I am already in a position to answer the rather befuddled or perhaps wary archivists who have been asking me the same question since last Tuesday: "You're working on what? Or on whom?" What they hadn't been able to understand was that I was then at a stage in my work where it was still impossible to answer such questions. But now I have Louis-François Pinagot, recalled from oblivion, and already I've put our meeting to good use. I know, for instance, that he was a woodsman, the son of a carter, an indigent *sabotier*, or clog maker, who lived on the edge of the domanial forest of Bellême. I know his height (1.66 meters, 5'5"), the places where he lived, and his marital status. But he is still just a name, a shadow cast upon documents whose interest in him is only as a member of a series or group. Obviously, I will never know what his face looked like or how he presented himself, and most likely I will never know about his youth, his love life, or the exact nature of his clientele. Nevertheless, his life holds the potential to reveal a range of emotion and a variety of human experience, owing to his longevity, the extent of his family, the variety of roles he played and places he lived, and the diverse nature of employment in the woodworking trade.

It is important to maintain a clear head, however. The distance—temporal, social, and cultural—between me and Louis-François Pinagot makes it difficult for me to understand him. By the same token, it would probably have been difficult for him to analyze me. Still, he had his key for understanding other people, just as I do, and it would have been of some use to him. Let us try at any rate to avoid whining on the one hand and condescension on the other.

Pinagot will be the invisible center, the unseen spectator of the portrait I intend to paint of his world as he might have seen it. My procedure will resemble that of a filmmaker who shoots a scene through the eyes of a character who remains off screen. I must do everything I can to reconstitute his spatial and temporal horizon, his family environment, his circle of friends, his community, as well as his probable values and beliefs. I must try to imagine his pleasures and pains, his worries, his bouts of anger, and his dreams. I will need to conjure up an image in the round from the shape of the mold, from what the very silence surrounding my quarry reveals.

Louis-François Pinagot lived a long life on the edge of the forest. His life span coincides with that of the great French Romantics. He was a contemporary of Lamartine, Hugo, Vigny, Michelet, and Berlioz. Of course, he was probably completely unaware of this. He lived under monarchs, between two invasions, in a milieu where the local history of the Ancien Régime and Revolution was often discussed.

Half of his life, a period of thirty-seven years, unfolded while one or the other of the Bonapartes was in power. For thirty-three and a half years he lived under the constitutional monarchy. From the time he was two until the time he was seventeen, France was first a Consulate and later an Empire. His youth, from age seventeen to age thirty-two, unfolded under the Bourbons, his maturity (age thirty-two to fifty) under Louis Philippe. His old age (fifty to seventy-two) began under the Second Republic and Second Empire, and senility overtook him between the ages of seventy-two and seventy-six under a still unsteady Third Republic. Such rapid political change would have been dizzying for anyone who attached real importance to the nature of the regime, but there is no evidence that Pinagot did. Since we know the outcome, however—the triumph of the Third Republic—we must make an effort to imagine the life of a man who was too young to have taken part in the Napoleonic wars and too old to have fought in the wars of the Second Empire but whose adolescence and youth were marked by two invasions, which link his life to the history of Europe.

Pinagot's long though obscure existence in a tiny commune in the Perche also coincided with a number of crucial historical processes: the collapse of the temporal structure of French society, the fabrication of new spaces in a countryside steeped in nostalgia (as was the case with the forest of Bellême), the inception and development of the sciences of man and of the social survey, the invention of the notion of traditional society and of the communal monograph, and of course the rise of individualism and the development of new modalities for the construction of self and citizen. To what extent was Pinagot aware of these processes, and what meaning, if any, did they hold for him? Or at the very least, to what extent did they shape the record of his existence?

As we shall see, Pinagot had experience of things that one might not at first sight expect: the exercise of the right to vote, the spectacle of modern war, and upheaval in the woodworking and textile industries, to say nothing of subtle changes in his identity. The son of a carter, he became a clog maker. Though indigent for many years, he belatedly came into property. Though perceived for a time as a son-in-law (Pinagot-Pôté), he had by the end of his life become an esteemed grandfather, whose eldest son was a member of the municipal council.

How—or as Lucien Febvre might ask, with what mental equipment—did he perceive and experience processes that would have been easier for him to see because they had a direct impact on him and the people around him?: the acceleration of the pace of life, the introduction of new means of communication and sources of information, the halting progress of literacy, and, more prosaically, the changes in the village of Origny-le-Butin and in the types of conflict and accommodation that existed in that impoverished commune. How concerned was he with honor and reputation? Was he deferential in his relation with patrons and other dominant figures? Whom did he hate?

The game we are playing here could of course be continued. If our goal is to reconstitute the world that Louis-François Pinagot might have lived in, we might think of expanding the effort to a collective one. It might not be absurd to set up a "Center for Pinagotic Research." This suggestion is not intended as an ironic pastiche of Jorge Luis Borges.

> June 1995. Within just a few weeks it has been possible to perform a series of resurrections, of collateral reanimations. A whole dense network of people around Pinagot has begun to emerge like the layers of a branching vine. He has brought any number of ghosts out of the darkness with him. A few of these already stand out because the record-keeping procedures for one reason or another favored them.
>
> In this way a hidden avenue of access to the nineteenth century has begun to open up. My sense is that a thousand pages on Pinagot, no matter how descriptive and overcautious in interpretation, would do more to satisfy the desire to understand this period than any number of minute studies of structures of protoindustrialization or hasty, pretentiously scientific comparisons of Percheron peasants with the tribesmen of New Guinea.

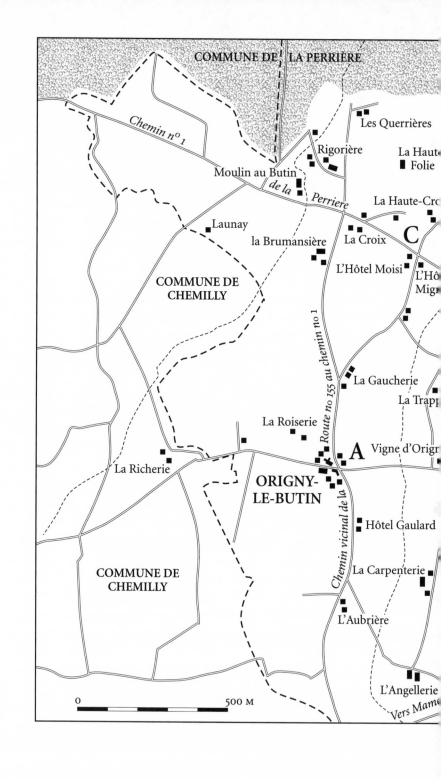

COMMUNE DE LA PERRIÈRE

Chemin n° 1

Les Querrières

Rigorière

La Haut•
Folie

Moulin au Butin

de la

Perriere

La Haute-Cr•

Launay

la Brumansière

La Croix

C

L'Hôtel Moisi

L'Hô
Mig•

COMMUNE DE
CHEMILLY

Route no 155 au chemin no 1

La Gaucherie

La Trap•

La Roiserie

La Richerie

A Vigne d'Origr•

ORIGNY-
LE-BUTIN

Chemin vicinal de la

Hôtel Gaulard

COMMUNE DE
CHEMILLY

La Carpenterie

L'Aubrière

L'Angellerie

Vers Mame•

0   500 M

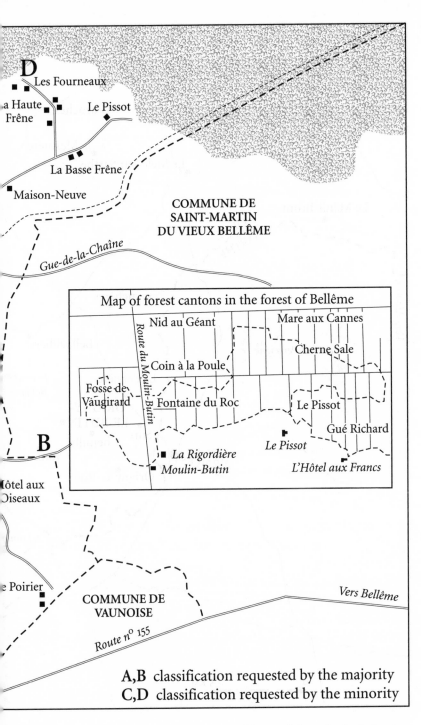

D Les Fourneaux

a Haute Frêne

Le Pissot

La Basse Frêne

Maison-Neuve

Gue-de-la-Chaîne

COMMUNE DE SAINT-MARTIN DU VIEUX BELLÊME

Map of forest cantons in the forest of Bellême

Nid au Géant

Mare aux Cannes

Route du Moulin-Butin

Coin à la Poule

Cherne Sale

Fosse de Vaugirard

Fontaine du Roc

Le Pissot

Le Pissot

Gué Richard

B

La Rigordière

Moulin-Butin

L'Hôtel aux Francs

ôtel aux
Oiseaux

e Poirier

Vers Bellême

COMMUNE DE VAUNOISE

Route n° 155

A,B classification requested by the majority
C,D classification requested by the minority

Map 1: Origny-le-Butin in 1872

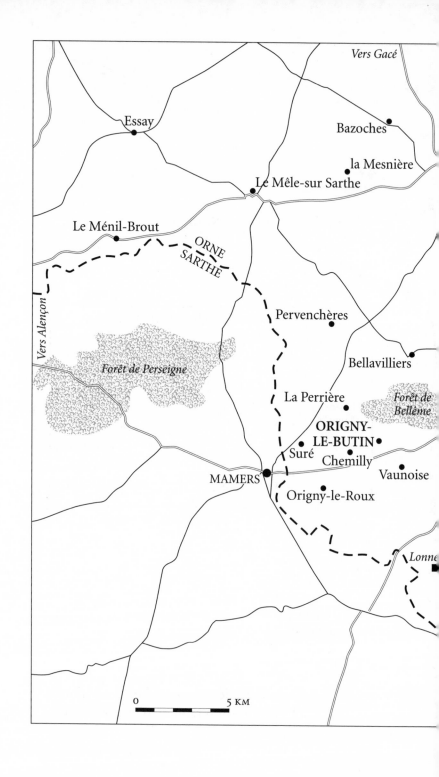

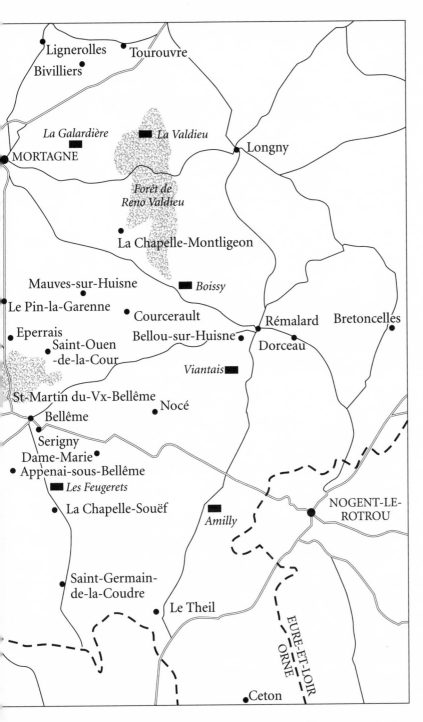

Lignerolles
Tourouvre
Bivilliers

La Galardière
La Valdieu
MORTAGNE
Longny

Forêt de
Reno Valdieu

La Chapelle-Montligeon

Mauves-sur-Huisne
Boissy
Le Pin-la-Garenne
Courcerault
Rémalard
Bretoncelles
Eperrais
Bellou-sur-Huisne
Saint-Ouen
-de-la-Cour
Dorceau

Viantais

St-Martin du-Vx-Bellême
Nocé
Bellême

Serigny
Dame-Marie
Appenai-sous-Bellême

Les Feugerets

La Chapelle-Souëf
Amilly
NOGENT-LE-
ROTROU

Saint-Germain-
de-la-Coudre
Le Theil

EURE-ET-LOIR
ORNE

Ceton

Map 2: Belleme Forest Region

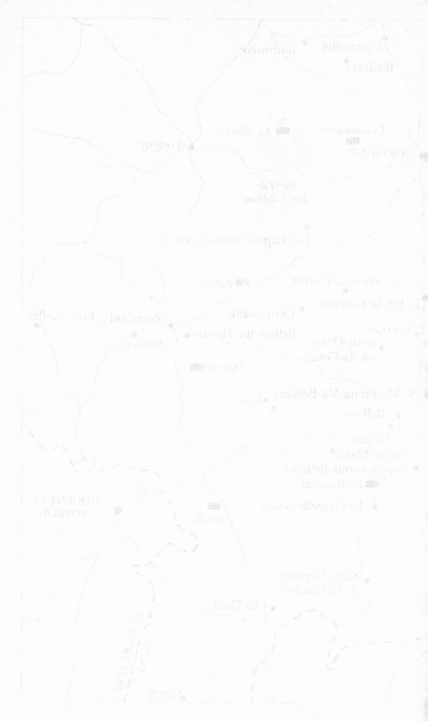

the life of an unknown

a lifespace

Apart from a brief stay in the nearby forest village of Saint-Martin-du-Vieux-Bellême immediately after his marriage, Louis-François Pinagot never lived anywhere but in the commune of Origny-le-Butin. His various residences—with his father in Haute-Frêne, in L'Hôtel-Migné, and for a lengthy period in Basse-Frêne (see map 1)—were located in the heart of a hilly section of bocages, or hedged fields, within a few hundred yards of the forest of Bellême. For a time he may even have lived in the forest itself, in a clog maker's hut.[1]

The walls of his house would most probably have been made of stone, in keeping with a by now well-established process of sedentarization of forest workers.[2] In Pinagot's case this choice may also have reflected uncertainty about his "geographical identity," for this man of the woods was also a man of the fields.[3] A clog maker, he was also at times referred to, or recognized as, a day laborer, and his father-in-law was a well-to-do farmer, Louis Pôté. His father, Jacques Pinagot, was a carter who also farmed a small plot of land. Thus it is likely that Louis-François, as the son and son-in-law of farmers, pitched in on the farm when help was needed, in return for which he would have received food when supplies were short.[4]

The proximity of the forest shaped the life of this working man, who lived in the heart of a region of serried fields separated by dense hedges. There was something vaguely foreboding about the landscape; gardens were vulnerable to damage by wild animals from the forest, and domestic animals occasionally reverted to a partly wild state.[5] But there were also many advantages to living near the woods: it was easy to scavenge for dead wood and forage for mushrooms, wild strawberries, and blueberries.[6] Poaching was easy, and herbs, leaves, and timber were there for the taking.

The benefits should not be overstated, however. The limits of the Bellême forest were quite clear. It was not one of those woods so vaguely defined as to encourage trespassing and filching, nor was it so vast as to threaten the surrounding farmland. In 1782 the engineer Jean-Alexandre Chaillou complained that the marking of the boundary was at best "intermittent."[7] It was therefore decided to renew the marking in the following year and to rebuild the "outer ditch."[8] Subsequently, this ditch was redug several times and reinforced with an embankment.[9] In addition, the hedges of the "enclosed inherited land" that rimmed the forest constituted "something like a rampart" preventing any tampering with the boundary.[10] This obstacle to the anarchic spread of woodland explains why the forest boundaries were so rarely challenged even in a region where disputes over boundary markings were common. The Bellême forest differed from countless others that have been described in the literature in that its southern edge was not contested territory. Because it was a domanial forest, moreover, the parties to any dispute would have been quite unequal, and this, too, tended to discourage controversy.[11]

Louis-François Pinagot, a resident of one of the "villages" that bordered the forest, is probably best described as a woodsman.[12] All his life, whenever he looked north from his house, he saw a dark line of trees. We would do well, therefore, to pause briefly to consider the forest of Bellême, through which Pinagot would have traveled frequently as a carter's helper and probably also as a woodcutter. Once he became a clog maker, he still would have gone to the forest to select his wood.

Because Bellême was a domanial forest, sole authority over it was vested in the administration.[13] Among the people who frequented these woods were timber merchants who purchased the right to cut trees under precise conditions specified in detailed bills of particulars. Toward the end of the Ancien Régime the forest consisted primarily of magnificent stands of oak and beech. In later years, descriptions of the forests of Normandy included obligatory passages of praise for these splendid trees, which the navy coveted. In 1803, Delestang, subprefect of the Mortagne district, drafted a description of the *département* for the Chaptal survey in which he waxed eloquent about these trees.[14] Adepts of travel writing joined the chorus of praise. Dureau de la Malle alluded in 1823 to "one of the marvels of France."[15] He quoted Napoleon to the effect that the forests of the Perche, especially that of Bellême, were among the most beautiful in Europe (the Perche, the region in which the forest of Bellême is located, occupies the western portion of the Paris basin and includes the eastern portion of the Orne *département* and the western portion of the Eure-et-Loir *département* as well as parts of the Sarthe-trans.). Scholars and antiquarians also had praise for Bellême's trees: in 1837, for example, Léon de la Sicotière vaunted these "superb timberlands."[16]

Bellême is a small forest: a hiker can cross it from north to south in an hour and from east to west in two hours.[17] There is no impenetrable thicket at its center. Although it did serve as a temporary refuge at times, including several periods of the Revolution, it was never truly a "sanctuary" for dissidents, as many other forests in western France were.[18]

The much-praised timber sprang from varied terrain. When Pinagot first began hiking in the forest as a child, it was dotted with small swamps and bogs, punctuated by quarries, and interspersed with moor and expanses of sand. Nevertheless, it was readily penetrable. A dense network of winding trails encouraged disorderly cutting that did considerable damage to the woodlands. In 1858 the network of trails was still as dense as ever.[19] A more rigorous development plan added a series of new logging roads, but during the Second Empire most of these new roads still were not improved with gravel. The Moulin-Butin road—the primary route from the forest to the Origny area—suffered as a result of this delay. Throughout Pinagot's lifetime the forest of Bellême served as a thoroughfare. The easiest route to the towns of La Perrière, Saint-Martin, and Bellême was through the woods.

Unlike the residents of the communes ringing the nearby hills of Ecouves and Tourouvre, the people who lived on the edge of the Bellême forest enjoyed no usage rights. The catalog of cantonal rights compiled in 1846 mentions neither rights of way nor rights of pasturage.[20] The only residual right was therefore the permission to gather dead wood.[21] This did not include the right to gather herbs or leaves, heather or fern for stable litter, or bundles of green wood.[22] The clarity of the norms explains the small number of recorded offenses in this forest, which experienced none of the problems caused elsewhere by sectioning and purchase of usage rights.[23]

The appearance of the forest of Bellême changed markedly over

Pinagot's lifetime, especially along the southern edge where he lived. As late as 1804, when he would have formed his earliest memories, the forest appears to have been seriously neglected. Specialists agree that serious damage was done during the Revolution.[24] Excessive grazing, "invasions" by neighbors out to profit from slackened surveillance, and overexploitation to meet the needs of war all took a toll. Devastation was greatest during the first two years of the Revolution (1789–1790) and toward the end of the Directorate. Meanwhile, however, a more modern system of forest regulation was being developed. One must be careful, however, not to be misled by the constant whining of administrators in the decades that followed what they saw as a period of torment. Prefects railed against the excesses of those trying times: overexploitation, unauthorized clear-cutting, and extensions of whitewood regions. At the same time, they stressed the importance of their own efforts to reorganize the forest and establish a new order, whose principles were to be codified in 1827.

In any event, the forests of the Orne, and that of Bellême in particular, were a subject of inexhaustible complaint for the prefect La Magdelaine. On his account, the forests had been in lamentable condition at the time of Pinagot's birth.[25] Because watchmen had ceased to be paid, they neglected their duties. "Lack of [road] maintenance forced wagons to seek more practicable routes through the woods." Houses in the forest had "generally deteriorated," and ditches were clogged. People living on the edge of the woods sought recognition of rights they had usurped. On 20 Frimaire, Year VI (1798), the prefect was pleased to announce that he had solved all of these problems. His administration had taken steps to reseed and repopulate the forest. Pruning along major roads allowed circulation of both people and goods to resume and introduced salubrious air and "public security" into a forest still "infested with brigands" (or *chouans*, rebels against the government of the Revolution), just like the dangerous forest of Ménil-Brout described by Balzac.[26] Later, "meteorological worries" in the Orne cast doubt on the forest's future.[27]

Thanks to the precision of the archival sources, we can follow the various stages of improvement and exploitation of the forest of Bellême in the nineteenth century in great detail. The forest code of 1827 did not really mark a new beginning, because the state was already deeply involved in forest management. During Pinagot's lifetime the organization of the forest was clarified. The limits of triages and sections, ambiguous at the turn of the century, were delineated more sharply. As a result, the outline of the forest became clearer.[28] While Louis-François was still young, the cuts specified in the improvement plan of 1782–1783 were carried out.[29] As a result, by 1834, when he was thirty-six, the forest no longer resembled the forest of 1782.[30] Between the two dates, 714 hectares of woodland were harvested, and areas of scrub expanded.[31]

For the next ten years (1834–1844) "woodland treatment" was interrupted. More of the forest was converted to scrub. Then, on September 12, 1845, a temporary regulation was instituted, putting an end to this confused period. The new regulation set limits to clear-cutting, provided for forest replenishment cuts, and instituted clearing procedures. The forest of Bellême again became "exploitable woodland." Efforts toward improvement were accompanied by development of the heath and bogs, once again altering the landscape.[32] In 1835 the forest of Bellême contained 281 hectares of voids and clearings. Maritime pine was introduced and then, when that failed, Scots pine. After 1852 swamps and bogs were drained, then seeded with spruce and ash. By 1859 the voids in the forest had almost been filled in.

By Pinagot's last years the forest of Bellême had regained its former beauty. "The stands of old trees, some more than two hundred years old, arouse universal admiration for their vigorous vegetation and for the beauty of the trees, some of which are more than 125 feet tall. All the woodlands are in good condition. Dead, dying, and stunted trees have recently been removed. The natural regrowth resulting from the thinning operations that have been carried out since 1822 is extremely beautiful."[33] In the following year Napoleon III signed the new improvement plan.[34] The forest of Bellême was to be treated "as full woodland" until 2059 and subjected to a rotation of two hundred years, divided into eight periods of twenty-five years each.

Consider the southern edge of the forest, which borders the bocage of Origny-le-Butin (see map 2).[35] This includes the number one triage area, known as "La Perrière," where the terrain was particularly uneven. Place names were quite picturesque; these not only described each area but reflected the wealth of local legends. Among them we find the Nest of Giants, the Pool of Cane, the Ugly Oak, the Preacher's Pulpit, the Chicken's Corner, the Fountain in the Rock, the Piss-Pot, the Bourgoin Pasture, and the "Vaugirard" (Girard's Calf). Cutting in this triage was intense when Louis-François was a child (1797–1803). It continued with lower intensity until 1818. As a result, the aspect of the forest as seen from Haute or Basse-Frêne changed dramatically, and wooded areas in the vicinity shrank considerably.

It is important not to view these changes with an unduly pessimistic eye. The purpose of the plan was to prevent the forest from dying out, and the dominant idea was still that of a cycle rather than alternation.[36] Looked at in this way, harvesting trees is not to be equated with destruction of the forest. This was the realm of eternal return. Cutting timber did not cause pain or elicit nostalgia; such sentiments belong to a more recent era and its obsession with protection. In any event, Pinagot always had magnificent timberland to gaze on, even after the most drastic clear cuts, most notably the one carried out in the "Ugly Oak" section in 1858, which covered twenty-two hectares.[37] The height of the oak trunks, measured with a dendrometer, ranged from 65 to 88 feet, while those of the beech ranged from 59 to 88 feet. Forty-eight oaks and nine beech trees had circumferences greater than 10 feet.[38]

It would be hazardous indeed to venture into the thicket of psychological effects that such an environment might have had on the mind of a nineteenth-century maker of clogs. We may assume, however, that Pinagot was sensitive to the rhythms of the forest, which would have exerted a strong influence on his sense of time and perhaps his way of thinking about society. The forest has no use for impatience. Trees by their very nature force us to take a long-term view. In the forest time is measured in periods of thirty years (the maturation time of trees suitable for making clogs), a hundred years (the maturation time of the kinds of timber used by industry), or even two hundred years (the maturation time of the sort of timber prized by the navy). Such time scales have nothing in common with those of the city dweller or even the farmer. Woodland was exempt from the acceleration of time that affected almost everything else in the nineteenth century. Still, Pinagot was a man of more than one identity, subject to other social time scales as well. Accepting the slower pace of forest time implied accepting the idea of deferred income, but in Pinagot's mind these long-run considerations probably competed with short-term views shaped by the liturgical cycle, the seasonal cycle of agriculture, and the stages of the family cycle, to say nothing of the unfolding of his country's history. Caution is therefore in order.

A similar approach is essential in dealing with "sonic space," or what has been dubbed the "soundscape." The elite sought not only to improve the forest as a productive resource but also to establish it as a "noise-free zone." Dr. Jousset spoke (at a relatively late date, to be sure, in 1884) of the "solemn silence" of the Bellême woods, which he found suitable for meditation.[39] Of course, the forest was a good place for listening; silent arrivals and sudden departures were common.[40] It was also good for spying on other people or keeping a discreet eye on them. But the forest was also a workplace for hundreds of people. All sorts of things were hauled through it. Hikers and strollers trod its paths. There is every reason to believe that, during the day at least, it was a noisy place, filled with chants, shouts, and the sound of woodcutting.

For our purposes, what matters most is probably Pinagot's immersion in a space where both animal and plant life could be observed, where keen attentiveness would have been an asset, and where a good sense of direction was essential. Obviously, he knew the soul of the forest. As a clog maker, he would have been an old hand at evaluating the quality of various woods, especially beech and birch, aspen and elm. He would have needed to be able to estimate the age of a tree.

Though not abounding with game (as we know because the man who purchased the right to hunt in 1858 tried to restock the forest), the forest of Bellême was home to roe deer.[41] It was full of beaver, marten, and skunk. People hunted boar, fox, and rabbit. Wolves were not unknown.[42] On May 23, 1834, Louis Massard, a logging contractor, found five wolf cubs in the Petit-Faux section. Under the mayor's supervision the animals were put to death and buried.[43] On May 13, 1849, Mme Vavasseur claimed a bounty of six francs for a male wolf cub roughly two months old, whose front paw and two ears she presented to the mayor of Saint-Martin. And there was no shortage of vipers in the forests of the Orne. In 1881, five years after Pinagot's death, the use of the scythe was prohibited and only the billhook allowed; this regulation led to the death of several indigents on the edge of the forest of Ecouves.[44]

Within the forest of Bellême opposing forces clashed: solitude versus sociability, silence versus noise, and the drive to exploit, improve, and rationalize versus the survival of a savage animality that made its presence felt along the edge of the forest, where many influences converged.

The changes in the landscape that Pinagot might have noticed over the course of his long life were not limited to those resulting from exploitation of the forest. The forest, its outlines transformed by agents of the administration, was subject to various measures of "beautification." At the turn of the nineteenth century, moreover, a plan was hatched to develop it as a therapeutic site. Various scholars drew on their erudition to bolster claims that the fountain of La Herse, on the opposite side of the forest from Origny-le-Butin, had been frequented by people of quality since 1607. Scarron had supposedly come for the waters, which nineteenth-century antiquarians insisted had been discovered in Gallo-Roman times.[45]

Be that as it may, the fountain owed its good fortune to Dr. Chaudru of Bellême, who noted its therapeutic qualities in 1777. Thirty years later, he drafted a scientific report summarizing the results of his experiments.[46] The text belongs to a genre common at the time. Its author invoked any number of medical theories in praise of a fountain that he hoped to see promoted as a medicinal hot spring with himself in charge.

For the time being, he conceded, "the spring is not in anyone's safe-keeping." His report continued: "I have prescribed the waters of La Herse internally for diseases of the kidney, liver, spleen, and other abdominal viscera resulting from swelling and even obstruction and in afflictions of the stomach due to debilitation. [Also] for very serious and refractory cases of scabs. . . . I have had great success with it. . . . I also had the satisfaction of witnessing the cure of a dropsical woman after she drank water *directly from the fountain.*" The good doctor added that "the waters of the Herse have aperitive and tonic properties." Indeed, "their preservation should be entrusted to enlightened individuals educated in the art of helping suffering humanity," for "they may be dangerous in ignorant hands." It would be useful, too, to "build an apartment for foreigners near the fountain," since the waters in question "are not capable of being transported."

At the time, the administrators were well aware of the spring's reputation. Local farmers claimed that the quality of the water it produced was a harbinger of the quality of the coming harvest. In 1803 Subprefect Delestang noted that the fountain's sweet, iron-rich water was indicated for various skin diseases.[47] In 1810 Louis Dubois gave assurance that the waters were indeed reputed, in Bellême at any rate, to heal the diseases enumerated by Dr. Chaudru.[48] He added fevers to the list. Pinagot's childhood coincided with the golden age of the health spa. Around the fountain common people rubbed shoulders with local elites. Cafés were set up nearby in the huts of clog makers. Here people sang, drank, and danced to the music of violins. Women, we are told, took advantage of the opportunity to pick blueberries. In 1884 Dr. Jousset, by then quite elderly, fondly recalled the festive ambiance of the fountain when he was a child.[49]

Nevertheless, the plan to develop a spa at La Herse came to naught. Antiquarians puzzled over inscriptions dedicating the health-giving fountain to Venus and Mars, which only added to the waters' reputation as a remedy for "women's ills and maladies of love." In 1839 Delassale expressed certainty that these sulfur-rich waters had once been credited with "a prolific and voluptuous virtue."[50] Still, the authority of the antiquarians proved insufficient to stem the fountain's decline.[51] Under the July Monarchy, La Herse became a picturesque spot, a harbinger of the coming "beautification" of the forest. The medicinal waters flowed "through a circle of lawn in which various exotic shrubs had been planted, surrounded by a sort of bower abutting the great trees of the forest. Through this bower run a series of verdant promenades, each ending in a stone stairway leading down to the spring."[52] Few sick people sought out the spring, however, other than women and girls with maladies of the lung, who came not to drink the waters of the fountain but to breathe the forest air.[53]

During the Second Empire there were sporadic experiments with new conservation and development techniques. The period also saw numerous projects of commemoration. At a time when the forest of Fontainebleau was being transformed into a "green museum," efforts were begun to turn Bellême into a tourist attraction for a new type of tourist.[54] Unlike the Fontainebleau project, however, the Bellême effort appears not to have been very successful.

Baron Boyer de Sainte-Suzanne, subprefect of the Mortagne district, had the waters of La Herse analyzed to determine their iron content. He then sponsored a plan to beautify the approach to the spring, although he realized that the flow was too small to sustain a spa of any size. Meanwhile, the *garde général* set out to restore the forest's crucifixes, said to have been destroyed during the Revolution. Thanks to his efforts, "each cross was given its own little square filled with sand and surrounded by a grass lawn, with improved access."[55]

This project, a part of the Catholic restoration of the period, was to prove ephemeral. A quarter of a century later, most of the forest crosses were gone, having been destroyed by the elements. The most prestigious of them, the Croix de la Feue Reine, restored in 1855 by a prominent Catholic family, provided the setting for a gala ceremony that year. On the night of

August 26—the first Sunday after Saint-Louis—it was solemnly blessed in the presence of parishioners of the four parishes on the northern edge of the forest, their banners flapping in the wind. The cross commemorated the passage of Blanche of Castille, who had come after the death of her husband, the king, to lead the victorious struggle against the duke of Brittany. On the day of the festival the cross was described as standing on "a long promenade that runs parallel to the Le Mans road and is lined on either side by gnarled old elm trees."[56]

The forest was abuzz at the time with rumors of treasure. From time to time, workmen would come upon heaps of old coins buried in the woods long ago by people who had gone there to hide out. The image of the forest as a place of potential profit was revived under the Second Empire by a government-sponsored plan to excavate the Roman camp at Châtelier. This was not surprising in view of the emperor's interest in archeology. Baron Boyer de Sainte-Suzanne had a map made of the camp with its ditches and embankments and two guard posts.[57] This site was located on the southern edge of the forest not far from Origny-le-Butin.

Particularly striking from our point of view was the interest in gnarled old trees and the myths surrounding them. Not far from Haute and Basse-Frène was the so-called *Chêne Saille* (or *Sale*: figuratively, Ugly Oak), which some people insisted was the famous Oak of Saint Louis. This was "an oak religiously preserved although it has been in a state of ruin for more than two hundred years, as a result of which it is popularly known as the Ugly Oak. It would be a good idea to restore the name attributed to this tree by legend and ancient documents rather than continue to apply a pejorative word to one of the most beautiful old trees in France. It measures 8 meters and 40 centimeters in circumference."[58] Saint Louis was supposed to have hitched his horse to the tree. In 1884, "this very old oak, hollow in its center and capable of accommodating three people inside its trunk, is still known as the Oak of Saint Louis," although some people continued to refer to it as the Ugly Oak.[59]

During the Empire it was common to single out remarkable sites in the most prestigious forests for commemorative purposes; legends grew up around these sites, and paths were established to provide easy access. What influence might projects of this sort have had on Louis-François Pinagot? Obviously we will never know. At best we can hazard an educated guess. The improvements made to the forest of Bellême and the marking of the territory made for novel forms of celebration and social encounter, quite different from those associated with markets, fairs, and inns. Social distances would have been maintained, however. In any case, there were certainly festive scenes in which Pinagot might have participated, such as the blessing of the Croix de la Feue Reine. Perhaps he or a member of his family worked on the excavation of the Roman camp.

Surely, Pinagot could not have missed the improvement and beautification of parts of the forest and the growing numbers of Sunday and holiday visitors. Whatever he may have thought of projects such as these (which he may have viewed with a jaundiced eye), his attitude toward his own origins was likely to have been affected. Indeed, it is not unreasonable to assume that these efforts to promote the forest made him feel rather proud of coming from a place recognized as having certain aesthetic qualities and respected for its wealth of monuments, rich legendary past, and historical depth attested by sylvan splendors.

The forest was not the only area that Pinagot frequented, however. As Abbé Fret noted in 1840, most of the inhabitants of the Perche "limited their horizon" to their own immediate neighborhood.[60] For Pinagot that neighborhood consisted, first of all, of the villages along the forest's edge in which members of his family resided: his grandmother, his father and mother, his aunts and uncles, his parents-in-law, his cousins, and eventually his children and grandchildren. With so many relatives nearby, he probably made short journeys nearly every day across fields and through gaps in the thick hedgerows. Relatives, neighbors, and friends helped one another out, and young men and women formed amorous relationships. Social relations of this short shaped the networks that developed in the region.

The town of Origny-le-Butin was too small to become a focal point of the region, as was common in the bocage in the western portion of the département. Of course, it took no more than a quarter of an hour to get there on foot from Haute or Basse-Frêne, but the likelihood of any significant social encounter was small. In 1831 the town's population consisted of just fifty people distributed among thirteen households.[61] Obviously, none of them was a member of the liberal professions, and none enjoyed a private income. There were no real shopkeepers. Until the middle of the July Monarchy, there was no inn in the town, just a baker, two weavers, a gelder, and a few craftsmen who occasionally also served drinks. By 1844 a grocer had set up shop, although we do not know exactly when this grocery was first established. In 1850 one clog maker also sold tobacco.[62] The town had no town hall during Louis-François's lifetime. The mayor's house probably also served as a "communal house." It was not until he was quite elderly that people began to discuss the possibility of building a schoolhouse.[63] What was called a schoolhouse during his lifetime was a building indistinguishable from any of the local dwellings.

In the center of the town stood a church, which, surrounded by a small cemetery, dominated everything else. During Louis-François's childhood and youth, this church was deconsecrated, despite which the former parishioners repaired and maintained it. In 1808 all religious functions were transferred to Vaunoise. Origny-le-Butin was not recognized as a branch church until 1820.

Shortly before mid-century a café and an inn opened their doors in Origny. By the time Pinagot reached the age of fifty, Origny was able to offer him a church, a cemetery, two inns, a tobacco shop, and a bakery.[64] Social relations developed around these various venues, especially when one of his sons-in-law, a weaver, set up shop near the church. Note, however, that Pinagot's name was never mentioned in any records concerning infractions for disturbing the peace at night or causing trouble in a tavern. Of course, he may by then have been too old to have been tempted by such offenses.

Since Origny had so little to offer in the way of distractions, Pinagot must have been tempted to visit the town of La Perrière, a mile and a half away. His family was centered there, and his mother, separated from Jacques Pinagot, seems to have gone there to live with her son-in-law. Of course, this may have alienated her from her son. As a clog maker, he may also have felt a need to visit the inns of Saint-Martin-du-Vieux-Bellême, which were not much farther from Haute and Basse-Frêne than the inns of Origny. Throughout Louis-François's childhood, the school, the parish church, and the home of the tax collector (it would be misleading to call it a tax office) were in Vaunoise; hence one might expect that he went there often, although winter storms would have made the journey difficult. There are many indications that this was not the case, however. Since he never learned to read or write, it is unlikely that he attended school. As for the catechism, petitions signed by the residents of Origny suggest that it was little studied, especially by children in the northern part of the commune. If Louis-François went to Vaunoise at all, whether occasionally or regularly, it would probably have been on Sundays to hear mass.

Beyond this inner circle of relationships, a clog maker who spent his entire working life in the commune of Origny would have been likely to form relationships with a somewhat wider circle of people who would have known him by name and reputation. The center of this wider circle was Bellême, the cantonal seat and former capital of the Perche, which was barely five miles away by forest trails. As a young carter, Louis-François must have gone there often. After he became a clog maker, he probably depended on merchants in or near the town. Although the Thursday market was mainly a woman's affair, Bellême's six fairs and Saint-Martin's two may have attracted him.[65] To be sure, he was neither a farmer nor a breeder of livestock, and he had nothing to sell. In those days, however, a fair was not just an occasion for buying and selling or showing one's wares.[66] The "Saint-Simon" fair in particular was an occasion for the initiation of the young, for meeting other people, for boasting and showing off, and perhaps for aggressive posturing and even actual fighting. And, of course, it was a place where young men learned how to hold their liquor.

Other fairs were within a day's travel, and these would have offered additional opportunities for entertainment and meeting people. Here a man could enjoy the discovery of new pleasures with some degree of anonymity. In Pinagot's twenty-second year, some thirty-three annual fairs were recorded within fifteen miles of Origny-le-Butin in the Orne *département* alone.[67] There were also the fairs of Mamers, a subprefecture of the Sarthe *département*, which was no farther away than Bellême. In the first half of the nineteenth century, however, departmental boundaries meant more than they do today.

Since Louis-François Pinagot lived in the heart of the Perche, we may think of him as "a Percheron," but what might such an identification have meant to him? Was he even aware of it? At this point in our investigation of the ways in which people constructed their identities, we must make a radical shift in the scale of our analysis. We must also touch on another history, of the construction of regional images by Parisian elites and local notables in the period 1770–1850. And then we must attempt the even more difficult task of gauging the influence of such imaginary constructs on the thinking of locals themselves concerning their membership in this or that community.[68]

In contrast to what we find in the case of Normandy or Brittany, in the Perche the perception of outsiders did not play a decisive role in the fabrication of local identities. The Parisian elites focused their attention on the more prestigious provinces, whose outlines were more clearly defined and better preserved. If they were aware of the Perche at all, it was because of the Trappist monastery in Soligny in the north of the ancient province, which led to its being thought of as an isolated region fit for silent retreat and meditation. In 1847 Chateaubriand described the "obscure trails of the Perche" as just such a place.[69] For historians and latter-day disciples of Abbé de Rancé, the Perche was a "wilderness," as it was for the faithful of the past. In Pinagot's time, however, the region did not yet suffer from the identification of its human with its animal population, as it did after the breeding of livestock began to flourish there. It is also worth noting that from the mid-seventeenth century on, the names of five French towns acquired comical connotations that made them the butt of frequent jokes: Pontoise, Landerneau, Quimper-Corentin, Carpentras, and Brive-la-Gaillarde. None of these towns was located in the Orne *département*.[70]

Before considering the construction of the region's image in Pinagot's time, we must first recall that under the Consulate and Empire the Perche was included in the vast descriptive tableau of France compiled under the supervision of interior minister Jean-Antoine Chaptal and based on a neo-Hippocratic reading of space. Delestang, the subprefect of the Mortagne district, responded with obvious pleasure to the order he received from the ministry along with the minister's compliments. He described the Orne section of the Perche as a region whose climate was determined by an "extremely bracing and dry atmosphere" not likely to "be encumbered by foul stenches since standing water is almost never encountered." Despite the abundance of rivers, the "medical constitution" of the region was therefore favorable. "*Le Perche ornais*" was a healthy part of the country, and Delestang noted "the almost total absence of contagious diseases or nefarious epidemics of any kind. This in turn accounts for the strong and robust constitution of the district's residents, who are generally tall in stature, sanguine in temperament, prone to love and pleasures of various kinds, yet hard-working although not to excess."[71]

This set of clichés, which filled the La Magdelaine survey, was in subsequent decades transformed into a series of leitmotifs.[72] In 1837 Leon de la Sicotière wrote that "thanks to the pure and bracing climate and to the absence of stagnant water and pestilential swamps, the inhabitants are generally strong and well constituted."[73] The Orne *département* belonged partly to the Perche and partly to the Armorican massif, and the same reasoning dictated a contrast between the Perche portion and the bocages of the Armorican zone, whose inhabitants were less well-educated, less hardworking, and more troublesome. Even within *le Perche ornais* this neo-Hippocratic thinking encouraged the view that the "cantons of the south," including that of Bellême, were better off than those of the north.[74]

Another consequence of these neo-Hippocratic categories was a stereotypical distribution of "temperaments." In the Perche, Delestang assured his minister, "the people live calm and quiet lives; they work hard, but not to excess." Joseph Odolant-Desnos thought of Percherons as "active, industrious, stalwart and intelligent, disposed to cleanliness, and less religious, less superstitious, and more law-abiding than [the inhabitants] of the west," that is, the western portion of the *département*.[75] As early as 1837, however, Sicotière, an excellent scholar, was directing his irony at this sort of analysis, which in his view led to description based on fiat rather than observation. He took malicious pleasure in pointing out that, regardless of the bracing climate and nature of the terrain, the Percherons of the Orne were greedy, stuck in their ways, hypocritical, and loose in their morals. Obviously, there is little to be gained from such descriptions beyond an appreciation of the categories that entered into their construction.[76] The truth lies elsewhere.

Locally, people quickly acquired a sense that their identity was ambiguous and threatened; indeed, they may have sacrificed their identity quite early on. Parts of the Perche were assigned to three different départements: the Orne, the Sarthe, and Eure-et-Loir. The region thus became associated with provinces whose strong identities were much more clearly defined: Normandy and Maine. Another province with a strong image, the Beauce, lay nearby. Three towns had claims to be considered the "capital" of the Perche: Bellême, Mortagne, and Nogent; in the nineteenth century, however, all three were sleepy little towns. Taken together, these factors no doubt contributed to the feeling that the Percheron identity was threatened. The danger of losing their identity stimulated local elites, who early on sought with little fanfare to construct an image of the province that grew increasingly substantial over the years.[77] Abbé Fret, the curé of Champs, who was born in the same year as Pinagot but died earlier, wrote forcefully of the need for a local identity. In 1838, in the introduction to his *Antiquités et chroniques percheronnes*, he railed against the "historical excommunication" of the Perche. He wrote of the suffering caused by the inability to understand the significance of local monuments, which stood in "eloquent silence." He deplored the "painful dearth" of local history. And he spoke of his "ardent desire" for knowledge, of his need to decipher the "symbolic language" of the vestiges of the past.

The love of one's birthplace, which the abbé called "patriotism," was a powerful sentiment that animated erudite elites throughout France in the early nineteenth century in their search for historical roots. This need "to illuminate the dark night of time" accounts for the abbé's use of primitive material and audacious reconstruction of the chain of time in his *Antiquités*. He understood his project as a search for the roots of a regional identity and its evolution over time. The temporal depth of this search made up for what it lacked in geographical breadth. His study was aimed at exorcising the danger of lost identity. At the same time, he was out to reclaim lost souls. Through scholarly research, he hoped not only to discover the roots of a provincial identity in the depths of the past but also to revive the lost fervor of a golden age. Recovering the "monuments" of a bygone era (including not just structures but also rituals and texts), along with burial places and customs, was part of a strategy predicated on the idea that all aspects of the local identity could be traced back to the spirit of Christianity.

What we see here, then, is different from what we see in Brittany, where local elites sought to establish a positive image of their region in contrast to the negative one foisted on them by Paris elites. The Percheron identity was created locally in the absence of outside influence. The process was complex. As in many other provinces, history was central.[78] Local historians invoked the names of the prestigious counts of Bellême. They cited a series of heroes led by Guillaume I Talvas and Robert le Diable, who figured in any number of verse plays. The Middle Ages dominated the reconstruction of the past. The same historians pointed out that until the Revolution, *le Perche ornais* had been distinct from Normandy, with its own customary laws and provincial estates, which met for the last time in 1789. It was subject, moreover, to the jurisdiction of the *parlement* of Paris, not that of Rouen.

Local legends also figured in the construction of a regional identity but probably came into play later than historical narratives, with which they were closely associated. The peak period for legends seems to have been around the time of Pinagot's death. We encountered the use of legend earlier, in our discussion of the crosses in the forest of Bellême. Since the geographical scope of such ventures was even more limited than that of local histories, there was a tendency to look even further back in time. There is "not a single crossroad that is not associated with some legend," wrote one scholar in the year before Pinagot's death. "At this one a crime was committed. At that one a battle took place. At yet another a supernatural apparition astonished the region's naïve rustics. To commemorate these events, wooden crosses were stuck in the ground at the places where they occurred. . . . Stone monuments were erected in other places, and in some cases names were given to these spots so as to perpetuate the memory of what occurred."[79] With all the references to medieval events and to episodes from the Wars of Religion and the Revolution, it is difficult in many cases to distinguish between history and legend.[80]

Rather paradoxically, such practices only reinforced geographic superstitions that the Catholic Church had attacked since the beginning of the Counterreformation. Louis Dubois listed a number of these in 1809, during Pinagot's childhood, and confirmed their influence.[81] In the evening, around the fireplace, Dubois claimed that people liked to tell stories about places where evil spirits revealed themselves: the spirit of the first night of winter, people supposed to enjoy influence over wolves, Mère Harpine, will-o'-the-wisps, werewolves, and goblins. In 1823 Dureau de la Malle discussed these same superstitions, which he claimed were still quite influential toward the end of the eighteenth century. He added the terror of ghosts, "glowing woods, strange stumps, and carcasses illuminated by swamp fire."[82] His most important point, however, was that such phenomena were on the decline. According to him, people "who travel by night" were now spared, among them, millers, livestock dealers, and carters (such as Pinagot's father). In darkness tamed by long familiarity, once terrifying objects came to seem familiar.

In parallel with this historical and legendary reconstruction, the geography of the Perche was described as a scenic wonder. The same thing happened all over France. To do full justice to the phenomenon would take us beyond the limits of this study. In the first half of the nineteenth century, the Perche was described in terms ordinarily reserved for mountainous terrain but suitably scaled down. In 1823 Dureau de la Malle wrote that the "land is generally hilly, difficult, and uneven." The "mountains" were nevertheless "accessible." They offered "a *full abridgment* in miniature of the

Alps and the Pyrenees."[83] In other words, descriptions of the Perche reflected, with a certain time lag, typical descriptions of mountains scenery. They reveal the role of this sort of writing in the emergence of new ways of looking at landscape.

Two examples will suffice to illustrate how this picturesque image of the region was constructed. The first is an album entitled *Vues pittoresques prises dans les comtés du Perche et d'Alençon, dessinées d'après nature pas Louis Duplat et suivies d'un texte statistique et historique par Jules Patu de Saint-Vincent* (Picturesque views of the Perche and Alençon, sketched from nature by Louis Duplat and followed by a statistical and historical survey by Jules Patu de Saint-Vincent). The work details the chateaux and manors of the region and singles out two scenic viewpoints: Bellême and La Perrière. Pinagot thus lived his entire life between two of his province's picturesque panoramas.

A few years later, Paul Delasalle published *Une excursion dans le Perche*, a modest account of a scenic journey that he began on September 5, 1839. The date of composition was sufficiently late that the author felt it necessary to ward off criticism by deriding the very genre in which he wrote. He therefore carefully distinguished himself from tourists, of whom he made fun because they "questioned natives about how they are born, marry, and die," made sketches, and "found in their [i.e., the natives'] dialect unambiguous remnants of the Ur-language and in [their] habits feudal or even druidic traditions."[84]

Accompanying this thinly veiled criticism of *Ancienne Normandie* (1820–1825) and of the attitudes of Charles Nodier and Baron Taylor was a weary allusion to the "thousands" of picturesque narratives. "The traveler makes many sketches and takes notes. He ascribes a purpose to a buried foundation, assigns a date to a cornice or window, and after three days of adventurous riding returns home laden with fossiles, decorative stones, old coins, and souvenirs-treasures that he promptly puts on display in his cabinet of antiques." But when Delasalle makes an "excursion" to the hamlet of La Trappe, he does exactly the same thing. His thinks of the journey as a pilgrimage and prepares carefully with the aid of an extensive bibliography. His text is therefore a prime specimen, and it, too, pays homage to the view from La Perrière, which overlooks precisely the area in which Pinagot's life unfolded.

Delasalle might make fun of it, but the scenic journey was closely associated with the recording of local customs. Travel accounts often went beyond their implicit neo-Hippocratic premises. For Abbé Fret, as we saw earlier, such writing had a proselytical purpose. As he saw it, the point of recording present customs was to criticize the collapse of earlier ones, to deplore the vanishing of a golden age. He wanted to use ancient customs to mock and if possible stem the tide of modernity. His method was to compose short playlets intended to be read in the evening around the fire. Known as the "Molière of the Perche," Fret, the author and editor of a modest regional almanac known as the *Diseur de Vérités*, evidently hoped that his message would reach people living in the country. It is said that he could imitate Percheron accents to perfection. The abbé was banking on his proximity to his intended audience. Unlike most scholars who recorded local customs, he did not look down on his subject from above. He was a strange combination of scholar, "antiquarian," observer with a flair for the comic, and country priest.

By contrast, Dureau de la Malle seems a less original figure. In a book published in 1823, this aristocrat, a member of the Académie des Inscriptions et Belles-Lettres, investigated the logic implicit in the customs of the Percheron bocage, which he saw as a region so isolated as to be almost changeless. He therefore treated it as a conservatory. His book is filled with references that had become commonplaces since the publication of Arthur Young's *Travels in France* and of Chaptal's survey, references to the "forests of North America" and the Hurons and Iroquois. He also created a new type: *le sanglier*, or wild boar, his term for the Percheron peasant whose temperament was formed, or so Dureau claimed, by the ubiquitous hedgerows of the bocage. "Once a week," he wrote, these rustics "take their produce to the closest town, where their high, brusque voices, crude dialect, *immobility in crowds*, gray clothes, and long, unpowdered hair have earned them the nickname 'wild boars.'"[85] Make no mistake, if Dureau de la Malle had run into Louis-François Pinagot in the Bellême marketplace, he would have seen him as one petrified animal among many.

Bocage dwellers, he assures us, "have little communication with town dwellers." At the market they "speak to the townspeople only to agree on prices."[86] Often they returned home without even "drinking or eating at the inn. . . . The Revolution passed over them as a torrent." It is important for our purposes to note the existence of such beliefs.

What might images of space such as these, elaborated on the scale and with the methods we have just examined, have meant to someone like

Pinagot? How aware of them might he have been? At best he may have had a vague sense that various people were working to construct a Percheron identity. Still, it was essential for us to pause to consider how systems of representation such as these were fabricated, because they structure many of the documents we shall be using to identify traces of Pinagot's existence.

As for Pinagot himself, we may speculate that on a smaller scale he too had an identity shaped by the forest and the area around its border. In support of this conclusion we may cite the tensions that divided the town of Origny-le-Butin, the forms of sociability and unrest associated with this sylvan society, and the many coherent features of this deeply impoverished region.

"the low multitudes"

When Louis-François Pinagot left his house on the edge of the woods to go to the town of Origny-le-Butin or to one of the other "villages" on the forest's rim, how did he perceive the commune in which he lived, which became a subsidiary parish (*succursale de paroisse*) in 1820? What notion did he have of its identity? If he thought of himself as a member of a community, what effect did it have on his personality? Once again, we are in the realm of speculation, if only as to the proper balance (or tension) between his sense of himself as a parishioner, or member of a church, and as a citizen, or member of a civil community. The relative importance of these two identities differed from region to region; it also depended on the intensity of the movement of parish restoration, which occurred during Louis-François's youth.[1]

In his eyes, and no doubt in his memory as well, any number of markers served to identify people of whose moral qualities and temperaments he was vaguely aware and whose social position, wealth, and reputation he had always known in a more or less confused manner. These included the way in which the land was divided up, the unchanging pattern of farm plots and the density of the hedges that indicated their limits; the situation and shape of the buildings on each farm; the features of those buildings' facades; the state of their gardens; the appearance of the livestock; the characteristic

The title of this chapter is taken from Victor Hugo, *Les Misérables*.

sounds of voices;[2] the calmness of the courtyard, or lack of it; the discipline of the children, or lack of it; the neatness with which things were stored, or lack of it. These qualities were intimately associated with the people who lived at each place, who inhabited each house.[3]

Thus, if we are to understand the impressions that Louis-François formed, to say nothing of the feelings he felt, we must consider what there was for him to see when he looked beyond the "solemnity of the forest." Origny-le-Butin was, to repeat, the tiniest of towns, but Louis-François was born there and knew that in all likelihood he would die there. Of course, at his baptism, in contrast to the baptisms of his parents and his children, no church bells rang, because in Year VI of the Republic the law prohibited any outward manifestation of religion. But did anyone ever tell him this? Indeed, the Orne clergy often flouted the ban on bell-ringing.[4] Every Sunday (except between 1808 and 1820) Louis-François could have seen the beautiful twin sixteenth-century baptismal fonts in which he had been baptized.

If we deduct the area covered by the domanial forest, the extent of the land associated with Origny-le-Butin, its *terroir*, amounted to just 114 acres. The insignificance of this territory is one reason why the commune's inhabitants had no nickname. Markers of identity were few: not much more than the church, together with its crypt, its *sonnerie*, or bells (partially preserved), a Renaissance Pietà, a retable installed at the end of the Ancien Régime, and a beautiful polychrome statue of Saint Germanus.[5] Origny-le-Butin celebrated its patron saint on July 31, but the commune had no fair or market. No chateau rose from its soil. The modest home of Fidèle, Armand de Bloteau, at La Brumancière was little more than a manor befitting a minor notable. Nor was there a mill or atelier on Origny's territory.[6] No road of any importance passed through the town.

This was a period during which France, recognizing its architectural heritage, began recording the history of its rural buildings and monuments, but here there was virtually no reference to the past.[7] There is no mention of any local custom that might aid in the construction of such a history or, at the very least, encourage awareness of the immemorial. Minutes of municipal deliberations are silent in this respect. Of course, there was the Ugly Oak, but the effort to make this tree a centerpiece of local legend came quite late and was initiated by elites outside the commune. Local scholars tried to explain place names in the commune in historical terms, but their arguments were rather nebulous, and we have no idea what, if anything, people in Origny thought about them. Jean-François Pitard went so far as to claim that the English had burned the town in 1449 after plundering it (whence the name Origny-le-Butin: *butin* means plunder—trans.).[8]

Cultivated fields dominated the picturesque and varied landscape that could be viewed from local trails. But this was not the "green Normandy" of a later period: it was not until the end of Louis-François's life that much of this land was planted with grass.[9] In 1825, when the cadastre was established, 92 of the commune's 114 acres were under cultivation, or some 81 percent of the total surface area. Wheat and barley were the dominant crops, despite their low yield.[10] Oats, rye, and *méteil* (mixed wheat and rye) covered a much smaller area. Some Origny farmers may have begun to plant potatoes, but it is difficult to be sure because there were only 20 acres of potato fields in the entire canton in 1852.[11] By contrast, the absence of hemp in the commune is mentioned several times.

In 1825 roughly 30 percent of Origny's fields lay fallow. This percentage shrank somewhat over the course of Pinagot's life, however. A quadrennial system of *assolement*, or crop rotation, had very slowly begun to replace the older triennial rotation.[12] By mid-century the new system structured the landscape. The first year was for *blé fumé*, or wheat fertilized with manure, the second for barley or oats, and the third for *jeune herbe*, often clover, while the fourth was the fallow year in the usual sense, during which "old grass" was allowed to grow.[13]

Still, the most striking feature of this tilled landscape with its predominance of cereal grasses was the ubiquitous hedges, thick, dense, and tall. Branches from these shrubs hung over the fields themselves, partially obscuring them with their shadows. Here and there a stile, fence, or gap hidden by a bundle of branches offered access to the interior of what looked to outsiders like a dense maze.[14] Indeed, these "timeless" hedges may have been the most important element of the commune's "architectural" heritage. They were pruned, depending on the rate of rotation, every eight or nine years, during the winter. Cutting was done during the "wheat year," so as to allow the hedge time to regrow and prevent it from being nibbled away by grazing livestock during the fallow year.

The land around Origny was also densely planted with apple trees. In the canton of Bellême in 1852, orchards covered as much area as there was natural pasture and artificial pasture (fields of oat and rye) combined.[15] At that time the agrarian landscape still bore the stamp of a civilization based on wood, cereal, and apples. The canton of Bellême produced over a million gallons of cider, or 110 gallons per person, and cider cost less than twenty-five centimes per gallon.

Dwellings in Origny were mostly scattered, but this vague general notion conceals a broad diversity in actual practice.[16] The commune included the town proper, where the sound of bells could often be heard; several bustling "villages," such as Haute and Basse-Frêne, Haute and Basse-Croix, La Renardière, and L'Hôtel-aux-Oiseaux, where one would have heard women's voices and the sounds of spinners and clog makers at work; a few isolated farms, such as L'Hôtel-Migné, Langellerie, and La Trappe; small farms at Le Pressoir, L'Hôtel-Gaulard, and Le Moulin-Butin; and a few houses built in solitude, such as La Vigne-du-Clos. To the eye and ear each of these locales appeared quite different. The "villages" were built around a common courtyard, shared by all. This common space was a source of considerable conflict in these highly sociable communities.[17] Here, firewood was stacked, wagons were parked while unloading, and manure from the barn was piled temporarily. Chickens wandered about, but ducks and geese were rare, because their feathers would have fouled the water of the pond used to water the livestock.[18]

In 1825 the taxable revenue from all developed property in Origny amounted to just 896 francs, a ridiculously small sum, little more than a clerk's annual salary. Houses were built low and had few openings (because doors and windows were subject to taxation); to us they seem quite dark inside. Of 124 dwellings in the commune in 1839, only one had a gate for a coach. Seventy-seven (63 percent) had only two openings, and thirty-one (25 percent) had only three.[19] Such was the norm in Origny. Again, however, we must be careful to avoid anachronism and pointless hand-wringing. Pinagot's contemporaries lived by hygienic standards different from the ones that outside elites sought to impose on them. Their attitude toward light and darkness, hot and cold, was different from ours. They did not have the same requirements for air and light and did not detest darkness and enclosed space as we do.[20] In addition, the buildings used for work were vast, as is evident from the number of troops that could be billeted in them.[21]

Almost all of these houses had gardens, which were an essential element of everyday life. A poor man who managed to lift himself out of poverty would first purchase a small cottage with a garden of 1,000 to 5,000 square feet. In 1825 plots of this size covered a total of 12 acres.

Given the partitioning of the landscape, the density of the bocage, and the poor state of road maintenance, which encouraged trespassing on adjacent land, rights of way were a fundamental fact of daily life. People could always cut across fields, but animals and vehicles needed permission to pass. Like disputes over boundaries, disputes over rights of way were common.[22] The primary vehicle in use during Pinagot's youth was a heavy, two-wheeled wooden cart. Light carriages drawn by horses that pawed the ground while waiting for their masters in the marketplace came later.[23] They were not seen in the southern Perche until 1836, according to the schoolteacher Arsène Vincent, but when they came, their effect was nothing less than revolutionary. The advent of the bicycle had a similar impact later on.

What the light carriage did was to hasten the pace of travel, thereby expanding the sphere of social relations and reshaping the ritual of the visit. In this region the two-wheeled cart, the light carriage, and the bicycle would remain the primary means of transportation for people and goods until the middle of the twentieth century. Until then, the reign of the cart, known locally as a *banneau*, guaranteed the importance of the cartwright, whose workspace extended beyond the confines of his shop into the public space of the town. In Origny there was one cartwright, but, oddly enough, no blacksmith or harness maker, so that farmers had to travel often to La Perrière or Saint-Martin-du-Vieux-Bellême.

The noise of these heavy carts was deafening, especially near the forest. Farmers went to the forest not only for wood but also for stable litter. In 1861 the farmer of Les Ecouvailleries, a small farm on the forest's northern edge, asked the authorities for twenty-five tons, or ten cartloads, of raw material for his dung heap.[24] They charged him one franc per fifty cartload. In addition, he had to pay ten francs to the five individuals he employed to cut heather, drag it to the cart, and load it. It took three or four horses to pull such a load. Cutting and loading heather was one of the jobs performed by forest laborers; Pinagot did such work for a time.

Around Origny it was common to hear the sound of commands being shouted to animals, or, rather, beasts of burden (the word *animal* was rarely used in French; for animals that pulled the two-wheeled carts and plows in use in the commune, *bête* was the common term). The sonic environment of the fields was quite different from that of the forest. In the woods, voices rang out in friendly banter and mutual encouragement. Speech or chanting was a rhythmic accompaniment to work, a way of pacing one's breathing. By contrast, the farmer's onomatopoeic utterances and plowing songs humanized or aestheticized the fields as opposed to the savage forest. Such sounds amounted to a sonic appropriation of the workplace. They kept others informed of the progress of a man's work, of his ardor for the job and his schedule. They stood as evidence of his moral qualities and enthusiasm. Of course, they were also a way of communicating with the animals, of issuing commands, of offering encouragement or administering a reprimand. In a commune with no shepherds, no flocks, no cowbells, and virtually no dogs, such voice commands were the primary form of communication between man and beast.

Every day Louis-François Pinagot moved back and forth between the sonic environment of the forest and that of the bocage. The two were linked by a stream of smaller two-wheeled carts known as *diables* as well as the large, heavy ones described above, which were drawn by horses, the only draft animal in use in the commune. In 1872, four years before Pinagot's death, there were thirty-nine mares in Origny, one stallion, four geldings, and three colts under three years of age.[25] At that late date the Percheron was the dominant breed. The number of horses was obviously rather small compared with the number of farmers, and many farms could not have functioned were it not for a complex system of exchange of services: human labor was traded for animal labor; barrels of cider and stacks of wood were bartered for a specified number of days of a horse's services. These people were perpetually in debt to one another, and the theoretical price of one day of a mare's labor served as a kind of standard of exchange. Pinagot would have needed to transport wood and batches of finished clogs. Hence horses would have figured among his concerns, as well as in his tacit accounts with relatives, friends, and business contacts.

According to an agricultural survey carried out in 1852, there were relatively few head of cattle in Origny, mostly of mixed Le Mans—Norman breed.[26] Once again, however, we must be careful to avoid anachronism. The countryside that Pinagot knew did not support a density of livestock like anything that we know today. In 1872 the commune's cattle growers together owned only 139 head: 1 bull (it was standard for a single bull to service all of a commune's cows), 81 cows, 25 steer, heifers, and bullocks, and 32 calves under three months of age. Obviously, the primary purpose of raising cattle in this way was to produce milk and replenish the herd with young animals. Cattle were not fattened for market, but steer, heifers, and young bulls were sold at fairs. In addition, some calves were sent for butchering.

Most cows were put out to pasture as well as barn-fed. By 1852, however, a minority were kept in the pasture full time. Therefore, despite the small size of the herd, Pinagot would have been accustomed to the sight and sound of milk cows in the fields, along with mares. In 1852 the typical cow gave birth to six calves during the course of her life and produced 366 gallons of milk per year. This was enough to allow some of the milk to be used for making butter and cheese (at the rate of 2 to 2 1/2 gallons of milk per pound of churned butter and 1.3 gallons of milk per pound of cheese.

Hogs (people in Origny were more likely to use the word *cochon* than *porc*) were less numerous than one might think given the number of books that have been written about the rituals of slaughter. In 1872 the commune had five boars, three sows, and nineteen suckling pigs. It therefore appears that salted meat was not an essential part of the diet. Sheep and goats were of little importance in Origny. The records for 1872 indicate only four rams, eight ewes, and seven lambs. Hence sheep were no more than a curiosity here. The same would be true of the twenty-three goats and their seventeen kids, except that these were a precious resource for a few poor households. Until the Pinagots of Basse-Frêne could afford to feed a cow, they may well have owned a goat or two.

Since there was no grazing on common land, no communal herd or flock, and no prominent resident wealthy enough to keep a pack of hunting dogs, there were very few dogs in Origny-le-Butin. Still, we should be wary of the report that there were only ten dogs in the commune in 1872. Many dog owners would have been tempted to conceal the existence of their dog in order to avoid the tax. The closeness of the forest and the fear of rabies (mentioned by the cantonal commissioner in 1855) discouraged the raising of dogs as pets.[27] The poverty of the locale, the absence of any major road, the small number of outside visitors, and the fact that everybody knew everybody else made watchdogs unnecessary. In any case, the barking of dogs was probably a less common sound in Louis-François's vicinity than the barking of commands to draft animals. As for fowl, which are notoriously difficult to count and therefore relatively easy to hide, their number seems smaller than one might expect: the records for 1872 mention 590 chickens, 136 geese, and just 16 ducks.

As he moved about from place to place, Pinagot would have run into any number of people. The land around Origny-le-Butin was relatively densely populated at the time. Hand signals and verbal greetings were common. The effects of a dense population on the presentation of self, the ritualization of encounters, and the theater of social interaction were not limited to the city.[28] During Louis-François's lifetime, however, the frequency and variety of such meetings declined, as we shall see later on. Even though it became easier to travel about, there was a certain tendency to withdraw into the family and the home.

The population of Origny-le-Butin decreased from 430 in Year VIII (1800) to 331 in 1876.[29] The greatest density was achieved in 1836, when the population reached 512. The change in the population reflected the pattern for other rural communes in the region, except that changes in Origny seemed to come earlier than elsewhere.[30] There was rapid growth in the first third of the century, but the demographic-economic equilibrium broke down here quite early, on the eve of the July Monarchy. By 1851, in the midst of the great mid-century crisis, Origny had already lost 9 percent of its population. The decline continued during the difficult early years of the Empire. By 1856 the population was down to 449.

During the Empire's heyday, the population stabilized (it was 426 in 1866) before dropping a precipitous 21 percent in the next decade. In the space of a generation (1836–1876), between the falloff in fertility of the Pinagot household and the death of Louis-François, Origny-le-Butin lost more than a third of its residents (36 percent). This happened, moreover, despite a sharp increase in the population of the town (as opposed to the commune as a whole), for the town was the first way station in the rural exodus. Some villages, including Basse-Frêne, where Louis-François lived, were literally emptied. Why did such villages wither away? Because forest people were mobile by nature, and because they refused to live in abject poverty.

The age pyramid seems to have been aberrant as early as 1836. The elderly, or, more precisely, people in the age group from sixty to seventy, were clearly overrepresented. As a child and young man, Pinagot lived among people who had known both the Ancien Régime and the Revolution. In 1836 there were still more than a hundred such people in Origny. The age pyramid for 1851 exhibits the bell shape typical of communities in decline. The one for 1876 is a textbook case of demographic disaster. In that year there were 111 inhabitants of the commune between the ages of fifty and sixty, far outnumbering the 48 children under the age of ten. In 1872, 18 of a total of 140 houses (13 percent) were uninhabited, and no new houses were under construction.

As an old man Louis-François was surely aware of this hemorrhage. Still, there would have been many other elderly people around, and this may have made it easier for him to indulge in the pleasure of remembering the past-something that demographers tend to forget in their haste to deplore the depopulation of the countryside. Indeed, it may be that communities of the elderly who know each other well are the most conducive to a happy old age.

At first sight, the residents of Origny would all seem to have been of roughly equivalent status. There were no notables,[31] no rich people, no people of unusual skill or talent. But scale is important here. The fact that differences were small and people's lives seemed so similar forces us to pay attention to subtle distinctions. One important distinction was that between farmers, who were in the majority, and woodsmen, who constituted a small minority. In 1831, when Louis-François went to live in L'Hôtel-Migné, 63 of 139 male family heads were listed as farmers. They employed 13 domestic servants, as well as 28 day laborers who worked both in the fields and in the forest. In that same year only 15 heads of household were woodsmen. There were also 18 artisans, a priest, and a gelder. Most women were also listed as tillers of the soil. Twenty-four were said to be spinners, that is, employees of textile manufacturers in Bellême or La Perrière.

Sixty-three farmers shared the 114 cultivable acres of the commune. Obviously, the farms involved were tiny. So were properties. In 1825 sixteen people owned two or more acres within the territory of Origny, and only four of them lived in the commune. Henri de Bloteau, who lived in La Brumancière, passed for a major landowner in these parts although he owned just over three acres. So did Jean Bourdon au Plessis, who owned two acres. Two other men, Jean Courapied of Aubrière and François Herbelin of Haute-Frêne, passed for well-to-do with an acre apiece.

Six of the twelve other largest landowners resided in one of three nearby towns: Bellême (three), Mamers (two), and La Perrière (one). The others lived in towns a short distance away: Chemilly (three), Origny-le-Roux (one), Pervenchères (one), and Rémalard (one). The largest property, which belonged to the widow Bry, a resident of Bellême, covered 3.4 acres.

Thus there is every reason to believe that the farmers of the commune farmed very small areas, even if they were able to rent land from several different owners.

By contrast, many people owned very small plots, a simple garden or *pièce de terre* (piece of land), as locals called it. Eighty-nine individuals owned less than a tenth of an acre, and thirty-one owned between a tenth and two-tenths of an acre—not enough to feed a cow. As the nineteenth century wore on, there was a tendency for very small parcels of land to be combined.

On December 14, 1839, Father Pigeard set out to take a census of his parishioners. In the parish register he drew a table in which he assigned each household to one of three "classes." The first group included mendicants (16 percent of the total) and other very poor people, regardless of the reason for their poverty. All told, 47 percent of households fell into this category. The second group consisted of households that "owned a cow or perhaps a cow and a horse." Twenty-eight percent fell into this class, including Louis-François Pinagot, the husband of a Pôté, who was listed as a "poor" clog maker. The third group included twenty "adult persons who own two horses and other animals." The priest's classification makes it clear that ownership of livestock was an important criterion in the perception of social status—a key symbol in this milieu.

Other criteria were also important, however. In the countryside around Origny (not including the town proper), many subtle distinctions entered into the judgment of a person's status. Did a man (or woman) own his (or her) own land, and where was it located? Did he own a small house, a garden, or a "piece of land." Was he in debt? How large was his family? Were his children girls or boys? Or was he at a different stage in the life cycle of the family? Could he count on the support of an extended family? Did he have any marketable skill? Was he a clog maker or a day laborer? Did he work for himself or others? Was he dependent on a merchant or manufacturer? Sex, marital status, level of education, and reputation were also important criteria.

Geographical origin counted as well. No foreigners lived in Origny-le-Butin. It was not part of "the mosaic France."[32] The only outsiders were those who came from another *contrée*, or region. Since the commune was not cut off from the rest of the country, there were a fair number of such people. To be sure, the vast majority of residents of Origny had been born in the Orne *département*. Despite the proximity of the Sarthe and Eure-et-Loir, some 85 percent of the residents in 1872 were natives of the Orne. By contrast, only a minority of the inhabitants were natives of Origny (Louis-François was one of them). In 1831, for example, 69 percent of the men and 71 percent of the women living in the commune had been born elsewhere. One such was Anne Pôté, Louis-François's wife, who came from Appenay, while her grandmother, parents, uncles, and aunts all came from La Perrière.

It was especially common for woodsmen and their wives to come from other communes; many were natives of Saint-Martin-du-Vieux-Bellême or La Perrière, the most populous of the nearby communes. The forest seems to have acted as a barrier, however: few residents of Origny were natives of communes on its northern edge such as Eperrais or Bellavilliers. Migration flowed laterally along the southern edge of the ridge. If Louis-François married a woman who had been born in Appenay, it was because she lived with her parents, who had moved to Origny-le-Butin. In short, the population of the commune in 1831 consisted essentially of people who had moved there from elsewhere. This could only have diluted the local identity and perhaps weakened the cohesion of the community.

People did not travel far to live in Origny-le-Butin, however, and they chose their spouses from within a limited radius. Movements were generally confined to the three communes of La Perrière, Origny-le-Butin, and Saint-Martin-du-Vieux-Bellême. The kinship networks of most of the small commune's inhabitants therefore extended well beyond its limits, into its two larger neighbors. This further diluted the local identity. Indeed, we have already had occasion to remark on the significant place that La Perrière may have occupied in Louis-François's heart and mind.

In 1841 Pinagot was living in Basse-Frêne, although we do not know precisely how long he had been there. He would remain there until his death thirty-five years later. He probably spent half his life there. Between 1831 and 1841 the character of the working population of Origny-le-Butin had changed dramatically, although it is difficult to say how much possible changes in record-keeping procedures affect our view of what happened.[33] For example, in 1831 we find sixty farmers, sixteen artisans, and twenty-eight laborers, but in 1841 there were thirty-eight woodsmen-twenty-five clog makers, seven woodcutters, and six long sawyers. This increase reflects the growing importance of clog manufacturing.[34]

The change is clearest when we look at the occupations claimed by, or at any rate attributed to, women. Thirty-seven are identified as *cultivatrices*, or farmers: these were no doubt the best off of the lot. Thirty-seven are called "domestic servants," and 110 are listed as "spinners." These late female participants in the allegedly declining protoindustrial movement are particularly numerous in the families of woodworkers and day laborers. The wives of all six long sawyers declared themselves to be spinners, as did six of the seven wives of woodcutters and fifteen of the twenty-eight wives of laborers. With clog makers the connection is less clear: only nine of their wives are said to be spinners. We should, however, include widows and daughters of men in these trades as well. In short, it was common in Origny for woodworkers to be married to spinners, and this was the case in the marriage of Anne Pôté and Louis-François Pinagot.

Spinning, however, was an activity that extended well beyond this milieu. Farmers' wives were also involved. Thus spinning established a bridge between the farmers and the woodsmen, because women in both groups did the same kind of work, traveled to the same places, and entered into similar relationships with manufacturers.

The 1851 census at last makes it clear that three-quarters of the "farmers" (*cultivateurs*) in Origny-le-Butin were in fact tenant farmers (*fermiers*). The proportion of tenants subsequently declined as some of them came to own property. Despite these purchases, however, tenant farmers were still in the majority (58 percent) in 1872. Leases in the canton ran for four years.[35] This duration accorded with the four-year cycle of crop rotation. Farm leases began on either March 1 or November 1, or, less often, on Candlemas (February 2) or Saint John's Day (June 24). They were subject to tacit renewal. Indeed, tacit arrangements were the norm in this society of few words, where "it goes without saying" was the general rule.[36]

In order to understand Pinagot better, let us pause for a moment to look at Basse-Frêne. If we wish to grasp his local identity, it is probably more appropriate to consider the hamlet (*village*) rather than the communal level. In 1841 the "village" of Basse-Frêne was situated in the poorest part of the département, centered on Saint-Martin-du-Vieux-Bellême. In that year thirty-one residents, or 8 percent of the population, of Origny-le-Butin declared themselves to be beggars.[37] This was a typical percentage.[38] But the rate of mendicancy in Basse-Frêne was much higher: it was the poorest place in the commune. The village at that time had thirty-four residents, of whom twenty-three were adults. Eleven women were spinners, while two were listed as "farmers." Four men worked as clog makers, two as woodcutters, and three as laborers. Only one man described himself as a farmer. Of these twenty-three adults, five were officially considered beggars.

In that year, in addition to Pinagot, his wife (a spinner), and their young children, twenty-nine other people lived in Basse-Frêne. Among them were Marie Foussard, a widow and a spinner, who lived alone, and Michelle Virlouvet, another spinner who lived alone. Marin Lebouc's family was in serious distress: the husband, a mendicant, was a disabled laborer "crippled in both hands and feet," according to the local priest; his wife was a spinner. She had taken in a child to nurse, as had six other women in the commune. The family of François Cottin, Louis-François's step-grandfather, also seems to have been quite impoverished. The husband, aged seventy-seven, was a laborer; his wife, Anne Germond, was a spinner and beggar. They supported two children. Louis Bellanget, a clog maker, and wife, a spinner, may have been somewhat better off. Like the Pinagots, they had two children, but their household also included Marie Barbe, a spinner and mendicant.

Since Pinagot was officially recognized as indigent at this time, only two households seem truly to have escaped misery: that of Trouillard, a farmer, his wife, a spinner, and their son, a woodcutter; and that of Chevalier, a woodcutter, who lived with his wife, a spinner, and their daughter.[39]

What can we know about social distance, relative status, authority, and charity in such a milieu? Here we glimpse the "low multitudes" evoked by Victor Hugo-multitudes in which the individual seems to vanish. Basse-Frêne was a melodrama staged out of doors: a Gorbeau cottage, a horizontal and rustic *Jacressarde*, a Lille cellar raised above ground. Within the limits of Origny-le-Butin it was not an exception, however. It was much like Haute-Frêne, located a few hundred yards away and at that time home to fifteen individuals: seven spinners, two clog makers, two long sawyers, a crossbar maker, and three children. This was the village of Uncle and Aunt Drouin. In Les Querrières, where Uncle Louis-Sébastien Pinagot lived with his poor and disreputable family, the poverty was just as bad. In short, many of Louis-François's relatives were mired in the grinding misery of the forest's southern edge.

Ten years later, the situation seemed even worse. Economic distress along the forest's edge peaked at mid-century. Basse-Frêne was just as densely populated as before: thirty-three people lived there. Its thirteen houses sheltered thirteen families. Cohabitation of several couples under one roof was unknown here. In ten years the professional structure had changed: only adult women described themselves as spinners, and they had worked in the trade for some time. Younger women said that they made gloves.

To be sure, the number of beggars decreased, but poverty and women living alone were just as prevalent as before. For example, Anne Germond, the widow of François Cottin, became a beggar. Louis-François, now a widower, was still mired in poverty. He shared his house with five of his children, one of whom was a clog maker and three of whom made gloves. All told, there are twenty widows and widowers, out of a total village population of thirty-three. Obviously, people in Basse-Frêne did not remarry. For the Pinagots the future took the form of a new arrival: Pierre Renaud and his family. Renaud was a clog maker of forty-six, his wife was a spinner, and their four sons were clog makers. Five artisans in one family constituted a workshop large enough to aspire to a more comfortable position.

During the next five years (1851–1856), which correspond to the last years of the Second Republic and the first years of the Second Empire, inexorable, unbearable misery drove the poorest residents and many young people out of Basse-Frêne. In five years the village lost sixteen people, or 48 percent of its population. Pinagot now lived with two of his daughters, both of whom made gloves. His third daughter married one of the Renaud boys. The young man's father still lived in Basse-Frêne, where he had bought a small house in 1854.

By 1866 the complexion of the village had changed sharply yet again. The prosperity of the Empire made its influence felt, though in a modest way. The population was the same as in 1851: thirty-three. But there were no longer any beggars: begging had been outlawed. Fewer women lived alone: there were only two widows in the village, the Rouyer woman and the widow Beauchet, a spinner. Pinagot now lived alone in a small house he had acquired ten years earlier. He was the only widower in Basse-Frêne. Pierre Renaud, the father-in-law of one of his children, had bought a second house and two gardens nearby in 1862. Renaud had also acquired three small fields, one of them in the village. There were two young families that had grown up in the village, and three farm couples with children. In other words, the situation along the southern edge of the forest had stabilized. But this proved to be a temporary plateau.

By 1872, following a terrible drought and a period of war and occupation, only twenty-three people remained in the village. This time the decline was apparently irreversible, because four years later, in the year that Louis-François died, only fourteen were left. Above all, the composition of the group had changed radically. Of the twenty-three people who lived in Basse-Frêne in 1872, ten were members of the Pinagot family and six of the Renaud family.[40] Between 1830 and Louis-François's death in 1876, the village, which had been settled originally by people from elsewhere (poor woodsmen and spinners accustomed to short-range mobility) had become the patrimony of two settled families. While the older members of these families lifted themselves out of poverty, the younger ones forged bonds of kinship.

During his stays in Haute-Frêne, Hôtel-Migné, and, for a longer period, Basse-Frêne, Louis-François Pinagot lived through, and was no doubt aware of, a number of evolutions on several different scales: the commune's demographic rise and subsequent decline, the growth in the number of empty houses toward the end of his life, the increase in the town's population, the modest expansion in the range of his activities at work, and the change in the structure of the population of Basse-Frêne and nearby villages. He himself gradually slipped into poverty but eventually pulled himself out with the help of his children. Here, the Second Empire was the decisive period, marking the end of misery.

But the "familialization" of Basse-Frêne and its increased prosperity (though only in relative terms), which came with the death or exodus of its poorest residents and part of the younger generation, can also be seen as an impoverishment or withering away of social life. The decline in the number of women living alone (and men, too, except for Louis-François himself) and the gradual disappearance from the village of widows, young female spinners, beggars, and young unmarried clog makers no doubt reduced the diversity of exchanges, dampened the spirit of evening vigils, and stanched the flow of everyday charity. In any case, by 1872 Basse-Frêne had become a respectable village of clog makers and farmers in which family feeling and family obligations supplanted the social relations and mutual assistance that poverty and charity had fostered. The village had become an extended family, but it had once been far more than that.

elective affinities and kinship relations

Because historical demographics, which relies on time series, reveals collective rather than individual attitudes, it is of no use to us here. Nor would it do us any good to borrow the methods that anthropologists use to study families. My purpose is to sketch the outlines of a man's life, to imagine the feelings and emotional relationships that might have animated him and the forms of sociability that might have shaped his days. Hence it makes sense tõ focus on a subgroup of Louis-François's relatives: those who lived nearby or worked in jobs related to his and who might therefore have had a significant influence on his life. Since he left us no autobiographical narrative, we must make assumptions about which relationships mattered; there is, of course, no certainty that these assumptions are correct.

Families of the authoritarian type, in which the elderly patriarch designates his heir or heiress, were unknown in the Perche. Nor did the region belong to the rather limited area in which we find "fratries" or other forms of extended family systems in which relations among family members were governed by oftentimes complex agreements. In the Bellême area it was rare for more than one couple to live under a single roof. In this region relatives tended to live in clusters of hamlets separated by short distances, and subtle customs regulated relations among kin. Louis-François Pinagot lived within a dense network of nuclear families scattered among "villages" along the southern edge of the forest of Bellême, from La Perrière to Saint-Martin-du-Vieux-Bellême. Bonds of kinship were loose, not to say tenuous. In the nearby Eure département, young people were often hired out to uncles or cousins, but that was not the case here.[1] Family feeling, the emotional bond that kinship fostered, did not preclude a considerable margin of liberty. Individuals moved by elective affinities or antipathies were free to enter into close relations with relatives or to keep their distance as they pleased; no structure of authority created indissoluble bonds.[2]

If family relations were relatively relaxed, relations with neighbors were quite important, especially for individuals living in actual "villages" (that is, hamlets). It was for this reason that we paid such close attention to the residents of Basse-Frêne in the previous chapter. The village provided the framework within which individuals and families built their reputations (in this region there was no strong belief in "inherited character").[3]

Louis-François Pinagot could trace his origins to two families of "outsiders," if we can apply that term to the Pinagots and Cottins, who came from La Perrière, and to Grandmother Tafforeau, who came from Serigny. None of his forebears was a native of Origny-le-Butin. At the age of twenty, moreover, he married Anne Pôté, also a child of "outsiders" (from Appenay) who moved to the commune eighteen years after the Pinagots.

On November 10, 1787, Louise Tafforeau, Louis-François's future grandmother, married for the second time and settled with her husband in Le Pissot.[4] Her first husband, Jacques Pinagot, with whom she had lived in La Perrière, had died in March 1786. With him Louise had had (at least) seven children, among them Jacques, the father of Louis-François, who never knew his paternal grandfather. In 1787 Louise Tafforeau married a much younger man, François Cottin. Two and a half years later, two of her sons, Jacques and Louis-Sébastien, joined her in Origny-le-Butin, and her daughters Françoise and Catherine probably came with them.

On August 2, 1791, Louise Tafforeau arranged for her son Jacques to marry her young sister-in-law, Jeanne Cottin. Jacques, who had been to school in La Perrière, could read and write. Both he and his wife were twenty-one. Louis-François was a product of their marriage. He did not know his maternal grandmother and had few memories of his grandfather, who died when he was seven. Jacques and Jeanne settled in Haute-Frêne, where Louis-François spent his childhood.

Until he was twenty-seven, he could have visited his grandmother Tafforeau, who died in Le Pissot in 1825, and even after that he could have visited his uncle Cottin, who was also his grandfather by marriage. Twenty-one months after being widowed, Cottin, then in his sixties, married his servant Anne Germond, aged thirty-four. He had a son by her, Victor, in 1828. Thus Louis-François was already in his thirties when his step-grandfather discovered the joys of fatherhood. Shortly thereafter, François Cottin and his wife moved to Basse-Frêne to be near their nephew. They remained there until François died in 1846, at the age of eighty. All of Louis-François's ancestors were small farmers.

His father, Jacques Pinagot, a carter and farmer residing in Haute-Frêne, thus married his stepfather's sister. The couple had four children between 1792 and 1808. At an unknown date, Jacques took a young mistress: Marie Goisdieux, the illiterate daughter of a carpenter. In 1822 he and Marie had a daughter, Jeanne. From the census of 1831 we know that at that time Jacques was living alone with Marie and her child. When did he separate from Louis-François's mother? There is no way to know. We may speculate that his wife was unwilling to live in a ménage à trois. She probably went to La Perrière to live with her son-in-law, who was a clog maker from that town and the husband of Louis-François's younger sister, Jeanne-Catherine-Rose. In any case, it was in this son-in-law's house that Jeanne Cottin died on October 19, 1833, at the age of sixty-five. Louis-François was therefore thirty-five when he lost his mother, who was then separated from his father. Until then, given the short distances that separated L'Hôtel-Migné, where he lived, from Haute-Frêne and the town of La Perrière, it would have been easy for him to visit her.

On February 4, 1834, barely four months after his wife's death, Jacques Pinagot married his servant-mistress. In the following year, forty-three years after the birth of his first child, his new wife gave him a son, Jacques-Louis Pinagot. So Louis-François, now thirty-seven, found himself with a new half-brother when his own eldest boy was already sixteen.

Until he was twenty, Louis-François lived with his parents in Haute-Frêne. He was able to help his father with transporting wood and cultivating his small plot. He may have taken part in various misdemeanors in the forest in which his father was involved (poaching, illegal wood gathering, and the like). Louis-François grew up alongside his three sisters. When he was eight and a half, on January 25, 1807, he suffered the misfortune of losing the eldest of the three girls, who was fourteen at the time. We know nothing about the middle sister, who was a year younger than Louis-François. As was mentioned earlier, the youngest sister, who was ten years younger than her brother, was to marry a clog maker from La Perrière.[5]

Louis-François's immediate family would be a tempting case for a pyschoanalyst. His mother's brother married his paternal grandmother. He saw his eldest sister die when he was still a child. His elderly father produced two more children after Louis-François was already grown. Five of his own children were older than his half-brother. His father and mother were separated, and his father lived for many years in a notoriously illicit relationship with his mistress.

Let us turn our attention now to Louis-François's in-laws. I suspect that they played a large role in his life. In the village he was known as Louis Pinagot-Pôté.[6] He was only twenty, and therefore legally a minor, when he married Anne, who was a year older. At that time his father-in-law, Louis Pôté, was already sixty. He settled in Origny-le-Butin on May 1, 1807, where he was described as a farmer. His wife, Louise Chevauchée, a much younger woman, called herself a spinner.

The Pôtés were remarkable for their longevity. The children of Anne and Louis-François were able to enjoy the affection of their maternal grandparents for many years. Louis Pôté died in 1838 at the age of eighty, and his wife, who went at that time to live with her son Jacques in La Mazure, was still there in 1856. Louis-François's parents-in-law were moderately well off. In 1823 Louis Pôté's name figured on a list of the commune's thirty top taxpayers.[7] For a time he held the power of attorney of Mme de Villereau, the woman who owned his farm. The family fortunes suffered a sharp reverse in the next generation, however.

Let us return once more to Louis-François's ancestors and collateral relations on his father's side. These formed the bulk of his kinship group in Origny. Among them, we will concentrate on those most likely to have influenced Louis-François's life or sense of his identity. There is little to say about Aunt Landier (Françoise Pinagot). Born in La Perrière in 1782, she was a domestic servant in Year XII (1804) when she married François Landier, a boy from Vaunoise (in Origny-le-Butin, outsiders married other outsiders). Landier was seven years older than his wife. He was a farmer living in Moulin-Butin, a few hundred yards from Haute Frêne. He died on September 18, 1827, at the age of fifty-three. A month and a half later, his widow gave birth, in her house in Moulin-Butin, to a posthumous son, Pierre Landier.

In sharp contrast to the enigmatic Aunt Landier, we have the substantial figure of Aunt Drouin (Marie-Catherine Pinagot). Born in La Perrière in 1784, Marie-Catherine would live to the ripe old age of eighty-nine, preceding Louis-François to the grave by a scant three years. Throughout his life he would have been able to visit this aunt, who described herself as a spinner when she married an illiterate clog maker in 1811. As we have seen, this pairing—clog maker married to spinner—was typical of the area, and Louis-François would emulate the model in his marriage to Anne.[8] Marie-Catherine's husband, Jacques-Augustin Drouin, was slightly younger than his wife and a native of the commune. His family had roots in Haute-Frêne, where he lived with his widowed mother and sister. He would remain there all his life. In 1824 he bought a small house and a barn in the village, along with a small piece of land (roughly a tenth of an acre) known as "Bidaux's field."

Uncle and Aunt Drouin—familiarly referred to as *les Gustins*—were a fixed point in a family whose members were for the most part constantly on the move (over short distances to be sure). Louis-François was thirteen, the age of apprenticeship, when his aunt married Jacques-Augustin. There is a good chance that it was Uncle Drouin who taught the boy how to make clogs. For years he would have been able to turn to this elder fellow trades-man for advice: his presumed mentor did not die until 1863, at the age of seventy-seven, when Louis-François was sixty-five.

Besides Aunt Drouin and her husband, there was also a poor uncle, Louis-Sébastien Pinagot, the patriarch of a large family whose history is a saga worthy of Victor Hugo. Like Aunt Drouin, Louis-Sébastien was born in La Perrière, on May 2, 1775. When he married in Year VI (1798), the year of Louis-François's birth, he was employed as a domestic servant in Basse-Frêne (this was not a promising sign). Louis-Sébastien never became any-thing more than a laborer and woodcutter. Like all his male offspring, he was a forest worker. The split between farmers and woodsmen divided Louis-François's family as well. With his wife, Françoise Deschamps, a spinner and the daughter of a laborer from Chemilly who was the same age as he, Louis-Sébastien settled first in Haute-Croix and later, for a longer time, in Les Querrières. The couple had many children and lived long enough to be miserable in their old age. Aunt Pinagot left her husband for a time and courted scandal by living with a mason by the name of Loitron. She died in Haute-Croix, in 1854, at the age of seventy-nine. Louis-Sébastien passed away two years later at the age of eighty-one. His aunt and uncle therefore figured in Louis-François's family drama until he was well advanced in years.

The Pinagot-Deschamps were wretchedly poor; without ever leaving Origny-le-Butin they moved from one house to another as their fortunes waxed and waned. Their children, who were treated as outcasts by the village community, tried to stay close to their father. We encounter a number of them at charity work sites. After a long period of residence in Les Querrières, Louis-Sébastien and his wife settled again in Haute-Croix (where their presence was recorded in 1846 and 1848). At that time they had taken in an infant to nurse. Five years later Louis-Sébastien was characterized as a "laborer-mendicant" in the census list of Port-Chopin. He was then seventy-six. He ended his days as a widower in Les Querrières, where his son Etienne had taken him in.

Louis-François was surrounded by cousins. Of these we shall focus on those who lived within a short distance of his various residences. The closest was Jacques-Pierre Drouin, eighteen years younger than Louis-François, who was also a clog maker in Haute-Frêne. He, too, married a spinner and fathered a son, Bazile Drouin, who grew up to become a clog maker in Haute-Frêne and to marry a glove maker. Three generations of clog makers married to spinner/glove makers thus succeeded one another in the Drouin family of Haute-Frêne. Jacques-Pierre Drouin was well respected. His fellow citizens made him a corporal in the national guard. In 1863 he bought a piece of land and a house in Haute-Frêne. In 1873 his name appeared on a list of the commune's top taxpayers. By the 1840s, then, Anne and Louis-François were living in Basse-Frêne among relatives with whom they had a great deal in common. It is a good bet that Louis-François would have felt at ease in the Haute-Frêne of his childhood, where his father continued to reside, especially after one of his sons, Pierre-Théodore, also a clog maker, came to live in the village in the 1850s.

The Pinagot cousins—sons and daughters of Louis–Sébastien—were numerous. Louis-François no doubt felt sorrow over Louise-Rosalie's death at the age of nineteen. A spinner, she was only a few months older than he. Her brother, Jean-Louis Pinagot, soon left Origny to work as a woodcutter, and we lose track of him at that point. Cousin Anne-Françoise, born in 1809, was seduced and abandoned. An unwed mother at the age of nineteen, she nevertheless found a man to marry her when she was twenty-two.[9] He was the son of a spinner from La Perrière. In 1853 we find her illegitimate son working as a clog maker in Haute-Frêne.

The most colorful figure in this family saga was none other than Cousin

Angélique-Julienne-Agathe Pinagot, who faced poverty courageously and thumbed her nose at what people said about her. She was born in 1812. After working at first as a spinner, she became a glove maker when the economic climate changed. An illiterate, she bore seven illegitimate children. Obviously men liked her. All of her children survived. Cousin Angélique was a fighter.[10] During the winter she gathered bundles of firewood in the snowy forest, which of course made her a habitual criminal. When not living with her father, poor Louis-Sébastien, who gave her and her brood a roof over their heads, she did spinning for industrious widows.

In 1833 she gave birth to Jacques Marin; in 1836 Louis was born; and in 1838 it was the turn of Louise-Marie, who grew up to be an unwed mother herself—illegitimacy was hereditary among the Pinagots—before marrying a weaver in 1862. At this point the intervals between births grew longer. Héloïse was born in 1844, Marie-Fortunée in 1846, and Estelle-Léontine in 1850. In that year Angélique left her father's home for a place of her own, where she lived with five of her illegitimate children.

Age slowed her down, though. In 1858 she married Louis-François Lorillon, an illiterate farmer originally from Chemilly but living at the time in Hautes-Folies. He was sixteen years younger than she, and he was certainly not the father of her first several children, the oldest of whom was by then twenty-five. Two years later, however, fertile Angélique gave Lorillon a son of his own.

In 1861 we find Cousin Angélique, now forty-nine, living in Les Querrières with her thirty-three-year-old husband, her daughter Louise-Marie— the mother of a seven-month-old baby—her five-year-old son, and a child she had taken in to nurse. In subsequent years she moved with Lorillon back and forth between Les Querrières and Les Fourneaux. When her children were old enough to be hired out as servants, she placed them with farmers in the area.

Compared with Angélique, her brother Etienne was a rather pallid figure. He was a woodcutter and farmer living in Les Querrières when he married a spinner. We know very little about him, except that in 1851 or 1852 he had a house built in Les Querrières and bought another in 1855. Like many of these poor woodworkers, he was keen to own a small dwelling of his own. In 1868, at the age of fifty-four, he was officially listed as a cripple. He and his wife had several children, little cousins for Louis-François's sons to play with: Benoît, a laborer and carter who lived in Les

Querrières, Virginie, a glove maker who would marry a clog maker, and little Isaïe.

Besides cousins, Louis-François had brothers-in-law and sisters-in-law whom he saw almost daily. Jacques Pôté, ten years younger, was a poor, illiterate laborer who moved from village to village within the commune: La Basse-Croix, Les Vignes-de-la-Coudre, La Renardière. It was he who took in his mother when she was widowed. At the age of twenty-nine, Marin Pôté, born in Appenay in Year XI (1803), well before the Pôtés moved to Origny, married a widow of sixty-three. Throughout his life he worked as a carter and laborer.[11] He was one of the few members of this generation of the extended family who could read and write.

There is every reason to believe, however, that the person to whom Louis-François felt closest was his sister-in-law Anne-Louise Pôté. A spinner who died in 1881 at the age of eighty-seven, Anne-Louise married Julien Courville, an illiterate clog maker originally from Saint-Martin-du-Vieux-Bellême, who was five years younger than she, the same age as Louis-François. In other words, the two sisters, Anne-Louise and Anne, found themselves in identical situations: both married clog makers born in 1798. After marrying, the two young couples lived for a time side by side in Les Vignes-de-la-Coudre. In 1845 one of Louis-François's sons, Pierre-Théodore, himself a clog maker, married Marie-Louise, a spinner and glove maker and one of the daughters of Anne-Louise and Julien Courville. Louis-François's brother-in-law, who was the same age and worked in the same trade, became his kinsman by marriage twice over. And Louis-François must have been proud of the connection, since Courville was a corporal in Origny's national guard unit. Anne-Louise seems to have been the only child of the Pôtés to have avoided downward social mobility.

Unfortunately, Louis-François's wife, Anne, remains quite mysterious. Born in Appenay on December 9, 1796, she was eighteen months older than her husband. Just before her marriage she was a "farmer" in La Croix, where she had gone to live with her parents on March 1, 1808. After her marriage she was always listed as a spinner. If we want to try to imagine what she looked like, it is worth saying a word or two about the stature of women in this milieu. The average (as well as median) height of the fifty-six female workers in Saint-Martin-du-Vieux-Bellême above the age of twenty was slightly less than 5'1" (based on an 1855 survey).[12] We know nothing about the married life of Anne and Louis-François, except that they stayed together, did not cause any scandal, and together produced eight children, all of whom were still living when their mother died on January 1, 1846, at the age of forty-nine in the poor hamlet of Basse-Frêne on the edge of the domanial forest.

The oldest boy, named Louis-François like his father, was born on July 2, 1819. His parents married on July 7, 1818, so there is no reason to think that theirs was a "shotgun wedding."[13] This slightly nearsighted youth grew up to be a relatively tall 5′4″ and learned to read and write.[14] He also knew clog making, which he probably learned from his father. Nevertheless, in 1841, when he was twenty-two, he was employed as a domestic servant in Le Plessis alongside his Cousin Fine (Joséphine), the eldest of the Courville daughters. When he married in 1843, he was again paired with a female servant four years older than he in L'Hôtel-aux-Oiseaux. Later, he would identify himself as a clog maker in the same hamlet. In the meantime, he and his wife seem to have moved in with one of the wife's aunts.

In 1849 or 1850 the couple left Origny-le-Butin. They lived in Appenay until 1866. On November 1 of that year, Louis-François Jr. moved with his wife to Haute-Croix after acquiring several pieces of land in the village and having a house built there.[15] He was in a position to become a minor notable in Origny, and we shall have occasion to encounter him again later on. The fact that he and his wife had only one daughter may have contributed to this success. Marie-Hélène, the oldest of Louis-François's grandchildren, was born when her parents were living in L'Hôtel-aux-Oiseaux. A grandfather at forty-six, Louis-François would continue to live in proximity to his granddaughter until his death.

In 1823, when the couple was living temporarily in Saint-Martin (an opaque episode in Louis-François's life), a second son was born: Pierre-Théodore. Of all the children, he was the one who would follow most closely in his father's footsteps. Deemed to be of weak constitution, he was excused from military service.[16] At twenty-two he married his first cousin, Marie-Louise Courville, a spinner and glove maker. After working for a while as a laborer in La Bonde, Pierre-Théodore made clogs in Basse-Frêne alongside his father. Later he would ply the same trade in Les Fourneaux and Haute-Frêne in proximity to his grandfather, uncle, and cousin Drouin, two of whom were clog makers. Pierre-Théodore had three children with his wife: Isaïe, Amandine-Olympe, and Félicie-Estelle. All three lived in Haute-Frêne, a few hundred yards from their grandfather.

Louis-François's third son, Eugène, was born in L'Hôtel-Migné in 1825. At twenty we find him working as a domestic in La Gaucherie alongside his cousin Fine Courville. Clearly, then, when the boys (other than Pierre-Théodore) were old enough to work, Louis-François and Anne placed them with nearby farmers to whom they were not related. Like all his brothers, Eugène was also a clog maker. Despite a "weak constitution" acknowledged by the military examiners, he drew a bad lottery number and was drafted into the Seventy-Second Infantry Regiment in Versailles. To be sure, he was a strapping lad of 5'6".[17] Obviously, the Pinagots were not wealthy enough to pay a substitute to do military service in place of their son. After Eugène's discharge from the military, we lose track of him.

The eldest daughter, Anne-Marie-Louise, was also born in L'Hôtel-Migné, in 1827, and lived with her parents while working as a glove maker. After her father was widowed, she went on living with him until she married a clog maker from the village, Louis-Pierre Renaud. Younger than his wife, he came from Saint-Martin and was able to read and write. The couple lived near Louis-François, to whom they gave five grandchildren.[18] In 1861 the Renauds took in a nursling. They also provided lodging for the youngest son, Victor-Constant.

The second daughter, Françoise, born in L'Hôtel-Migné in 1830, lived with her father and was still unmarried at the age of twenty-five. Then she drops out of sight, perhaps because she married outside the commune.

The fourth son, Evremont, born in 1832, suffered a more tragic fate. Despite what military examiners termed his "weak eyesight and sallow complexion," to say nothing of his illiteracy, he was a tall boy at 5'4" and deemed fit for military service. As a private in the Fifth Regiment, he died in the corps infirmary at Boulogne in November 1854 shortly after being recruited.[19] It is easy to imagine the sorrow of his father, who was then a widower living in Basse-Frêne.

Julienne-Philomène, born in 1837, also lived with her parents and then her father until her marriage. (Her first name indicates that she was placed under the patronage of a saint conjured up out of thin air in the nineteenth century.[20]) A glove maker, she learned how to read and write. In 1859 she married not a clog maker but a weaver from the town of Origny. Louis Bourdin, her young husband, was the son of a laborer. The couple settled in the commune's center, unlike all the other members of the extended family. Four children were born of this marriage between 1860 and 1870.

Louis-François's youngest boy, Victor-Constant, born in 1841, also suffered from a "weak constitution."[21] Declared unfit for service because of his brother's death, he became a clog maker in Basse-Frêne and later in Maisons-Neuves. Unlike Julienne-Philomène, Victor-Constant was illiterate. In 1865 he married a glove maker from Basse-Frêne, the daughter of a laborer and a glove maker who were born in Appenay, the commune from which her husband's mother's family came originally.

This portrait of Louis-François's immediate and extended family illustrates what these people would have known about one another's backgrounds. It calls for several remarks, in no particular order. The first is biological in nature. The reader has no doubt been struck by the longevity of many of these desperately poor people. The younger Pinagots were surrounded by any number of elderly relatives. Thus distant memories would very likely have been passed on, and values, customs, and traditions handed down from generation to generation. Louis-François himself, his father, Grandmother Tafforeau, Grandfather Cottin, Aunt and Uncle Drouin, Uncle and Aunt Pinagot, Louis-François's in-laws (the Pôtés), and Cousin Courville all lived to be at least seventy-five, and some lived far longer than that. The fact that different generations of this extended family lived together within a very small area was an essential characteristic of everyday life.

The Pinagot women were spinners and/or glove makers. The men were clog makers, woodcutters, or, less often, farmers. To some extent they were also laborers. As adolescents, many of the boys and some of the girls were placed with farmers as domestic servants. In short, a certain versatility was required: all the men in the family were apt to work in the forest during the winter and as laborers whenever local farmers needed extra hands; this was in addition to their work as clog makers.

The reader will already have noticed the high degree of social and professional endogamy in this extended family. Here, there was no escaping one's milieu. There was a monotonous regularity in the choice of a spouse. Clog makers, woodcutters, and carters (all of whom were laborers on the side) married spinners, some of whom later became glove makers after having worked as servants in their youth. Louis-François's father-in-law, Louis Pôté, and his son-in-law Bourdin, a weaver, were exceptions to the rule, as was his eldest son, who devoted himself entirely to agriculture in his mature years. Marriage did not provide a true opportunity for upward social mobility to any members of this clan, male or female.

Furthermore, geographical endogamy was just as significant as social and professional endogamy. The Pinagots chose mates from their immediate proximity. Two of Louis-François's children found happiness in Basse-Frêne, where they lived, while one son went all the way to Haute-Frêne, a few hundred yards away, to seek a wife. Nevertheless, the person chosen was often the son or daughter of an "outsider." In most cases the young bride was slightly older than her husband.

Toward the end of Louis-François's life, there were more than fifty members of his extended family living in Origny-le-Butin. All lived in the country, except for the Bourdins, who lived in town. They were concentrated in the villages along the forest's edge, especially Haute- and Basse-Frêne—where Louis-François spent most of his life—Haute-Croix, and Les Querrières. The Pinagots rarely left these few hamlets except when they held jobs as domestics. One exception was Louis-François Jr., the eldest son of our Louis-François, who went to Appenay to make his modest fortune. In other words, the family's horizons were limited. The only opportunity for broadening would have been in visits to or from the uncles, aunts, and cousins living in La Perrière.

Proximity (social and professional as well as geographical), together with the large size of the family and the complexity of relationships among cousins, probably fostered a certain solidarity and facilitated the exchange of services that has to be taken into account when gauging a person's status and position. Family ties may have been instrumental in arranging apprenticeships, transportation of goods such as wood, harvested crops, and finished clogs, loans of animals, and barter of labor and food. Mutual assistance was no doubt required in certain seasons as well as in times of scarcity. The cohesiveness of the family unit could only have been reinforced by joint poaching expeditions and socializing among cousins. And then, of course, there was concern for the family's honor, although this seems to have been much less of a factor here than in regions where the authoritarian structures of the stem family were paramount.[22]

A network of friends further extended these types of mutual support. The time has come to turn our attention to it, and to that end we shall have to make do with the list of people invited by Louis-François, his parents, and his children to witness marriages, births, and deaths. Of course, some of these were merely incidental witnesses, honored with invitations simply because they lived in a certain place or enjoyed a certain social status. In the cases that concern us, however, these seem to have been relatively rare.

Two models of friendship existed, one early, the other late.[23] In Louis-François's generation, the usual practice was to invite large numbers of family members living nearby, and if additional witnesses were needed, to invite fellow woodworkers. For instance, Louis-François invited Louis Bellanger, a clog maker in L'Hôtel-Migné, to serve as a witness on three different occasions; Louis Baveux, a cartwright at L'Hôtel-des-Oiseaux, was invited once. Or he might invite some of the wealthier farmers such as François Herbelin and Julien Boutier. Some of them belonged to the municipal council, and to invite people such as this connoted not friendship but a desire for respectability. Only two of the fourteen people invited as witnesses were from the town: César Buat and the weaver Nicolas Bosse, both of whom counted as minor notables.

In the next generation, when Louis-François's daughters and sons married and when their children were born, the friendship network was wider. Of a total of twenty-one witnesses, only four were family members: three Pôtés and one Pinagot. Fourteen were people from the town. César Buat, the mayor, and his son were invited five times; the tobacconists, Félix de Bloteau and Nicolas Basse, were invited twice; Louis Frénard, the baker, and Louis d'Aubert, the tailor, once each; and one laborer and one sawyer also received invitations. The three other witnesses were farmers who lived outside the town: Daboineau of L'Hôtel-aux-Oiseaux, Louis-Tranquille Printemps of Saint-Eloi, and Chevallier, who lived by "Richard's Ford."

This evolution suggests a loosening of parental authority, greater independence of choice on the part of the children, and the growing influence of the town. Two prestigious friendships bridged the gap between the early model and the late one: one with the Bloteau family and the other with the Buat family. Armand-Fidèle de Bloteau, a former officer in the royal army and former mayor of Origny-le-Butin, was a witness at Louis-François's wedding in 1818.[24] The date fell between the former émigré's removal from office and his arrest. Later, Félix de Bloteau was called upon when that family moved down the social scale. Still, it was the Buats—father, son, and grandson—who seemed to be called most often, unless the frequent invitations to César Buat can be explained simply by the fact that he was mayor.

If we look at the godparents connected with the second generation, the diminished dependence on family members becomes even clearer. Half of the twenty-six godfathers and godmothers of the thirteen of Louis-François's grandchildren who were baptized in Origny-le-Butin were members of the family: two grandfathers, four uncles, three aunts, and four cousins. The others—five godfathers and eight godmothers—were neighbors or friends, and after 1860 these non-family members were in the majority.

As one might expect, the sexual relationship between Louis-François and his wife remains a mystery.[25] They seem to have practiced some form of birth control, but we cannot be certain of this since we have no idea whether or not the taboo on sex during breast feeding was respected. The intervals between births suggest that the efficacy of any birth control measures was spotty. Not until 1832 is there any evidence that it was effective, but after that date we note an interval of three years and eleven months between the birth of one child and the conception of the next. After 1841 Anne conceived no more children, but by then she was forty-four.

Cousin Angélique would not have given birth to seven "natural" children if her various partners had regularly practiced coitus interruptus. Of course, she had a reputation for being "easy," so that her lovers might not have felt the need to take precautions. Among the Pinagots of Les Querrières, illegitimacy reached record heights. Angélique, her sister, and her eldest daughter all conceived children out of wedlock. We do not find evidence of illicit sexual relations in other branches of the extended family, however, except for the adulterous affair between Jacques Pinagot and his servant, Marie Goisdieux. This was the only illicit couple other than Angélique and her lover Lorillon.[26]

The time has come to get back to Louis-François Pinagot. His life was difficult throughout. By the time he was forty-three he had eight children to support, and when he was forty-seven his wife died. He was lucky in one respect, however: in the conscription lottery he drew the number 55.[27] This allowed him to marry at the age of twenty. When he and his wife were living in L'Hôtel-Migné, their situation deteriorated with the birth of each new child. What we know about incomes in the clog-making and spinning trades suggests that the most difficult period came between 1830 and 1832, when the couple was supporting five or six children, the eldest of whom was not yet old enough to work. It was at this point that Louis-François was officially declared to be indigent.

In Basse-Frêne Louis-François's circumstances remained straitened until 1855. When he was widowed in 1846, he had seven children to support (his eldest son had aleady married). By then, however, Pierre-Théodore was twenty-three and working alongside his father making clogs; Eugène was in the army; and Marie, his eldest daughter, aged eighteen, and Françoise, the next eldest, aged fifteen, both spinners, were able to take care of the three smallest children. Louis-François's years as a widower were certainly not the most difficult time of his life.

Between 1846 and 1861 his burden gradually lightened as his children established lives of their own. He managed to put aside enough money to buy a house, in which he lived alone. In fact, his solitude was more apparent than real: five of his children settled in Origny-le-Butin. Three of them lived near their father, either in Basse-Frêne itself or in Haute-Frêne close by. Thirteen of his grandchildren also lived in the commune.

We must be careful not to paint too idyllic a picture, however. Although death spared most of his children (only Evremont and Louis-François Jr. died during his lifetime), we have seen that his male offspring were found to be of "weak constitution." Four of his school-age grandchildren figured on a list of indigent pupils compiled in November 1871, including three who lived near him in Basse-Frêne.[28]

The family met with numerous disappointments. Up to the time of Louis-François's death in 1876, we detect no upward social mobility other than in the case of the eldest son, mentioned earlier. To be sure, we detect no downward mobility either, if such a thing was even conceivable. The children of Anne and Louis-François received very little education. We know for certain that two of them learned to read and write, as did two of their sons-in-law, while three others remained illiterate.

Let us try to imagine Louis-François as he would have been in his later years—between 1871 and 1874—that is, between the departure of the Prussians and the two deaths that occurred in the family just two years before Louis-François's own death.[29] He would have been surrounded by his offspring, most of whom were concentrated in Haute- and Basse-Frêne, Haute-Croix, and the town of Origny. His children and grandchildren lived within overlapping circles of cousins. We can easily imagine the games these young people played, their social visits and treks across surrounding fields. But we have no idea how these sons and daughters of poor woodworkers might have related to the children of farmers.

True, we know that in Normandy the influence of the family was not as strong as it was in many other regions. Still, everything that has been said thus far forces us to recognize the crucial importance of the family circle in the life of Louis-François Pinagot. Not only the fabric of his interpersonal relations, the substance of his conversation, and the nature of his work but also his honor and reputation, his attitude toward his hamlet community and its attitude toward him, would have been influenced by his large and growing extended family. So would the "affective geography" structured by the grouping of his relatives along the forest's edge. All these people, related by blood, would have beaten joyful and familiar paths to one another's doors—unless, of course, hatred turned the family into a nest of vipers. This seems unlikely, however, since no record of any such hatred has been preserved in the archives.

the language of the illiterate

We know nothing about Louis-François Pinagot's physical appearance other than that he was 5′5″ tall. For this time and place, in other words, he was a tall man.[1] Support for this assertion comes from records of the size of conscripts from the Mortagne district in the period 1802–1809[2] and of youths from the canton of Bellême in the cohort of 1819.[3] Unfortunately, the lottery lists for conscripts of Pinagot's cohort (1818) have been lost.[4] As a result, we do not know the particulars of his appearance.[5] Had his record survived, we would know the color of his eyes and hair and any infirmities from which he may have suffered. As it is, we know only that he drew number 55, which was apparently a lucky one (unless he was exempted from service for some other reason). In any case, he married in 1818 at the age of twenty, which he would not have done had he been called to the colors.

It is worth noting, however, that the young men among whom he grew up appear to have been reasonably healthy compared with the national average.[6] The young men of Bellême did not suffer from genetic pathologies, diseases associated with dietary deficiencies, or physical deformities. Of the 147 young men of the class of 1819 who were examined, only 26 (or 18 percent) were exempted for any reason other than "deficiency of height." Only one "pronounced goiter" was detected, along with one epileptic and "one man with a limp." Two were deaf and four stammered. Three suffered from hernia, and three others had a withered arm or hand.

Only one had a "deformity of the feet." Other exemptions were granted for varicose veins, ulcerated or "flat feet," or "weakness of constitution."

By contrast, we know for sure that Louis-François Pinagot was illiterate, as was his wife. Many documents attest to this, including all civil records that mention his existence.

Jacques Pinagot, Louis-François's father, could sign his name and probably read and write a little. Why did the level of instruction decline from one generation to the next? The reasons are obvious. The father grew up in La Perrière during the reign of Louis XVI. Louis-François was born in Origny-le-Butin at the end of the Revolution, hence he would have lacked the means to acquire the rudiments. He should have attended school from 1805 to 1811, but during that period it would have been difficult for him to do so.[7]

It is unlikely that there were any teachers in Origny-le-Butin in those years. To be sure, we cannot prove that this was the case. But we do know for certain that "there [was] no school in this commune" in 1819; "the children [were] sent to the teacher in Chemilly."[8] This meant traveling a distance of two and a half to three miles. Furthermore, "the school [was] sustained by contributions from the parents," which would have put it beyond the reach of the son of a poor carter-farmer from Haute-Frêne, a village even farther from Chemilly than others in the commune. Of seventy-one children from Origny-le-Butin "eligible" to attend school in Chemilly in 1819, only twelve (or 17 percent: eight boys and four girls) actually did so. The other fifty-nine, we are told, were "deprived of instruction."[9] A comparison of the two communes, roughly equivalent in size, reveals a great disparity. Of the seventy-five school-age children in Chemilly, twenty-four boys and six girls, or 40 percent of the total, attended school.

What was it like to be illiterate during Louis-François's lifetime? Was illiteracy seen as a debilitating handicap likely to diminish a person's self-esteem? How important was literacy among the people with whom he would have come into contact? The answers to questions such as these depend on which phase of his life we are considering.

When Louis-François was growing up, most of the residents of Origny-le-Butin could neither read nor write. In this respect he was no different from any other conscript from his commune or, for that matter, from the rest of the Perche.[10] The fact that the son of a carter-farmer who worked as a laborer and apprentice clog maker was illiterate would have surprised no one, and it would have caused Louis-François little pain. Did he even want an education? There is no reason to believe that he did. Reading and writing did not become essential skills until later. Even more significant, the minor notables of Origny whom he might have met during his childhood—the wealthiest landowners and farmers—were not much better educated than he was.

The records of the deliberations of the municipal council offer detailed information about thirteen of the fifteen most highly taxed individuals in Origny-le-Butin. On August 28, 1804, when Louis-François was just barely of school age, five of them could neither read nor write, two "could sign their names a little," and three were capable "of reading a little and writing very little." Michel Virlouvet was "well versed in reading and not so well in writing."[11] In other words, only two of these fifteen people could read or write at all well. This report is unusually interesting because it did not classify individuals according to preestablished criteria. The document reveals subtle differences that would have emerged only after long familiarity with the notables in question.

By 1872, four years before Louis-François's death, the status of illiteracy in this community had changed. If we take the census results for that year at face value,[12] the majority of young people in Origny-le-Butin could read and write.[13] Yet only 30 percent of adults above the age of twenty possessed both skills, and only 16 percent were able to read but not write.[14] The literacy rate among adult women lagged behind that of men, moreover; this was not the case among the young.

A study of the nearby Cher and Eure-et-Loir *départements* has shown that the literacy of different occupational groups began to improve at different times but progressed in all cases at roughly the same rate.[15] It was not until after Louis-François's death that laborers and domestics in these départements began to acquire literacy at a rapid rate. This suggests that even late in life he would have felt comfortable among his peers and would not have felt glaringly inferior to others.

Did he want his children and grandchildren to receive an education? There is every reason to believe that he did. Close study of the sources reveals that he sent his progeny to school whenever possible, even if the benefits they derived from their education varied according to the quality of instruction, their abilities, and no doubt their diligence as students.

The history of the school in Origny-le-Butin appears to have been a tortuous one. It was a patchwork creation that bore little resemblance to the kind of school envisioned by the central administration or described in official minutes. As a result, the gap between Origny's school and other nearby schools grew rapidly.[16] Until the eve of Louis-François's death, the municipal council steadfastly and vehemently refused to buy or build a schoolhouse. Until 1869 it opposed spending any money on education. The community undeniably lacked interest in the subject and justified that lack of interest on grounds of poverty.[17]

For years the councilors claimed to be happy with the services of the commune's schoolmarms, lay teachers who were compensated by voluntary contributions. Local officials evinced little concern with these women's educational attainments or other qualifications for their work. They liked having teachers known to make few demands and content to live on the modest tuition paid by the parents of their pupils. This, after all, was what the councilors were familiar with, and to some extent that familiarity accounts for their preference, which in any case they repeated often. They worked hard to persuade the central administration to put up with, and if possible sanction, teachers deemed unqualified by government school inspectors. None of the commune's teachers belonged to the teaching congregations, whose members preferred larger towns. When the administration proposed assigning a teacher's college graduate to the local school, Origny's councilors flatly refused, for it was clear that she would not be as compliant as the usual volunteers.[18]

In 1836 the population of Origny was 512. In theory it should have been covered by the provisions of the Guizot Law, but in practice this was not the case. From 1832 on, the members of the municipal council responded to all proposals regarding teachers, no matter who made them, in the same monotonous way: Origny-le-Butin already had the only teacher it needed. She was Suzanne Bouquet, who had been on the job since at least 1828. She owed her position to an "arrangement," not unlike the arrangements that governed all social relations in the commune.[19] She took her salary from the sums contributed by parents, who "all told do not pay [her] 160 francs." In addition, the local curate "has for four years [that is, since 1828] paid the rent of fifty francs rent and the tax on the house used for the instruction of the children."[20]

In addition, some parents from one section of Saint-Martin-du-Vieux-Bellême, probably the La Chaîne section, sent their children to Mlle Bouquet and also had them attend catechism classes in Origny. These were the same families that attended the local branch church. Because of this unexpected boon, the councilors asked that this dissident section be joined to their impoverished commune, but their plea went unheeded.

Mlle Bouquet remained in her post until 1850. Thus she taught an entire generation of the commune's children, including the children of Louis-François Pinagot. Clearly, Origny was pleased with her, but then she never asked for much. In 1841 she expected only one franc per month per student and offered free instruction to eleven indigent children, including Françoise and Evremont Pinagot. At the beginning of the July Monarchy the situation in Origny was not as bad as one might think, since 247 communes of the Orne still had no teacher in 1835.[21]

In 1846, on the eve of the serious crisis that struck France at mid-century, the mayor was pleased to note that a "private individual has charitably devoted herself to teaching and for some years now has been serving this commune as a teacher without a salary" or housing allowance.[22] Such was the conception of schooling in Origny at the time: a school was an institution based on charity, devotion, beneficence, and benevolence. In that year, however, Mlle Bouquet increased her demands. She was willing to continue teaching if the "commune sought approval of her position and granted her a stipend of 60 francs 84 centimes."[23] She also asked for an additional twenty-five francs to buy a stove to heat the classroom and ten francs to purchase books. The municipal council, which still staunchly refused to accept a teacher's college graduate, got its way: Mlle Bouquet was finally accepted by the academic administration.[24]

According to the report of the school inspector who came to the commune in 1850, Mlle Bouquet, who was not married, was a woman of upstanding morality. She was respected by the parents of her students and was on good terms with everyone. Fifteen boys and fifteen girls attended her elementary school during the winter, and seven boys and ten girls during the summer. The average tuition for each student was one franc per month. Thus their teacher earned 200 francs per year, less than a laborer but more than a spinner. Mlle Bouquet was an undeniably zealous teacher. She used the simultaneous method. Her school's texts were approved, but her abilities were deemed weak.[25]

Teaching was interrupted in the years that followed, which were among the worst of the century.[26] On May 16, 1854, the mayor complained that the

children of the commune were deprived of education, "which is most prej-
udicial to proper behavior and civility." He hoped that "a female schoolteacher" would come to Origny, for a woman "would be much more suitable" to the commune than a man.[27] He estimated, moreover, that of the
fifty children in the commune between the ages of six and fifteen, only sixteen were for the time being "in a position to pay." And "where else will
they go to school?" he wondered. The condition of the roads was too poor
to allow them to attend school in nearby communes. In short, Louis-
François's grandchildren, who lived in the wretched villages of Haute- and
Basse-Frêne and some of whom had indigent parents, thus found themselves in the same deplorable situation that their grandfather had been in a
half-century earlier.

The mayor proposed a solution in keeping with Origny's traditions.
"Previously," he stated, "there was a schoolteacher who provided her own
housing and was content to live on the students' tuitions. At present there is
in this commune a Mlle Charron, a laywoman of good moral character and
steeped in religious principles, who would like to assume responsibility for
teaching the children as her predecessor did."[28] He asked that she be
approved until the commune could provide a teacher with housing and supply a room.

This request was repeated in 1855. Mlle Charron was at that time the
head of a school whose fate we do not know. In any case, the academic
authorities now took a firmer line than in the past, and the subprefect issued
a sterner warning. By 1857–1858 a new school was in operation in Origny.
Admittedly, it was not much of a school, since that year it had only nine
male and six female students. The teacher was Théodore de Bloteau, a victim of "great misfortunes" whose precise nature remains a mystery.[29] In
1859 the administration approved him as "interim instructor." The size of
the school increased: the student body now consisted of fifteen boys and
four girls, from seven to thirteen years of age.[30] Nevertheless, the commune
still refused to provide the teacher with housing on the grounds that he also
had a license to sell tobacco and was therefore not without resources of his
own.

On November 5, 1860, Théodore de Bloteau received a visit from the
school inspector.[31] This married Catholic struck the inspector as a "very
honorable" man, "worthy of interest for his misfortunes," and apparently
quite diligent as a teacher. He enjoyed respect and was on good terms with

his fellow citizens. His income amounted to a total of 526 francs, including a base salary of 200 francs plus 116 francs in tuition at the rate of 1 franc 25 centimes per student per month. The remainder consisted of miscellaneous income, probably from the sale of tobacco. But he was not a graduate of a teacher's college and had no teaching certificate. The inspector's final judgment was that he was "not very able but quite devoted." He rented the house that served as a school for sixty francs per year. The premises were not suitable, according to the inspector, and the state of maintenance was poor. The classroom was just over 172 square feet for thirteen boys and twenty girls. The furniture was inadequate and in poor condition. And, of course, the inspector deplored the fact that there was no separation between boys and girls and "only one door for both sexes." Fortunately, however, it did contain a crucifix, an image of the Virgin, and busts of the emperor and empress.

By the following year Théodore de Bloteau had obtained a third-degree teaching certificate. But his school was in jeopardy, as the student body had dwindled to just eight boys and thirteen girls. This would be the school's last year. Even though the teacher was a local man and not a teacher's college graduate, he was not as successful in Origny as his predecessor, Mlle Bouquet.

From 1862 to 1870 Origny-le-Butin found itself once again without a school. Children from the commune had to travel to classes in Chemilly or La Perrière. Ultimately, however, the municipal council came to feel that the situation was intolerable. People's thinking had changed, and they no longer insisted on a volunteer female teacher. By unanimous vote on December 1, 1869, the councils asked the prefect "to assign a teacher to direct the school that we propose to establish in the center of the commune" (establish did not necessarily mean "buy" or "build"). They also emphasized the need for a teacher to "take care of the municipal records," for which he would receive a base salary of fifty francs.[32] For the first time the council had voted to spend money on a schoolteacher.

By February 1870, seven months before the fall of the Empire, the new school was in operation. The archives of the municipality were transferred to the schoolhouse. There would be no further challenges to the school's existence. Parents of children under the age of seven paid one franc per month; parents of older children paid one franc fifty.[33] Seven indigent children were accepted without tuition, including Isaïe Pinagot and the Renaud children. Thus in the final six years of his life, Louis-François had the pleasure of seeing the youngest of his grandchildren attend school in Origny-le-Butin, as his children had done before them. Thus the teaching of reading and writing to his progeny was not a steady process but one that was interrupted several times during the course of his life. This accounts for the varying levels of literacy they achieved.

We can easily imagine how he might from time to time have turned to his father or to certain of his children or grandchildren when he needed help in deciphering one of the few texts that for one reason or another he needed to understand. Yet there is no proof that he did so. It is sometimes assumed that people without the benefit of former schooling might have learned the rudiments of reading and writing from children who did go to school. This was not the case with Pinagot, who remained illiterate throughout his life. At most he may have heard one of his children or grandchildren read from a book or almanac during an evening gathering.

Attendance at catechism class and at religious services may have compensated for the clog maker's illiteracy. Unfortunately, the parish archives are poor, so that we have no way to gauge the degree of Louis-François's religious fervor. It is not very likely that he would have regularly attended the catechism classes taught by the curate of Vaunoise after the branch church in Origny-le-Butin was closed in 1808. On the other hand, there is every reason to believe that he had his children baptized within the canonical period, since we know that the two youngest, Julienne-Philomène and Victor-Constant, received the sacrament on the day after they were born. The parish archives also tell us that the time limit was observed in the baptisms of thirteen of his grandchildren. Four of them received the sacrament on the day they were born, five the next day, and two the day after that. Emile Renaud was baptized on the third day and Auguste Bourdin on the fourth.

In Louis-François's family, the priest was sent for at the hour of death. In this milieu anything else would have been almost unthinkable. Uncle Cottin died at eighty-one, "provided with all the sacraments." The same was true of Aunt Catherine Pinagot. If Louis-François's father-in-law, Louis Pôté, "only confessed," it was "because death caught him unaware," according to Father Pigeard. Louis-François Jr., the eldest son, was buried two days after his death, "provided with all the sacraments of the Church." As for Louis-François himself, there was no extreme unction, but he died "with the sacrament of penance." Perhaps like his father-in-law the Grim Reaper took him by surprise. His agony may have been brief.

Nevertheless, any number of signs suggest that even if the Pinagots respected the rites of passage, they were not very fervent. Only six of Louis-François's fourteen grandchildren made their first communion, and only one of his granddaughters, Amandine, received the sacrament of confirmation.

The fact that Louis-François had no choice but to communicate orally makes it all the more imperative that we try to imagine how he spoke. To that end, we are fortunate indeed to posses documents that date from his childhood and adolescence. Eager to obey orders set forth in a memorandum from Minister of the Interior Montalivet, Monsieur Delestang, subprefect of the Mortagne district, gathered information that would help him to respond to the questionnaire sent out by Coquebert de Montbret and translate the parable of the prodigal son into the vernacular.[34] In so doing, he revived the idea of a "statistical analysis of spoken language." In particular, he turned to the mayor of Bellême, who called upon the services of Beneuil, the commune's schoolteacher.

Of course, we must be careful not to overestimate the validity of the results obtained. At the end of the century the archivist Louis Duval was critical of the method. The investigators should "not have relied exclusively on townspeople, on semibourgeois; they should have established direct relations with peasants and initiated themselves into their language and above all their habits of pronunciation."[35] In his opinion, this was too much to expect of Delestang, who had delivered a speech in the presence of Empress Marie-Louise her return from Cherbourg in 1811. The criticism was too harsh. The survey documents show a real familiarity with the language of the people. Their rich content did not escape the attention of scholars. At the prefecture, Louis Dubois, the author of the departmental monograph attributed to the prefect La Magdelaine, relied on this survey for his "Glossary of Norman Patois," which was published in the *Mémoires de l'Académie celtique*. In 1822 Dureau de la Malle, a learned historian of local customs, presented Subprefect Delestang's "vocabulary" to the Academie des Inscriptions et Belles-Lettres.

Documents that discuss the regional speech of this part of the Perche before 1860 invariably reflect the same prejudices that we have already noted in the imperial survey. The peasants' language is described as "crippled French." Their bad, or "defective," pronunciation is repeatedly deplored; their accent is said to be harsh and "disagreeable to the ear." The "corruption of words" and use of archaic turns of speech is lamented. This obsession with the "defects" of peasant speech is for us a distraction, however, since what we want to know is how French was spoken in the Bellême region during Pinagot's adolescence.[36]

Delestang begins his report with a series of comments on the defective pronunciations and "incorrect constructions" that grated most on the investigators' ears.[37] He notes, for instance, the use of the first-person singular pronoun with a verb in the first-person plural: "*j'avons, je faisons, j'allions*" (instead of *j'ai, je fais, j'allais*, as in standard French—trans.). According to Delestang, all the peasants of the district spoke this way. He was also struck by the use of endings in *as* and *ant*, even though this contradicted the previous remark: "*j'allas, je venas, je faisas, is venant, is demandant.*" The vowel *a* was often replaced by the diphthong *ai*: *fourmaige* instead of *fromage, passaige* instead of *passage*. By contrast, *ai* was often replaced by *a*: *agu* instead of *aigu*. *C* became *que* or *ke* (*queroisée* or *keroisée* instead of *croisée, queroix* instead of *croix*). *Che* became *j*, for example in *j'va*, which was used instead of *cheval*. *O* became *en*, as in *enrée* for *orée*. The words *veau, beau, eau* became *viau, biau, iau*, and the *l* was often palatalized, as in *bié* for *blé*.

Remarks such as these help us to imagine the sound of French as spoken by Louis-François and people like him. So does the list of words that Subprefect Delestang found "incomprehensible," such as *gourer*, which meant to deceive or swindle, and *baiser*, which meant to catch someone. Obviously, it would take far too much space to reproduce the entire glossary of the report, and in any case it would be pointless. Yet I could not have written this book without consulting it and other, similar documents.

Take one example among many: the vocabulary of femininity. A woman or girl was a *créiature* or *fumelle*.[38] More precisely, according to Abbé Fret, young women were known as *créaitures* in the vicinity of Mortagne, Mauves, and Pin-la-Garenne in 1842.[39] In other cantons of the Perche, people spoke of *Kériatures* or *criatures*. A *guenette* was a woman of loose morals.[40] A pleasant young woman was a *gentrouillette*, but if she amused herself too much she became a *gigaleuse*, especially if she allowed herself to *lichouaner*, or kiss frequently. *Ils se lichouanent toujours*, they're always kissing. Or *piaufrer*, to kiss greedily: *je n'aime pas qu'on piaufre ma fille*, I don't like anyone to kiss my daughter greedily. If she liked *la gobine*, she was debauched.

The same investigators also deplored the inertia of the local language, and in particular the inability to assimilate the metric system. Other innovations inspired by the Enlightenment and enacted into law during the Revolution met with similar resistance. Did Louis-François Pinagot know how to count? Probably, for at the very least he would have needed to estimate the number of pairs of clogs he made. How did he measure and therefore evaluate his environment? Fortunately, this aspect of his "mental equipment" (to borrow a phrase from Lucien Febvre) is rather easy to imagine.

Take, to begin with, the measurement of surface area. In 1825 the cadaster of Origny was established in metric units. According to a study of local customs in the canton of Bellême that was carried out between 1844 and 1846, when Pinagot was in late middle age, area was still measured in *perches* (1 *perche* = half an are, 100 ares = 1 hectare = 2.471 acres), *quartiers* (that is, a quarter of an *arpent*, 12.5 ares, somewhat more than a quarter of an acre), and *arpents* (1 *arpent* = 1/2 hectare, somewhat more than an acre).[41] A *journal*, the amount of land that could be plowed in a day, measured 40 ares in the vicinity of Bellême but 44 near Mamers. Land was also measured in *hommées*, or 33 ares. The *journée de fauche* was 25 acres. A *toise* of masonry referred to a parallelepiped 40 meters long, 1 meter high, and 50 centimeters thick. Clearly, by this date, despite the inertia of the vocabulary, the metric system had quietly begun to influence the way in which people estimated and represented areas.

This was not true of measures of volume, however, at least not in all cases. A *boisseau*, or bushel, may have corresponded to fifty liters, but a *meule* (or stack of hay) weighed one metric ton plus forty kilograms. A cord of wood was three feet thick, eight feet long, and four feet heigh. A *pipe* of apples or cider was equivalent to twelve bushels, or 600 liters. As for the *faix a col* (a bundle of wood or other merchandise carried on the back) and the *somme* (a load to be carried by a horse or mule), the size depended on the nature of the merchandise. All of these units were in everyday use by forest workers. We shall have more to say about the *somme* as applied to clogs later on.

We know even less about units of currency. There are no studies of this region as detailed as the ones we have for the Landes and the Nivernais.[42] These case studies nevertheless lead us to suspect that Pinagot would have used only copper and nickel coins in his infrequent dealings on the market-place. For him, the most important transactions involved the exchange of services or barter of goods.

How large was the circle within which he would have been able to carry on a genuine conversation. Or, to put it another way, what was the maximal range of communication for a person who spoke the local "patois?" Of course, we should not assume that one way of speaking excluded others or that a given individual could express himself in only one way. In practice, verbal exchanges are intermittent. Many people were able to judge the use-fulness of speaking in a certain way in relation to the person they were speaking to. There were subtle gradations of speech that governed the con-versations Pinagot might have had with more cultivated people.

At the time, mastery of "good French," meaning correctness of gram-mar and/or pronunciation, did not imply that the speaker could not also manage "patois." The linguistic novelties taught at school did not impede conversation between social classes and generations. The ability to move back and forth easily between "good French" and "patois" could be used to ingratiate oneself; at times it even served as a mark of distinction. Hence it is wrong to think that either way of speaking excluded the other, and it is wise to use caution in interpreting the simplistic statistics compiled on orders from the central administration, especially those resulting from the well-known Duruy survey of 1864, where the goal was simply to ascertain the maximal level of performance.[43]

The inspector for the Mortagne district explained this quite clearly in a report written in 1855. This report repeats the usual litany of complaints about the use of "corrupt" expressions and "acquired poor locution." According to the author, there was, "strictly speaking, neither an idiom nor patois in the district. People speak French badly." Indeed, "rural patois is nothing more than a few corrupt and disfigured words that came originally from the French language and are by no means unintelligible." This "famil-iar language of peasants and farmers" was understood by everyone, and nearly everyone could speak it, but unfortunately it was "impossible to reform."

"The truth of this assertion is confirmed by the fact that many relatively well-to-do farmers know the rules of grammar and pronunciation but use that knowledge only when speaking to educated people. They succumb to habit, to established usage, in their region and revert to the patois they spoke as children in their parents' home. So strong is this habit that when a man of the fields moves to town, he corrects and perfects his language, but when he returns to his fields, he takes up his old idiom again along with his plow and spade. In the communes with the best schools, a few elite students speak their language correctly with the teacher, the curé, and a few educated notables, yet one cannot persuade them to speak purely with their parents, servants, and friends." Indeed, "education does nothing to correct the rural man's speech, and he really uses his instruction only when writing." In this respect at least, elementary education thus had "little or no influence outside the schools."[44]

In the 1860s, within a small circle of members of the local elite, attitudes toward the vernacular changed (later here than elsewhere). As usual the change was spurred by a feeling of loss. As early as 1849 Edélstand Duméril was deploring the fact that "our patois dies a little with each day that passes."[45] Thirty years later, Louis Duval called attention to its clear "attenuation." But this was not the crux of the matter. In 1865 Achille Genty tried to promote the use of "the Percheron idiom" by the cultivated elite.[46] For him, that idiom was not a corrupt form of French but the remains of the original *langue d'oïl*, which predated that of the eleventh century and was closer to Latin than was the Norman dialect.

This primordial tongue, supposedly associated with an "old Gallo-Frank pronunciation," was alleged to have been corrupted later on by the influence of Norman patois and French into a confused amalgam. So, once again, we have a process of degradation, but now interpreted in the opposite sense. According to Genty, the right thing to do was to try to recover this lost primitive language, to return to the pristine beginnings of a now forgotten tongue. The Perche offered the ideal laboratory for a new kind of linguistic research. Its peasants had been protected by their isolation from the corrupting effects of French.

Behind this attempt to promote a hitherto denigrated form of speech lay an aesthetic impulse. Achille Genty was full of praise for the work of his father (1770–1820), a self-educated blacksmith who could not write and barely knew how to read but who, according to his son, had spontaneously composed very beautiful poems.[47] One of the son's tactics in extolling his father's work was to distinguish the regional idiom of the Perche from the Norman "patois" to which his father had never succumbed, even though he lived in a place that was "insufficiently *percheron*."

A restoration of this sort would surely have had no impact on Louis-François Pinagot, who was by then a poor old man still holed up in Basse-Frêne. This was just one of many attempts to give substance to a Percheron identity perceived as under siege. Nevertheless, the new admiration for the local dialect may have changed the way members of the elite heard it and therefore changed their attitude toward the peasants. Be that as it may, the idea of the "Percheron idiom" as the survival of some primitive tongue seems to have evaporated fairly quickly. It was a late conception, and this made it vulnerable to attack by scientific philologists whose work was based on a more solid foundation.[48]

We turn now to the very tenor of spoken exchange, to the nature of conversation itself. In the end this is what matters. Indeed, I want to insist on the relevance of the concept of conversation to the study of milieus other than salons, circles, and cafés. Certain forms of wit and ways of wielding words served as important criteria in defining a person's temperament, quality as an individual, reputation, and self-image.

How did Louis-François Pinagot express himself? Was he voluble or taciturn? Was he a simpleton and therefore the butt of jokes or a wit quick with a lethal jibe? Such questions are impossible to answer. The best we can hope for is to try to imagine the kinds of verbal exchanges in which he would have been immersed. He would have had four types of occasion in which to display his aptitude for conversation: (1) fortuitous encounters on the road or outside the church, episodes that would have been highly ritualized and dependent to a large extent on proverbs; (2) bargaining, or, more generally, "arrangements," negotiated in the confusion or perhaps din of a tavern; (3) visits, primarily to members of his extended family; and (4) evening gatherings and other family conversations. Mention should be made as well, of course, of the very texture of silence, of the exceptional weight of the unspoken in a world that attached so much importance to tacit understandings.

We shall try to resurrect two of these four situations that promise to be most useful for our purposes. To that end we shall rely on texts published by Abbé Fret: *saynètes*, or playlets, which he included in *Le Diseur de vérités*, the almanac he edited. These playlets were clearly intended to edify their readers, as is evident from their naäve dramatization of everyday life. Since they were also addressed to a number of different audiences, their author was inclined to wink now and then in the direction of his more urbane readers.

For our purposes, however, these texts have a number of virtues. They have little in common with the conventional representation of peasants in classical French comedy, because they were intended primarily for local rural people and written in part to be read in the evening around the fireside. The author was therefore required to aim for a certain level of plausibility, especially in the conception of his situations and the texture of his dialogue. As in classical comedy, the target of derision was "the other," but because of the primary intended audience, the tables were turned: the other was now the Parisian, the student, the petty notable, the rural mayor. The peasants in Abbé Fret's playlets are never the butt of laughter; at most they may occasion a smile now and then. In other words, his oeuvre offers an ideal illustration of the inanity of the superficial distinction between high culture and popular culture. When the "Molière of the Perche" adapted a prestigious genre to a popular theatrical form intended to be read in public to diverse audiences, the result was a subversion of social boundaries. Social distance in Fret's texts turns out to be quite a subtle quality.

Take, for example, two of the situations mentioned earlier. Let us first consider the family visit, or, more precisely, the visits to relatives that people traditionally made during *les jours gras*, that is, the three weeks preceding Lent. This, according to the abbé, was an "age-old custom," although it had been on the wane since the beginning of the century. The scene is set on Monday, February 6, 1837, near Mortagne. A pig had been slaughtered the Friday before.[49] At the appointed hour, "eleven-thirty on the dot," the guests, all extended family members, arrive, and a *pignoche*, or tap, is placed in a keg of cider.[50] Before entering the house, the men remove their capes and the women take off their traveling caps. All are wearing their Sunday best, whose style varies from generation to generation.[51]

Once inside, everyone embraces, the three customary kisses on the cheek are exchanged, and the conversation begins. Each person's position in the family tree is reviewed. Even godparents are identified, and the new arrival's ability to recognize everyone present is put to the test. "Oh, hallo, my poo' father, my poo' mother. Hallo, my brother, my sistah, my uncle, my aunt, my nephew, my niece, my cousin, my godfather, godmother, child's parent in-law," and so on. The frequent use of the word "poor" is a sign that these people's lives are hard. It is an implicit compliment to those who face adversity with courage. It is also a way of warding off the danger that would attend an ill-considered assertion of good fortune or newfound wealth.

These intertwined litanies would then be followed by ritual phrases of welcome expressing pleasure in the visit and setting the terms of hospitality.

"Hey, there, how goes it?" [The French dialect has a savor of its own, which this English rendering is not intended to reproduce. —trans.]

"Well! And you?"

"Not bad, thanks. I'm so glad to see you, I was afraid you wouldn't come in this rotten weather."

"Oh, my poor children, only for you would I have made such an effort."

At this point the conversation proper begins, beginning with stories about the trip. This leads to a discussion of how tiring the return trip is likely to be and of the date and time of the planned departure. The dialogue then takes the form of a game, or, rather, a negotiation, in which the guest eventually gives in and the terms of surrender are spelled out: "Are you happy now?" The whole conversation is punctuated with standard formulas, feigned indecisiveness, and mock contradiction:

"You'll wait until the weather lets up a little before going back, I hope."

"Well, we'll see about that."

"You feel cold, you must be frozen. Come over here and warm yourself up."

"I'm not as cold as you might think. Walking warms a body up, doesn't it?"

After snacks are served to warm the visitors, the table talk can begin. There are frequent interruptions, as food is offered and guests are urged to "take a little bit more, just a taste." As dishes are served one after another (soup, sausages, grilled meat, stew, and boiled meat, all washed down with cider), the discussion turns to general topics of a more elevated nature than those discussed at evening gatherings. Fun is poked at "fancy reasoning," and someone says that "they'll never make country folk believe that." The present (*annui*, for *aujourd'hui*, today) is compared unfavorably to the past.

Was Pinagot a man of high enough social status to take part in such feasts and ritualized encounters? In Origny-le-Butin this kind of socializing was more likely to be associated with farmers than with woodsmen. It might well be that he socialized mainly with fellow clog makers around a bottle of cider at the inn. Yet there was no shortage of farmers in his very large extended family, including his father, his father-in-law, and his eldest son. So it seems likely that he would have participated in family visits of this kind, particularly during the season before Lent.

In any case, evening conversations around the fire must have been a more familiar pleasure. With the exception of L'Hôtel-Migné, the tiny out-post where he lived for a few years, the villages in which he resided, Haute-Frêne during his childhood and Basse-Frêne during the second half of his life, were ideal for organizing evening gatherings. The nature of the hous-ing lent itself to the practice, as did the substantial number of residents, the proximity of their social positions, the presence of different age groups, the approximate equality in the number of men and women, the fact that nearly everyone was an artisan of some sort, and especially that spinners and glove makers were used to conversing on the job. All these conditions were met until at least 1870. Still, the truth of the matter is that we have no proof of any of this, and no description of an evening gathering except from outside observers.

Abbé Fret wrote in 1842 about a gathering he says took place on Decem-ber 23, 1840: "In every village there is a place designated for the regular evening gathering. This is sometimes a habitable dwelling but more often than not a cowshed belonging to the wealthiest or most obliging of the vil-lagers. People from nearby hamlets, which have no gathering place, some-times join in. Immediately after supper, which takes place at six or seven o'clock, each participant gathers up his or her work and goes to the com-mon workspace. A candle (*chandelle*) of sixteen or twenty (centimeters) for a cowshed, or, for a house, an *oribue* (probably a torch) held in place with a piece of iron or split wood in a corner of the fireplace provides the only illumination," bathing the scene in a light that is "weak and pale."[52]

In *le Perche ornais* men and boys made baskets, models, or oblong ham-pers known as *raisses*. "The youngest ones kept busy making *logettes* (cages) or nets for catching birds when the weather was snowy or foggy. Women and girls, called *criaitures*, mended the clothes of their husbands, fathers, children, or brothers and then their own clothing [note the insistence on this order]. More often, however, they spun linen or hemp either for themselves or for linen makers." The evening unfolded amid the "hubbub" of spinning wheels.

Such occasions offered a context for speech quite different from that of the family visit. Conversation was not confined by the rituals of hospitality. People were less reserved in their use of language. This was a place to "gos-sip." Women, in particular, felt more at liberty to express themselves. These gatherings, held in the off season (September 15 to March 15) during the evening or even into the night, were an ideal occasion for mockery and deri-sion. Jibes and jokes, sometimes cruel, poured out in endless succession.

This was not a place for tact. It was a time to *endêver* others: to make them angry. It was also a place for young people to make their mark and try out their wit, meaning essentially their capacity for repartee, their talent for verbal invention, their facility in producing merriment, and their ability to judge other people's temperament and gauge their status. Ultimately, the goal was to figure out who was attractive to whom.

On the night of December 23, 1840 (in the imaginary scene set before us by Abbé Fret), "they got Jeanneton into a lather about her abortive marriage to Renot Guittard, who dumped her for Marion Lamberde, who works for Master Guespin." (Note that young domestic servants referred to their employers as "master.") The girl shows a gift for repartee in responding to her would-be tormenter: "You've been with at least twenty girls, you'll soon have run through every girl in the canton and spent more than three years of your wages buying *glorias* [coffee mixed with spirits], *petits pots*, bottles of wine, and gold rings and earrings. And still you've gotten nowhere with your crooked mouth, your heron's neck, and your bandy legs. You've already been engaged to three girls, and not one of them wanted to kiss you."

While the young played at courting and seduction, the adults indulged in "tittle-tattle" and gossip. During evening gatherings or in daytime at the wash house, women made and destroyed reputations.[53] Sometimes the discussion turned to politics. It was here, Fret tells us, that the myth of Napoleon was created, along with the dark side of the Napoleonic legend, in which the emperor was painted as a Lucifer (*Lucifai*) who was overly ambitious (*ambitionneux*).[54] More frequently, however, the conversation was likely to be about recent events in the area, such as a fire or murder. The news vied for attention with the stories bandied about by "wicked gossips." In Haut-Perche games were played (Giroflin, hunt-the-slipper, *défourner la galette*). Riddles were posed. And spinning wheels were stopped long enough to practice songs to be sung at upcoming weddings.

Louis-François Pinagot would have attended such evening gatherings at every stage of his life. We would like to be able to hear him laughing with his wife and children, playing games, giving his opinions about people, things, and events. But as we come to know him little by little, the best we can do for now is to sketch with as much detail as possible the sonic and linguistic ambiance in which he would have savored his familiar, everyday pleasures.

the clog makers, the spinners, and the glove makers

Louis-François Pinagot's adolescence remains totally obscure. It is possible that his parents placed him temporarily with a friendly farmer, as was commonly done in their circle. Or perhaps before learning his own clog-making trade, he helped his father, a carter. In any case, the work that his father, Jacques Pinagot, did obviously influenced his upbringing.

In those days there were two kinds of carters. One transported merchandise from town to town along major highways. The other carried goods over short distances only. The elder Pinagot was a carter of the second type. His job was to "pull" loads from the depths of the forest (*tirer*, "pull," was the term used). He hauled bark, boards, and timber or stacked wood for dealers in Bellême, and above all La Perrière, his birthplace. On September 6, 1836 (by which time Louis-François had long since moved out of his father's house), Jacques Pinagot was sentenced to pay a fine of twelve francs for allowing three horses to graze at night on two- to three-year-old saplings. He was employed at the time as a carter by a Sieur Cavalier, a wood dealer in La Perrière who owned the "contractual right to cut wood in the section of forest where two of the three horses were found."[1]

Jacques Pinagot lived in Haute-Frêne, and because of the nature of his work it seems likely that Louis-François would have acquired early knowledge of the forest, its paths, the people who worked in it, the rituals and practices around which they organized their lives, and perhaps also the petty crimes they committed. At his father's house or at work sites in the forest, he would have met wood dealers and master clog makers when they came to arrange for shipments. He would have witnessed the negotiation of deals with farmers and clog makers. In his youth he probably worked on occasion with woodcutters and laborers, if only while loading his father's wagons. He may even have received substantial tips, since it was customary at the time in the canton of Bellême to pay the deliveryman sixty centimes for each cord of wood delivered.[2]

At first Jacques Pinagot hitched his wagons to a team of two horses. Of that much we are certain. As a young man Louis-François would surely have learned about working with the animals. In 1812 and 1813 his father's horses were white and gray, whereas in 1818 both were bays.[3] At the time the administration was attempting to regulate hauling and carting. La Magdelaine, the prefect of the Orne, took an active role.[4] A new regulation prohibited hauling during periods of thaw. It fixed the width of fellies, or wheel rims, and the maximum weight of wagons and payloads. And it required every vehicle to carry an identifying plate, probably the first time in history that such public identification was made compulsory.

These measures were draconian but, as the prefect himself admitted, unenforceable. Exceptions were inevitable, as they were wherever the administration attempted to impose regulatory controls.[5] Thus Jacques Pinagot very likely enjoyed a certain latitude when it came to obeying the law. For example, "occasional (*accidentel*) transport" of large trees and stones, something that would have been of great concern to him, was authorized, provided no major highways were used. The transport of food for humans and animals to homes in town was totally unregulated, as was the transport of clay and farm products to processing sites. An ordinance of June 7, 1814, prohibited "carters and wagoners" from "loading" or "making deliveries on Sunday"; the punishment for violating this ordinance was a fine of one hundred francs. It is very difficult, however, to determine whether this law was ever enforced in Origny-le-Butin.

Hauling cargo did offer the possibility of earning a decent living. At the time, freight charges in the *département* amounted to one franc sixty per (metric) ton for a five-kilometer haul. But Jacques Pinagot needed to graze his horses. Since he lacked sufficient pastureland of his own, he deliberately allowed his horses to eat saplings in the forest. Nine of the citations he received for violating the regulations against this are preserved in the archives.[6] The judges of the district court considered him a "habitual crim-

inal." His horses ate grass, young shoots, and green branches in the La Perrière *triage*, or, more precisely, in the cantons of La Mare Bouillie and Le
Coin à la Poule, near Haute-Frêne.

Jacques Pinagot was not the only carter to feed his horses this way. For
decades Sieur Clotet of Saint-Martin-du-Vieux-Bellême had no compunc-
tion about allowing his mules and horses to graze in the nearby forest. But
Louis-François's father was a sly old fox. For a time he lied about what he
was up to, but later he realized that he couldn't fool the judges and took a different tack. On December 15, 1812, a warden spotted his white horse munch-
ing on the branches of young oaks.[7] Pinagot pretended "that [the animal had
been] wounded by wolves, which chased it and nipped at its flesh," and
offered to provide proof that what he said was true. At the next hearing he
produced a certificate from the mayor of Origny. The judge refused to
believe him, however. The certificate did "indeed state that several horses
and mules had been victims of the ferocity of these animals," but it did not
confirm that Pinagot's horses had "been attacked and wounded." On March
27, 1813, another warden spotted two horses belonging to the carter of
Haute-Frêne grazing on saplings less than one year old in the canton of La
Mare Bouillie.[8] The owner of the two horses declared "that they had gone
astray and were there against his will." Furthermore, "he had gone to fetch
them after the warden" identified them. On June 17 of the same year, Jacques
Pinagot again claimed that his two horses had "escaped and gotten lost in the
forest." To be sure, this claim was not implausible since the forest was
nearby, but Pinagot subsequently confessed.

As the foregoing makes clear, Jacques Pinagot was more talked about
than his son Louis-François, who, so far as we know, was never found guilty
of any misdemeanor. But this does not tell us much about why he chose to
become a clog maker. All we know is that both father and son were in frequent contact with artisans, who worked either in or around the forest of
Bellême, and that Uncle Drouin worked as a clog maker in Haute-Frêne.

Louis-François probably began working, like most other boys he knew,
when he was twelve. In his canton clog makers worked twelve-hour days
"when the weather was good and the hours of daylight were long."[9] The
work day ran from five in the morning until seven at night, with two hours
off for meals. In the warm season the worker, "who normally works out of
doors, . . . has little fear of the rain." Many questions remain, however.
Where did Louis-François work and under what conditions? What net-

work of commercial contacts was he a part of? Such questions are difficult to answer because of the wide range of possibilities, the imprecise nature of the documents, and the fact that clog makers often went unnoticed (they were not mentioned in surveys undertaken during the Consulate and Empire, for example).

Let us begin by considering his place of work. Did he make clogs in the forest itself or at home, first in L'Hôtel-Migné and later in Basse-Frêne? In the many works devoted to the clog makers of the past, we find descriptions of cottages, huts, shacks, and shanties. Rudimentary structures of this sort did exist in the forest of Bellême, particularly in the area belonging to Saint-Martin. They are pictured in late nineteenth-century postcards, but this may simply be a sign of nostalgia for picturesque vestiges of a bygone era.[10] Admittedly, there were many clog makers' huts in the forest of Bellême during the Empire and Restoration, as we know from judicial archives. We still find some in cases dating from the middle of the century, in the early years of the economic crisis. After that, however, they are seldom mentioned.

In September 1846 Louis Riday, a dealer in clogs from Saint-Martin-du-Vieux-Bellême, claimed that he was owed thirty francs by Julien Courville of Origny-le-Butin, Louis-François's brother-in-law, in return for twelve *gaules* (poles or sticks) that Courville took from him "in the forest for the construction of his workshop."[11] These clog makers' huts have often been described.[12] They were wooden structures built on a platform—when the terrain allowed—and equipped with a fireplace. In nearby Sarthe, their roofs were made of broom. In the Bellême forest in the early nineteenth century, it was common for several clog makers to work together in a hut belonging to a dealer or master craftsman. By working close to the source of the green wood they used in their work, they avoided the cost and difficulty of transporting their raw material. The huts measured about 270 square feet. Wood was stacked outside, along with shavings, known locally as *calots* (the pile of shavings was called a *calotier*).

Huts could be used in more than one way, however. The clog maker could come out to the woods for his day's work and then return home, or he could move in for the season. He could live alone, or he could share the space with fellow workers or with his wife and children. Instances of each are found in the judicial archives. Where clog makers lived in villages along the forest's edge, however, it is highly unlikely that they would have used the huts as dwellings. Unlike the relatively small number of workers from other areas, the local clog makers were more apt to use the huts as workshops during the day only. The fact that many clog makers were married to spinners is an additional reason to doubt that families lived in these huts even temporarily, although it may be that women who normally worked as spinners also spent part of their time scraping and finishing clogs. This is unlikely, though, since clog making (*saboterie*) was essentially a man's trade. The term *sabotière* (female clog maker) does not appear until 1835, and a parlement-sponsored survey of industrial labor in 1848 mentions just ten *gratteuses de sabots* (female clog scrapers) in the entire canton of Bellême.[13]

Let us look now at some specific examples of rudimentary structures in the forests of the Perche in the early nineteenth century. On March 14, 1819, forest wardens searched clog makers' huts in the Lignerolles section.[14] In the huts of Messrs Lameray and Gervais, known as Jeannet, they "found, inside the huts and in the shavings pile, twelve *bougons* [a local unit?] of green beech . . . [and] any number of pieces of a recently felled beech." Both of these master clog makers were in their huts that day. In the same year, a clog maker from Appenay was found guilty of having built a hut in a forbidden part of the forest. He gave assurances that he would destroy it once his work was finished.[15] On October 31, 1825, two master clog makers, one of whom lived in Tourouvre, used freshly cut branches of beech to seal up their huts.[16]

Apparently, some clog makers had more than one residence. On September 24, 1822, wardens found that three beech trees had been felled in Le Coin à la Poule (Origny-le-Butin) and subsequently removed. They located the illegally harvested wood among brambles nearby. "We went to a hut that remains standing . . . in which resides Nicolas Meslay, a dealer in clogs (or master) [sic], where we found twenty-two assorted pairs of clogs in freshly cut green wood and two lengths of split logs for making two other pairs that we recognized . . . as coming from the same beech. In front of the door of the aforesaid hut were two piles of shavings evidently from the foot of the same tree, which was more than a yard in circumference. The wife and daughter lived together in said hut[17]. . . . We also ordered a young man named Guillin, who carves clogs for the aforementioned Meslay and his daughter, to leave the premises immediately and take his tools with him, which he did."[18] But Nicolas Meslay, a dealer in clogs, had his primary residence in La Perrière, where he lived with his wife and daughter; his home was searched on October 8.

At about the same time, certain manufacturers on the southern edge of the forest of Bellême ordered clogs from clog makers who worked at home rather than in forest clearings. On January 22, 1836, Auguste Clotet, a carter from Saint-Martin, claimed that he was owed 24.90 francs by Armand Chrétien, whose "workers" had ordered "cartloads of wood delivered to their homes."[19] There were also self-employed clog makers who worked at home either alone or with a colleague. On February 2, 1824, Jacques Geslain, also known as Renotin, "a self-employed clog maker residing at Le Carouge" (in Saint-Martin, near Origny), attacked a forest warden who attempted to prevent him from cutting up a recently felled beech.[20]

On October 31, 1854, at six in the morning, François Herbelin, the mayor of Origny-le-Butin, inspected his town. He found an untended fire in a pile of shavings on a piece of land owned by Lemay. It had been started by Maury, "a clog maker employed by Lemay . . . at the behest of his master, for the purpose of smoking clogs."[21] This fire was just ten feet from "the hut owned by the aforementioned Lemay." This shows that *loge* (hut) was synonymous with *atelier* (workshop) and that huts existed even within town limits.

More convincing than these case reports, perhaps, is the testimony of eyewitnesses. On February 1, 1815, the commandant of the Fourth Legion of gendarmes, who bore responsibility for overseeing the forest of Bellême, reported that 293 of the workers employed in the forest were clog makers. "They do not participate at all in the cutting or exploitation of timber. They are sedentary workers who practice their profession either in their homes or in nearby huts."[22] Much later, in 1867, it was reported that the clog makers in this forest "work at home."[23]

These observations support our assumption that Louis-François's workshop, or hut, was somewhere near his home, especially during the long years he spent in Basse-Frêne. There he had a father who was a carter and a father-in-law who was a farmer, both with the means to make deliveries. Several other clog makers lived in the same village. Wood was readily available nearby. The structure of his family, the diversity of his relatives' occupations, and the tendency throughout the region for artisans to leave the forest and settle in villages where they could be more fully integrated into the community—all of these things tend to confirm our hypothesis.[24]

Still, we cannot be certain that it is correct. He may have worked in a hut in the forest before he was married and only later decided to set up shop closer to home. In either case we have a fairly good idea of what his working day was like. He would have worked at all times in the vicinity of a smoldering fire that was used for "smoking" clogs. With a ready supply of wood shavings he would not have suffered from the cold, even though the fire "used for smoking clogs [was] a fire without a flame."[25] We can imagine what his workshop and twin workbenches looked like. Clog makers generally worked close to sources of light and heat. Wood was stacked in the darker portions of the work space.[26] Finished clogs were prominently displayed. When the weather was good, the work moved outdoors among piles of billets and scattered wood shavings.

The clog maker's first concern was to procure good wood. Sometimes wood was supplied by the master craftsman or manufacturer for whom he worked. If not, it was purchased at the cutting site through an arrangement between one or more workmen and the wood supplier. Two craftsmen from the same village often went in together on these deals. Most clog makers were capable of cutting their own wood if need be.[27] The master craftsman or journeyman clog maker would then have to strike a deal with a carter or farmer to haul the logs or billets. This sometimes involved a complex exchange of services. On February 4, 1852, a forest warden spotted two men following a horse-drawn wagon along "a forbidden trail." The wagon belonged to Jacques Heuzé, a farmer from Bellême, who had been summoned (*requis*) by Pierre Josse, a clog maker, to "transport wood for clogs that he had purchased at cutting sites in the forest."[28]

Several different species of wood fulfilled the clog makers' requirements.[29] Birch was light and cheap and could be used to make clogs that were cool in summer but a little cold in winter. Alder was also light and good for making open sandals. Elm was less slippery than other woods. Best of all was beech, which was hard and solid and good for making the creamy white clogs favored by farmers—the perfect material except that it was not very warm in winter and tended to split in wet weather.

There is every reason to believe that Pinagot, like other clog makers in the forest of Bellême, used mainly beech and to a lesser extent birch. Beech was among the dominant species in the forest and suited the needs of his clientele. Nearly all the recorded offenses committed by clog makers from Origny-le-Butin involved the illegal cutting of beech. In 1834 the prefect alluded to "the clog making industry and the production of a variety of objects that require the use of beech."[30] In 1858, the author of an improvement plan for the Bellême forest went into some detail about the uses to which its wood was put:

> There is a substantial number of beech trees, and those that are perfectly straight and more than 65 feet long are purchased by the merchant marine . . . the rest are used for making splints, shovels, dishes, and clogs. Branches up to 16 inches in diameter are used for the latter. . . . In natural and artificial clearings clogs are made from beech, birch, hornbeam, and alder as soon as the branches reach 16 inches in diameter (or 10 inches for children's clogs).[31]

The trees were cut when the moon was waning or, better yet, during the old moon (when the sap was descending).

Like all clog makers, Louis-François worked with green wood. It had to be dried somewhat, however, in order to avoid splitting in the finished product, which would then require banding. Logs were split with a wedge into billets (*pelotes*), usually quarters five or six inches wide and fairly thin. In order to prevent splitting during drying, the woodworker "always eliminates the heartwood." In the Haut-Perche it was customary for clog makers to work with two benches, one facing the other. The first was used "to rough out and dress the exterior of the clog," the second "to hold it in place during the hollowing-out operation."[32]

There were three stages in the making of a clog. The first was to rough-hew the billet to resemble the desired final shape. The tool used for this purpose was known as a *doloire*, or adze, and with nine strokes a good workman was supposed to be able to carve the outline of the object and raise the sole.[33] In the Bellême region, the tool had a long wooden handle, which was curved and shaped in such a way as to relieve the wrist.[34] "To begin the cutting of certain arches, one should use an *assot* or *herminette* with a curved blade and cutting edge perpendicular to the axis of the handle."[35]

The second operation, hollowing-out, was done on the second bench, on which the roughed-out clog was placed in a notch to fix it in place. The craftsman began by boring a hole vertically into the part of the clog that was to remain uncovered. Then he bored an oblique hole into the covered part. He then enlarged both cavities with a set of very sharp gouges. Then he chiseled away the wood between the two holes. The front of the clog had to be hollowed out to within an inch of the desired size. The craftsman then used a scraper called a *rouanne* to finish the insole. This consisted of a short, curved blade attached to the end of a long steel rod inserted into a wooden handle. The woodworker had to "scrape the inside of the clog to eliminate any roughness in the wood."[36]

Then he finished dressing the sole, shaped the edges, upper, and heel, and ensured that the two clogs in each pair looked alike. For this he used a *paroir*, a long, sharp blade with an iron hook attached to the opposite end of the handle. This hook was inserted into a ring attached to the bench. Once the dressing was done, all that remained was the finishing and, if desired, decoration. In finishing the workman made fine cuts with the *paroir* to eliminate any irregularity in the shaping. The interior was smoothed out with the aid of the *rouanne*. Sharp edges were rounded off with a *dégageoir*. Then the clogs were pierced with a *percette* to assemble the pair.

During drying, which extended over a period of three to five months, the clogs lost half of their weight and shrank slightly. Allowance therefore had to be made for this shrinkage. Throughout the drying period the clogs were kept out of the wind in order to keep them from splitting. The procedure just described, used for making covered clogs, was also used for clogs with pads or straps. Some clog makers were adept at making lightweight clogs for Sunday use and wedding clogs, which were uncovered and finely decorated, but there is no evidence that Louis-François was one of them.

How did Louis-François learn the many skills required to perform these delicate operations? The only training available at the time was apprenticeship of son to father or disciple to master. Louis-François may therefore have taught the trade to his children and son-in-law, but he himself must have acquired his skills in the workshop of his uncle Drouin or of some other clog maker from outside the family. It is safe to assume that most of what Louis-François would have acquired in the way of technical, gestural, "somatic" culture would have come from the art of clog making. The trade required a good knowledge of wood species and ages. Louis-François would have needed to be a keen student of the smell and consistency of green wood and would have had to gauge the relative hardness of different billets. He also would have had to take account of the wood's color and pattern, predict its likely shrinkage in drying, and judge the quality of the finished clog by eye or by listening to the sound the wood made when tapped.

He also would have needed to know how to use a wide range of tools for cutting, drilling, and scraping, some straight or tapered, others curved.

Cuts were a constant hazard, and he had probably long since become inured to the pain. In the course of his work he would have learned a series of gestures that undoubtedly influenced his everyday bearing. His trade would have given him a strong wrist, a steady hand, and an accurate eye. His business was to shape three-dimensional objects day in and day out, piece after piece. Did he specialize in one of the three basic operations: rough-hewing, hollowing-out, or dressing? It is likely that he was skilled at all three, but when he worked with one of his sons or with his son-in-law in Basse-Frêne, each task may have been assigned to the person most skilled at performing that particular operation.

It was probably the master clog maker who decided what type of clog Louis-François made. There was a heavy demand for covered clogs made from beech, however, so it is plausible to assume that this was his primary product. Did he work exclusively for a dealer or manufacturer, or did he also have a local clientele of his own? There is no way of knowing. It is possible that relatives, friends, or fellow residents of Origny ordered clogs from him. If he had clients of his own, he would have needed additional skills. He would have needed to know about feet—how to measure them, how they curved, how sensitive they might be, and how they could be misshapen. We know that many village clog makers knew the foot size of each of their clients.

If we really want to understand Louis-François Pinagot, what we need to fathom is his intuitive grasp of how the clog fit into rural civilization, of the idea of peasant life it symbolized. Let us therefore pause for a moment to examine what this footwear meant to this society, which will shed new light on the clog maker's importance in the social imagination.

The clog implied a certain repertoire of gestures, a certain somatic rhythm, a certain type of behavior. It made casual walking and rapid running impossible.[37] It was heavy. It prevented the foot from bending. It did, however, stabilize the foot on most terrain by enforcing a certain type of gait. It protected the foot from impact, cuts, and burns and preserved it from water, mud, and snow. In winter it was stuffed with hay, which felt warm, and in summer with ferns, which felt light and cool. Clogs hardened the soles of the feet, which were left bare, whereas shoes imprisoned them. And the clog was also a tool. With it one stepped down on the spade.[38] And a simple kick was enough to break up a compact mound of dirt.

The country air resounded with the clack of clogs, declaring one's own presence and revealing that of others. Clogs pounded out dance rhythms and when necessary drowned out unwanted voices. It is no accident that clogs figure prominently in popular song. They were also a time-saver: unlike boots, which are difficult to put on and even more difficult to take off, clogs can be put on without bending or sitting.[39] They are also easy to clean. They made it possible to go out to the garden, the well, the barn, or the stable without getting one's feet dirty, assuming that mattered to the people who wore them. And on occasion they could become a fearsome weapon, as we know (to mention just two examples) from the terrible events of August 16, 1870, in Hautefaye and, long before that, the massacres in the Orne in the summer of 1792.[40]

Clogs identified their wearers and revealed their presence. Left outside a door, they gave notice of the presence of a person inside, whether the busybody or the beloved. In the country, "people were announced by the sound of their clogs." The rhythm of clacks was slow for the elderly, more rapid for the young, while the tired field hand returning from the harvest tended to drag his feet. And the light, bustling step of a woman in clogs was immediately distinguishable from the calm, heavy sound of a man. The clickety-clack of clogs was thus as much a feature of the sonic environment as the sound of work songs and familiar voices that told who was coming, even if their words could not be understood.[41] After an arsonist set a series of fires in Lower Normandy in 1830, a man was sentenced to death because a witness testified that he had recognized the sound of his footsteps.[42]

Clogs were thus an intimate part of the peasant's world. He listened to the sound they made as he walked.[43] He smelled them while they "smoked" at a corner of the fire. He watched them wear out as he worked, reminding him of and preserving his past. Because clogs identified the person, those of the dead were religiously stowed away. Even more than the clothing of the deceased, they served as a permanent memento.[44]

Pinagot would have been aware of all this in a more or less confused way but probably would not have been familiar with what the clog symbolized in the eyes of the better-educated. This was a fairly small circle, at which we will want to take a closer look later on. Of course, he would have seen the point of various proverbs that mentioned clogs—proverbs that were often repeated by people he knew. In particular, the erotic significance of clogs came up frequently.[45] The nakedness of the foot in contact with hay, fern, or wood bestowed a sensual value on the clog. Its shape was somehow reminiscent of the female sex, as was the way one inserted one's foot. For a girl to allow a man to remove her clogs was to surrender to his desire as much as if she removed her apron string.[46] To "break one's clog" was to lose one's virginity. To "change clogs" was to take a mistress. Any number of anthropologists have remarked on such analogies.

Beyond these banalities caution is in order when it comes to the clog as a symbol of poverty, limitation, and subordination. To the elite, indeed to townspeople in general, clogs symbolized the common people. Any assembly of people in clogs evoked memories of the *levée en masse* of patriots (or of Vendéens) during the Revolution. The *Trésor de la langue française* attests to the ancientness of this image. To anyone who had risen in society, the clog signified the bottom rung of the social ladder.

I doubt, however, that it had any such meaning for Louis-François Pinagot. Indeed, he would have had many reasons to look upon the clog as the symbol of a dynamic class. People took great care in decorating their clogs. They proudly showed them off on holidays. Their footwear expressed their identity almost as effectively as a coat of arms. Clog production increased rapidly, and the number of clog makers grew accordingly, though most remained mired in poverty. Especially in the 1860s, when rural society in Normandy and the Perche seemed in full blossom, Louis-François must have felt proud to be a man who made clogs, then so much in demand. After all, it was the clog that set the peasant apart from the *va-nu-pied*, who, as the term implies, went barefoot.

The symbolic value of the clog in the city was, of course, the opposite of what it was in the country. To townspeople the clog designated failure. It smacked of the provincial. It was a focal point of the derision directed at all things associated with rural life. If one wished to disparage something, the way to do it was to link it somehow to the "clog." But in the country, throughout Pinagot's lifetime, the clog represented the highest value.

Let us return now to what it meant to be a humble clog maker in the forest of Bellême. What kind of business relationships would a man like Pinagot have entered into? Social relations in the region were typical of what sociologists have called "protoindustrial society."[47] This model has been described often, and I shall make free use of it here, although it is always wise to be wary of concepts in which the idea that historical processes have predetermined outcomes is implicit. There were clog manufacturers and licensed master clog makers in Bellême, Saint-Martin, Mamers, and La Perrière. Some of them lived in fairly small towns, for example, Sieur Lemay in Origny-le-Butin. The licensed master clog makers were a widely scattered group, and there were quite a number of them. In Year IX (1801), Delestang counted 193 in the Mortagne district.[48]

Less concentrated than spinning, clog making in this area was in fact dominated by dealers, who decided what type of clogs should be made and what masters to deal with. According to Raymond Humbert, a clog manufacturer in the Orne would have dealt with fifty or sixty workers, and a Paris dealer would have commissioned work from twenty-five master clog makers.[49] These figures are, of course, just estimates and probably on the high side for the first two-thirds of the century, during which the industry was apparently not quite so concentrated, to judge by the ratio between the number of clog makers working in the forest of Bellême and the number of licensed masters in the small towns mentioned above.

What matters to us, however, is what kind of relationship existed between the master clog maker and his "workers."[50] The judicial archives shed a good deal of light on how workers were hired to work in the forest huts. On September 13, 1822, Pierre-Nicolas Germond, a licensed clog maker from Bellême, and René Faucon Jr., a clog maker from Origny-le-Butin, appeared in court. On that date Louis-François Pinagot was twenty-four years old, and it is fair to assume that in previous years, before his marriage, his situation was quite similar to Faucon's. "By verbal contract," young Faucon "allegedly agreed to make clogs in the workshop of the aforementioned Germond, and on his behalf, in the forest of Réno [note the distance traveled], at an agreed price for each load of clogs until the next sale of government wood."[51] Now it was alleged that "without legitimate cause" Faucon "had decided to quit the aforementioned workshop to work elsewhere," to the "detriment of [Germond's] business." Germond was therefore asking that Faucon be forced to return to his shop and resume work "with an obligation to pay an indemnity of fifty francs."

Faucon stated that he had never entered into any contract. If he had, Germond would have paid him the customary advance. He acknowledged that he had "in fact worked for about three months in [the master's] shop but that he had since discovered that he could earn a higher price elsewhere and had gone there to work." Germond claimed that five months earlier they had "agreed on a rate of seven francs per load, including one franc's worth of wine for each load." By leaving the shop, Faucon "had put the man with whom he worked out of a job." Sieur Chrétien, a clog maker from Saint-Martin-du-Vieux-Bellême, testified as to the verbal agreement. When Faucon came to Germond and asked him for work, the master had said that he "paid [his] other workers seven francs per load." Faucon "accepted these terms and *left his tools*, which he had caused to be transported to [Germond's] shop," in which he had worked for three or four months. In the end he was sentenced to pay damages of five francs.

On August 1, 1827, Louis-Julien Lemaire, a licensed clog dealer from Bellême, filed a complaint against Julien Choplain, a clog maker from the same town. Accord to the complainant, Choplain was alleged to have "agreed to make clogs for him for one year in exchange for a signing bonus of ten francs for wine, paid in cash, plus eight francs per load of finished clogs. Three months' after his engagement, the aforementioned Choplain had left the shop without cause of any kind."[52] The defendant claimed that Lemaire had "left him without work." He had kept the ten francs as an indemnity for periods of unemployment. Furthermore, he had been required to cut down an ash and on several occasions had been obliged to "carry . . . wood to the shop on his shoulders." These chores had not been part of the original agreement. Nevertheless, the court ordered him to repay the ten francs.

If Louis-François worked in a hut when he was young or even after his marriage during his stay in Saint-Martin, he would have had to enter into an agreement of this sort—an "arrangement" like any other. The procedure is clear: master and workman made a verbal contract in the presence of a witness. They agreed on the price to be paid for each load of finished clogs and on the amount to be paid in advance or "for wine." The workman agreed to work for a certain period of time (for example, until the next sale of cutting rights by the government). Having done so, he would then have his tools brought to the master's hut or workshop, perhaps in town or else in the forest. From that point on, the master was required to provide the workman with the opportunity to work. The presence of other manufacturers in the area made it possible for the workman to pressure his employer by threatening to take a better-paid job elsewhere. Once set up in the master's shop, the worker could vary his income by adjusting the pace at which he worked. Finally, it seems that there was some form of specialization within the workshop: a hewer, a carver, and a finisher divided the labor among them.

In both L'Hôtel-Migné and Basse-Frêne, Louis-François probably worked at home. Another case will shed light on the somewhat different type of bargain that was struck between a manufacturer and a self-employed clog maker who worked at home. On July 16, 1819, Jacques Evezard, a licensed wood dealer from Bellême, and Mathurin Guillin (whom we met earlier), a partner of Jacques Geslain, also known as Rustin, clog makers from Le Carouge, a village of Saint-Martin, not far from Origny-le-Butin, appeared in court. It is quite likely that Louis-François knew these two workmen and that he himself entered into the kind of arrangement that we are about to describe. "In the hope that Guillin would work for him, [Evezard] advanced him the sum of 90 francs 80 centimes in a loan guaranteed as well by the aforementioned Geslain. Unable to repay this sum, they allegedly promised to give [*sic*] the aforementioned Evezard two and a half loads of unfinished clogs at the rate of 32 francs per load, [which comes to] 80 francs, and twenty-seven pairs of clogs yielding 10 francs 80 centimes at the rate of 40 centimes per pair; of which only one load of clogs was delivered, minus one pair, on April 27, 1818; which gives 31 francs 60 centimes to deduct from the said sum of 90 francs 80 centimes."[53]

Evezard therefore asked for 59 francs 20 centimes. The court recognized this debt and sentenced Guillin and Geslain, also known as Rustin, to reimburse him. It also sentenced Guillin to pay 18 francs 80 centimes "for the price of clogs that were never smoked."

Here the agreement was simpler than in the previous case: the master submitted his order and advanced the clog maker a sum of money to allow him to do his work. The clog maker agreed to deliver the finished product, namely, a smoked clog. The fact that there were so many manufacturers, and each one needed to find workers with home workshops, suggests that in this period of expansion for the industry the ordinary clog maker was not totally defenseless on the labor market. Note, too, that the master could have wood delivered to the workman's home shop, which seems not to have been the practice in the previous case.

With terms such as these, it is difficult to estimate how much a workman such as Louis-François might have made. In 1809 Louis Dumbois estimated that a load of clogs cost forty-eight francs.[54] In 1819, in Bellême and Saint-Martin, a dealer paid a worker forty centimes per pair and thirty-two francs per load. At first glance, therefore, it would appear that the price of a pair of clogs had declined over the ten years, from 1809 to 1819. But there is no assurance that the "load" (*somme*) is the same in the two cases. It may be, moreover, that the first estimate is of the selling price of the clogs and not the buyer's purchase price. In any case, information such as this does not enable us to measure the clog maker's profits, because we do not know how much he paid for raw materials (when not provided by the dealer) and transportation. All in all, the seven or eight francs that a hut worker received for each load of smoked clogs is probably a more accurate indicator, although we do not know how long it would have taken to produce the required number of pairs.

Owing to complexities such as these, economic statisticians for a long time refused to include clog makers in their reports. The only detailed information we have is from 1834. In that year, Odollant-Desnos tells us that the clog makers of the Orne completed on average fifty pairs of clogs per week "at twenty centimes per pair."[55] This works out to a gross income of 1.43 francs per day. Unfortunately, no supporting details are given.

The first estimate of the average daily income of clog makers in Bellême and Saint-Martin dates from 1855, when it was 1.08 francs.[56] Incomes ranged from 0.75 to 1.5 francs per day, depending on each man's know-how and ardor for the work. Thus the clog maker earned roughly the same amount as the laborer, although the clog maker's employment was probably more regular. If we believe the results of a survey carried out in 1862 by the mayors of the Orne under the supervision of justices of the peace and cantonal commissioners, the clog makers of Origny-le-Butin earned from 1.75 to 2.25 francs per day.[57] Five years later (in 1867), the daily income of clog makers in the Bellême region ranged from 2 to 2.5 francs.[58] The inescapable conclusion, then, is that Louis-François Pinagot's personal income probably rose sharply during the Second Empire. Lending further credence to the figures is the fact that the mayor of Origny-le-Butin responded to the survey of 1862. In the last decade of the Second Empire, clog makers earned significantly more than laborers.

This improvement in the situation of the clog maker was a result of the favorable economic climate. Demand for clogs was high, and the market was quite extensive. In 1858, according to the author of a study of the forest of Bellême drafted as a preliminary to a new management plan, "clogs are shipped to Paris. Surplus production is consumed locally, in Mortagne, Bellême, Mamers, Nogent, and Le Mans."[59] Bear in mind, moreover, that "wood shavings are easy to sell."

Clog manufacturers turn out to have been in a paradoxical situation. During the first two-thirds of the nineteenth century, the economy of the Perche failed to make the transition from protoindustrial society to modern industrial society.[60] During the first decade of the Second Empire, in particular, the center of Orne industry shifted from the Haut-Perche to the bocage country of the western hills. Against this background of general failure, however, clog manufacturing paradoxically expanded. The trade therefore gained greater visibility in statistical reports, and along with that visibility went an increased respectability. At the same time, the canton of Bellême proved to be an exception: because of the expansion of clog making, this canton experienced "delayed protoindustrialization" during the first half of the nineteenth century.[61] Thus, as the Perche in general deindustrialized, the canton of Bellême industrialized. In the history that concerns us here, everything depends on the scale of the analysis.

Throughout his life Louis-François Pinagot was, in a sense, swept along by this favorable economic wind, this useful and paradoxical delay, which saved the area in which he happened to live from the de-industrialization that affected surrounding areas. The decline of the clog making industry did not occur until the 1880s, after his death. Of course, the improvement that he saw took place over the long term, and it was not linear: like other forest trades, clog making experienced periods of severe depression.[62]

The benefits of delayed industrialization were amplified by the unanticipated expansion of the glove-making industry. Louis-François's family was buffeted by a number of contradictory trends, about which we shall have more to say later on. His wife, Anne Pôté, and his eldest daughters, who were spinners, were victims of de-industrialization. The decline of the spinning trade led to a sharp drop in the income of a family already threatened by indigence owing to the large number of young children. After the crisis of 1846–1848, however, the rise of the home-based glove and net industry led to a wholesale shift in the type of work performed by local women in their homes. This favorable climate began to affect Louis-François's family just after the death of the mother.

Louis-François was no doubt aware of the fact that the clog industry was prospering and employing growing numbers of workers, if nowhere else but in Origny-le-Butin. This may well have persuaded him that the status of his trade was on the rise. We should be careful not to assume that he would have seen himself as bearing the stigma of an ancient and ineluctably declining occupation.

In all the forests of the Haut-Perche in general, and along the southern edge of the forest of Bellême in particular,[63] we find that, despite the impression of disorder resulting from a veritable "chaos of statistics,"[64] employment in the clog industry rose more or less steadily until after Louis-François's death. It would be misleading, however, to consider his occupation alone, since he was the head of a household whose members worked in a variety of trades. Until 1846 his wife and daughters identified themselves as spinners. As we have seen, spinning was one of the major occupations of poor women in Origny-le-Butin. It was a trade open to unwed mothers like cousin Angélique, widows, abandoned wives, and woodworkers' daughters. Working women in Basse-Frêne spun hemp for manufacturer-dealers in Bellême. The manufacturers supplied the raw material and took delivery of the finished product.[65] At one time the industry had prospered. According to Subprefect Delestang, 4,000 women worked as spinners in the canton of Bellême when Louis-François was a small child. By 1811, however, when an industrial survey was carried out, only 600 spinners remained in the Mortagne district. By 1834 the employment figure had risen again to around 2,000.[66]

For most women, spinning hemp was only a seasonal or occasional activity, in any case a secondary employment. Caution is in order, however. Hemp spinners did perform their "immemorial" labor when home alone during the off-season. Typically, they spun only half the year, according to the records of a survey carried out in 1812.[67] The same was true of linen spinners in the northern part of the district, who worked "so little of the time that the products of this type of industry do not warrant being taken into account."[68] However, the writer of the report added this concerning the spinners of the Bellême area: "There are a few, though, who spin all year round." Was this not true of Anne Pôté, the wife of a landless maker of clogs?

One of three hypotheses about her must be true. Either she spun all year round, in addition to her household chores. Or she worked with her spinning wheel only on occasion and helped out by doing finish work on clogs. Or she spun during the winter and worked in her father's or father-in-law's fields during the harvest season. Harvest work must have been tempting because it paid four times as much as what a spinner could earn. We will never know which of these three hypotheses is correct. She and her daughters may have experienced all three modes of work at one time or another.

Another point needs to be clarified: not all the spinners in Origny were employed by manufacturer-dealers. Some worked for a relative, friend, neighbor, or straightforward client. Many domestics spun for their masters, especially during the off-season.

On September 25, 1823, Françoise-Marie Martin, a domestic servant, filed a complaint against her former master, Henri de Bloteau, a farmer from Origny-le-Butin.[69] Louis-François must have known the Martin girl because they were roughly the same age and she worked for a landlord who had given Pinagot's father his power of attorney. Marie Martin asked for twenty-one francs in wages for the past year and ten francs for two months of the current year. She stated that in September of the previous year she had accepted employment with M. de Bloteau until midsummer for the sum of thirty-nine francs. "Finding herself pregnant, she withdrew to the home of the aforementioned Brodin, where she gave birth and thereafter remained for three months. Although she was no longer living in Sieur de Bloteau's house, *she did spinning for him*, in return for which he gave her board. She had been promised that she would not be charged for that board, but when she closed the account at midsummer, de Bloteau deducted a month's wages." Her master claimed that he owed her nothing for the three months; that he had "supplied her with what she needed to spin out of humanity; that because of this small labor he had paid her board at Widow Brodin's and provided her with necessities." The court found in his favor at the conclusion of a case that makes clear just how complex such arrangements could be.

Spinning was part of the complex system of service exchanges that governed social relations in Origny-le-Butin. Take, for example, a case from November 1853 that involved a sister-in-law and a brother-in-law of Louis-François and that also tells us about the working routine of one of his fellow workers.[70] Louise Pôté, the wife of Julien Courville, a clog maker in Vigne-de-la-Coudre, a commune of Origny-le-Butin, spun for Sieur Riboux, a farmer from Le Plessis. She spun a total of 17.6 pounds of hemp for a sum of 8.5 francs. When she went to claim what she believed was due her, Riboux "said that he did indeed owe her 8.5 francs for spinning thread, but that her husband [Courville the clog maker] owed him at least that much for plowing" two plots of land. He had intended to ask the clog maker for 10 francs in exchange for this service, "but, hoping to avoid a lawsuit, he had agreed to the mediation of notable individuals, including the deputy mayor of his commune."

Courville countered that he had had plowing done by a number of different farmers, including the mayor of Origny-le-Butin, and that everyone agreed that he owed Riboux no more than six francs. In the end the judge found that the two services were equivalent. So it may be that Anne Pôté and her daughters worked in exchange for hauling logs or billets of beech.

Spinners earned ridiculously low wages. In 1812 their earnings were estimated at twenty-five centimes per day, barely what a child could earn working in a factory.[71] The situation was no better in 1848: "The daily wage of a spinner who eats her [own] bread and is at her wheel twelve hours a day cannot be more than twenty centimes," whereas a "a dress maker, an adroit seamstress, or even a washer woman earns forty to fifty centimes a day beyond her board."[72] In 1855 spinners in Bellême and Saint-Martin were still earning just twenty-five centimes, compared with sixty-five for glove makers.[73] This makes it easy to understand the transfer of workers from one trade to the other.[74] Between 1851 and 1861, the number of spinners in Saint-Martin decreased by 45 percent, while the number of glove makers above the age of fourteen increased by 70 percent.[75]

From the early days of the July Monarchy, administrators continually lamented the decline of spinning in the canton of Bellême and the wretched condition of female workers, who had been plunged into the depths of misery. Along the forest's southern edge, the spinning wheel was often associated with begging. Louis-François's neighbors—Cousin Angélique, Widow Virlouvet, and Widow Foussard—exemplify this tragic fate. As mentioned earlier, moreover, the decline of spinning only hastened the Pinagot family's descent into outright indigence. The logic of this development is worth exploring. Jacques Pinagot, a carter and small farmer who held the power of attorney of a minor notable, seems to have avoided poverty, and the elder Pôté was among the Origny taxpayers who paid most at the turn of the century. It might, at first sight, seem surprising that these two men allowed a son and a daughter to sink into such wretched straits if we did not know about the declining fortunes of the Pôté family, symbolized by the pitiful condition of the brother, Marin Pôté, and the apparent selfishness of Jacques Pinagot, who worried more about his servant-mistress than about his wife, who left him, or his son, who was probably a hardworking fellow.

In the aftermath of the lengthy period of difficulties that marked the middle of the century, Louis-François, by then an indigent widower, witnessed an improvement in his family's situation. The number of glove makers living on the forest's southern edge continued to rise sharply. In 1862 there were 1,860 in the canton of Bellême alone, scattered among seventeen firms employing anywhere from 29 to 475 workers.[76] In Origny-le-Butin thirty-five women and fourteen children were employed in the making of net gloves, among them two of Louis-François's daughters. In this commune "female workers are empoyed by manufacturers in Bellême and Mamers." In 1867, 8,190 women and 1,410 girls were listed as glove makers in the district census.[77]

Glove making called for "steadier, less part-time employment of female workers" than did old-fashioned spinning.[78] The industry did not like disorderly methods. In conjunction with the clog industry, it formed a more coherent domestic system than did the earlier association of clog making with spinning. This was indeed a case of protoindustrialization as defined by Mendels. Still, within the domestic partnership consisting of Louis-François and his daughters, two dissimilar types of work coexisted. Clog making, no matter how prosperous it may have been, was merely a matter of survival. By contrast, the glove industry was a modern enterprise, a response to the demand created by Paris fashion. It was largely dependent on the capital, which provided leadership, financing, and a market. It also reflected a new concept of femininity unlike that associated with spinning, which was still practiced by the elderly, especially elderly widows. Young women and new brides looked upon net gloves and accessories as embodying the prestige, indeed the fascination, of luxury. Whereas rough linen fabrics, which featured a local raw material, at best hinted of an austere trousseau painstakingly accumulated over many years. By the end of the century, the proliferation of milliners and seamstresses only confirmed this fundamental shift in representations and desires.[79]

Gradually, the sound of the spinning wheel gave way to the silence of the shuttle used for making gloves, mittens, and hairnets. Silence made conversation easier and liberated feminine speech.[80] Our task is to imagine how this changed the climate of everyday life in Basse-Frêne.

The glove makers, as true industrial workers, proved better equipped to press their demands than the spinners. On January 6, 1855, nine of them were questioned by police in Bellême.[81] That morning, "a fairly large crowd had gathered . . . in the upper section of the Rue de Paris." The working women insulted a woman by the name of Pontoise "because she was responsible for the fact that their compensation for making a pair of gloves had been decreased [by five centimes per pair] by Maître Fribourg in Paris." The court found in favor of the workers and characterized the plaintiff's attitude as provocative.

The manufacturer, after receiving an order from a Paris merchant or wholesaler, selected and purchased raw materials. He provided his workers with thread, which was carefully weighed before delivery. And he chose which models the glove and net makers were to use. "Traveling from town to town according to a prearranged schedule, he 'received' visitors every two or three weeks in a village café or at the home of one of his workers."[82] He also employed factors or *entrepreneuses*, who lived in the same rural towns as the workers and served him as intermediaries. When he "received" his guests, he took delivery of finished goods and paid his *façonnières* for their work. He also monitored the amount of thread used, checked on the quality of the goods, noted the skill of each worker, and set their wages accordingly. At home young girls quickly acquired the dexterity needed to make gloves. They began by setting up shuttles for their older siblings. Then, when they reached the age of eight or nine, they learned to make the basic gauze material. It's likely that this is the way things worked in Louis-François's household.

Although there were many complaints about the work, the glove industry brought comparative prosperity to the countryside. In 1864 La Sicotière estimated that the typical glove maker earned from sixty to eighty centimes per day.[83] Other studies confirm this rate of pay, with some minor variations.[84] The differences in the estimates no doubt stem from the fact that glove making was skilled labor and workers were compensated in proportion to their skills. In any case, when we look at all the data, what is striking is not the fact that incomes increased but the fact that starting wages were three times higher than for spinners.

Combine this with the fact that the profits from clog making also increased, and it becomes clear how Louis-François Pinagot and his children slowly emerged from the poverty in which they had been mired for so long—in fact, during the entire lifetime of Anne Pôté. When Louis-François and his wife still had small children at home, their annual income could be calculated as follows:

313 working days × 1.05 francs = 329 francs
156 working days × 0.20 francs = 31 francs
or a total of 360 francs to feed seven people.

Under the Second Empire, Louis-François, by then a widower, lived with two of his daughters, who worked as glove makers. Their annual income was:

313 working days × 2 francs = 626 francs.

313 working days × 2 × 0.6 francs = 375 francs

or a total of 1,001 francs to feed three people.

Now, according to a study of the canton of Bellême commissioned in 1848, "a family of four (husband, wife, and two young children) requires at least 500 francs to avoid begging, stealing, or suffering from hunger."[85] The vast majority of workers could not attain this level of income and had to make do with cheese, brown bread, and cider. If we are right about Louis-François's income, his family remained below the poverty line for a long time. It would very likely have been necessary for both him and Anne to do harvest work in order to make ends meet. In the second half of the century, after enduring periods of dire poverty between 1846 and 1855, Louis-François and his children would have been earning enough to lift themselves out of misery and alter their pattern of consumption. Unfortunately, his wife died too soon to reap the benefits of the changed economic climate.

Beyond the family's newfound prosperity, it seems likely that the daughters' position within the household would also have improved markedly, and not only because their father was now a widower. The glove industry enhanced the status of women and girls enough to elicit diatribes. Writing of the "confection of gauze" and the "sewing of gloves" in 1868, the subprefect of Mortagne noted that while "these two branches of commerce have supplied mothers with additional resources, they have not had the most beneficial effect on public health or morality. Girls prefer this independent though less remunerative work to the more robust labor of agriculture and even to household chores, and since their daily pay is insufficient, they seek the resources they lack elsewhere, all too often in immoral behavior. This has resulted in an increase in infanticide and illegitimate births along with the inevitable procession of unwed mothers."[86]

This new perception of youthful desires, of the fears aroused by the intensification of dreams and the proximity of luxury, tells us how much things had changed. If Anne Pôté had lived, there surely would have been a greater distance between her and her daughters and daughters-in-law than there was between Louis-François and his younger sons, who still shared their father's trade.

the pleasure of "arrangements"

The only way for us to understand how Louis-François Pinagot and people like him used the domanial forest outside of work is to consult the judicial archives. Unfortunately, this approach to understanding what people wanted and how they went about getting it poses a fundamental problem: it tells us only about those accused of committing crimes. There were relatively few criminals in the forest cantons that concern us here, and most of them were "repeat offenders."[1] Louis-François was not among them: in my exhaustive study of local court records, his name never came up. Nevertheless, by taking a close look at the minor, seemingly insignificant offenses that were committed in the forest of Bellême, we will gain a better understanding of what it was like for him to live nearby.

What I hoped to find out was what people wanted and how they spent their time. A dry, statistical study of delinquency seemed unlikely to answer these questions.[2] Tabulating various classes of offenses would have drained the life out of them while shedding little light on how people related to the forest. Yet it would have made no sense to pick a few cases at random and study only them. I therefore decided to confine my attention to a very small number of villages, those that Louis-François would have visited often, and to focus on friends of his and members of his extended family. I gathered evidence about misdemeanors that he must have been aware of and that were almost certainly discussed by people he knew. Some of these incidents would have affected him directly, moreover, because they injured the reputations of his relatives.

The crimes committed within the limits of Origny-le-Butin and the adjacent forest cantons were, not surprisingly, banal.[3] For the most part, the delinquents were people who worked in the forest, knew its most obscure trails like the backs of their hands, and could observe the comings and goings of forest wardens without difficulty. They were clog makers, loggers, long sawyers, carters, and wood sellers. Among them were a few farmers and artisans, but they were usually the receivers of stolen goods, people who profited in one way or another from crimes committed by others. Sometimes, however, they took part in criminal escapades themselves.

No less banal than the crimes committed was the geographical distribution of those crimes. Among the villages involved we find not only Haute- and Basse-Frêne, of course, but also Haute-Croix, Hautes-Folie, Haute-Roche, Les Querrières, Verger, and Vignes-de-la-Coudre, to name a few. Forest workers lived in these villages. Some of them, in particular the clog makers and bucket makers, relied on wood from the forest for their work. Widows and single women who depended on the forest to ease their misery also lived in these places. The presence of trees and brush made it relatively easy to hide and transport stolen goods. The woods also served as a convenient refuge when the wardens came looking for someone. By contrast, the town of Origny-le-Butin had little to do with forest crime.

In truth, these desperately poor offenders did not rely on the domanial forest for much in the way of resources. They did occasionally allow animals to graze on forest land. As we have seen, this was especially true of carters such as Louis-François's father, Jacques Pinagot. But widows and single women, some of them reduced temporarily to begging, would sometimes allow a goat or two or a few sheep to graze among the trees. Their children sometimes helped out. On June 18, 1811, a forest warden by the name of Rouzé came upon children tending four cows in a fifty-year-old stand of trees belonging to the canton of Le Châtelier. One cow belonged to a long sawyer, another to the clog maker Lemay, and the remaining two, along with a goat, to a farmer who was also a wood dealer.[4] All these people hailed from the same village, Le Gadet, a part of Saint-Martin-du-Vieux-Bellême. I mention this rather atypical case because it shows that it was possible for a clog maker to own a cow. In addition, the episode reveals the existence of at least a rudimentary village herd, thereby demonstrating genuine solidarity among neighbors.

On June 23, 1818, the widow Fontaine, also known as Brodinne, whom we have met before and will meet again, was spotted "at seven in the evening" in a stand of trees fifteen or sixteen years old in the canton of Pissot in the vicinity of six lambs, six sheep, and four goats, "which wandered about and grazed under the eye of the aforementioned Widow Fontaine, another woman named Biardeau [the wife of a clog maker], and youngsters Boutier and Moisy," a woodcutter and a farmer, all from Origny-le-Butin.[5] Brodinne and Mme Biardeau admitted that their goats were within the limits of the forest but claimed that they were merely nibbling on a hedge that belonged to Cottin, Louis-François's uncle and grandfather by marriage, who lived in Le Pissot.

On June 18, 1823, Widow Maillard of Hautes-Roches was caught red-handed by Warden Dupuis while tending a goat in an area of regrowth (aged seven years) in the canton of La Mare Bouillie, where Jacques Pinagot often allowed his horses to graze. Furthermore, she was carrying on her back "a pouch full of oak and hornbeam saplings," which she had just cut.[6]

Women (and, on rare occasion, men) also looked to the forest for dead leaves and ferns to use as stable litter, grass and acorns for animal feed, and, above all, wood for heating. Sometimes they bundled fallen branches or, less often, filched wood shavings from scrap piles. They carried this contraband on their backs in pouches or sacks that fastened around the shoulder.

During the economic crisis that marked the middle of the century, this sort of offense became increasingly common. On June 17, 1850, the home of Louis-François's cousin Angélique Pinagot in La Rigorière was searched under the watchful eye of Nicolas Bosse, the deputy mayor. In the unwed mother's loft the wardens, assisted by the *cantonnier*, or trail keeper, found two sacks of wood from a recently felled Chablis beech that had been stripped of its branches. Angélique confessed to having "taken the wood for heat."[7] This episode cost her 5.70 francs, or the equivalent of ten days' labor. Her crime was quite similar to that of Mélanie Barbet of Les Quer-rières. On November 28 of the same year, she was spotted by the wardens in the canton of the Chêne Sale, in a twenty-four-year-old stand of wood, in the process of "loading a sack with green branches from an oak that collapsed under the weight of the snow." Her fine was 2.20 francs.[8]

During the same winter, residents of Basse-Frêne, whom we have met before, were also reduced to similar petty crimes. On December 22, Anne Germond, Widow Cottin, Widow Bouquet, and the unfortunate Leboucs—a sampling of the poorest residents of the poorest village in the area—were caught red-handed while transporting three "sacks of branches broken by the snow."[9] On February 1, 1851, Widow Bouquet repeated the offense and was fined 5.60 francs, a fortune for a poor spinner who earned only twenty centimes per day.[10]

There were other forms of gathering as well. On August 4, 1812, Warden Beaumont spotted a woman by the name of Mouton from the town of Origny-le-Butin in the woodland section of the Vaugirard canton. She was gathering leaves to use as litter for "her cows and other animals" and had filled three sacks, for which she was fined three francs.[11] Her "pouches" were confiscated. As an owner of livestock, she was in a different category from the criminals mentioned previously. So were Mme Chevallier, the wife of a woodcutter from the village of Les Croix-Chemin, and Mme Bosse, the wife of Louis Bosse, a farmer, whom a warden found at four in the afternoon one day in 1827 "with a sack full of grass they had just cut with a sickle in a section of six-year-old trees."[12] On November 6, 1844, the warden saw the wife of a clog maker from Saint-Martin gathering acorns.[13] This tells us that at least one clog maker's wife kept a pig.

Most offenses involved more substantial pieces of wood, however. People surreptitiously chopped down trees or cut branches off them to build a hut or shed, to make fence posts for marking the limits of a parcel of land, or to make clogs. Beech, oak, and birch were "dishonored" by forest workers, that is, stripped of their best branches. On January 29, 1842, a warden filed this report: "We saw Pierre Landier, the minor son of Pierre Landier, a farmer from Gros Chêne" and a first cousin of Louis-François Pinagot "who had just dishonored a green oak more than three feet in circumference by cutting off all its major branches from top to bottom."[14] The tool he used was a billhook. For this offense he was fined thirty-seven francs, more than he could earn in a month.

Some women committed crimes by themselves, others with their husbands or other men. Take, for example, Brodinne, the widow Fontaine. On October 27, 1819, accompanied by Lemay, a young clog maker, she used a billhook to prune two branches of a green oak more than three feet in circumference. The two delinquents then carried the wood away on their shoulders.[15] On June 13, 1823, Brodinne again dishonored an oak. Warden Dupuis spotted her in the canton of Le Pissot, together with her daughter, the wife of clog maker Mathurin Guillin, also known as Fanfareau, one of the "habitual criminals" we met earlier in the hut of Master Duclos. The two women had stripped the branches from a green oak more than four feet around and filled five sacks with the wood thus obtained.[16]

Some of the Pinagot women were as determined as Brodinne. The wife of Uncle Louis of Les Querrières, the scandalous aunt and mother of Cousin Angélique, lived with a master mason by the name of Loitron (or Louatron). On March 21, 1823, in the canton of Le Coin à la Poule, Warden Dupuis saw Loitron using an axe to chop down a tree more than six feet in circumference, "from which he had obtained at least a horse load (*somme d'un cheval*) [of wood]. He had in his company the wife of Louis Pinagot, his nearest neighbor [in Les Querrières], a woman who abandoned her husband and children [including Cousin Angélique] several years ago [i.e., during Louis-François's adolescence] in order to live as the concubine of the man Louatron [or Loitron]. When he saw us, he ran off as fast as he could with his axe."[17] The warden then issued a summons to Pinagot's wife and asked her to "inform her favorite," that is, her lover.

On the first day of the same month, Warden Dupuis caught in the act another delinquent female whose reputation was no better than Uncle Louis's wife's: "Marie Louénnard [or Louanard or Loinard], the wife of Fleury, 'living disreputably' apart from her husband although no divorce has been granted [divorce having been abolished seven years earlier]. She makes her home by herself in the former presbytery of the commune of Origny-le-Butin."[18] On this particular day she had "climbed to the top of a green beech" more than three feet in circumference and "was pruning branches as she climbed down." As a result, the tree was "repeatedly dishonored." Mme Fleury was equipped "with a billhook, a belt, and a hook behind her back, like a regular woodcutter. . . . We ordered her to climb down from the tree, and she made as if to obey."

Even lawfully wedded couples engaged in crime. On February 18, 1844, Warden Coquart, a clever detective, discovered Mathurin Biard and his wife, Marie Chauvin of Les Ricordières, in a stand of 160-year-old trees in the canton of the Chêne Sale. "The man had just climbed two green beeches and cut down some of their branches."[19]

Clog makers were the most common delinquents. They needed wood, and Louis-François had probably watched them obtain it in ingenious ways from the time he was a young child. On March 18, 1812, a band of clog makers from Le Carouge, accompanied by Widow Guillin, a laundress, cut down a beech.[20] On April 28 Warden Beaumont caught another band from the village of La Croix (Haute or Basse?) in the act. Jean Biardeaux (also known as Bierdeaux), a clog maker, and Louis Marchand, a charcoal burner, accompanied by Pierre Chevallier, a wood cutter from Les Vignes, had damaged three beech trees. After a search supervised by the mayor of Origny-le-Butin, a faggot was found in Marchand's house, while eight aspen pickets turned up in Biardeaux's house and a load of beech at Chevallier's. As always on such occasions, the men were absent, and it was their wives who gave explanations to the authorities.[21]

On November 24 of that year, the same warden determined that someone had cut down two birches and ten small oaks the night before in the canton of Le Coin à la Poule. Hidden beneath a bed in the home of Dupont, a clog maker from L'Hôtel-aux-Oiseaux, the authorities discovered a green birch "split by splints" that the warden officially identified as one of the trees he was looking for.[22] In that same year, Aunt and Uncle Drouin (pronounced *Deroin*), who owned property in Haute-Fresnaye (or Frêne), were searched. In their home the wardens found "a sack full of green beech." The authorities found another sack in the home of François Borel, a laborer from Basse-Frêne.[23]

Some of these offenses were quite serious. In the family of Jean Lorillon, a bucket maker and wood splitter who was an acquaintance of Louis-François's, there were some brave souls.[24] In May 1831 Lorillon cut down a beech more than three feet around. On October 19, 1839, he and his son François sawed up four aspens. On July 19, 1844, a warden accompanied by Deputy Mayor Bosse searched the home of Pierre Lorillon, the future father-in-law of Cousin Angélique, who worked as a wood splitter in Hautes-Folies. In a shed the searchers found two Chablis oaks more than twenty-one inches around and thirty-nine to forty-five feet long, along with a beech that they recognized by its bark.

Laborers were no slouches when it came to petty crime. On March 15, 1817, the wife of a laborer named Ricordeau was caught in her home "heating her wash with wood of dry oak, freshly cut and split" as well as a "horse load of the same wood hidden behind a chest."[25] On April 3, 1828, three laborers from the village of La Bonde chopped down a beech more than two and a half feet in circumference in the canton of the Chêne Sale and split it "into pieces" before transporting it to their homes.[26] On December 11 a warden came upon Pierre Renard, a laborer from L'Hôtel-aux-Oiseaux, and Pierre Guijason, a "framer," once again in the canton of the Chêne

Sale. "With a saw they were cutting a beech almost four and a half feet around into lengths and splitting it into pieces with an axe so as to carry it home more readily."[27] It is easy to imagine the kind of camaraderie that would have had to exist among these woodcutters of fortune.

Jean-Louis Ruffray, the man reputed to be the biggest criminal in the commune, lived in Haute-Fresnaye. On March 22, 1837, his home was found to contain twenty-one pieces of beech split with an axe, and a search of a nearby field turned up three billets of beech, one of them more then six and a half feet in circumference, from Le Coin à la Poule. On September 8 Ruffray cut up an oak and a birch with a billhook. On January 7 of the following year, Warden Coquart saw him using his tool on a beech more than two and a half feet around.[28] On February 3, 1839, near the same spot, in Haute-Fresnaye (or Frêne), at the home of the laborer Jean Biardeaux, searchers found under the bed and next to the fireplace wood from three green birches, freshly cut in the canton of the Chêne Sale.[29]

What kind of relationship did Louis-François have with neighbors of this sort? Did he admire them? We have no way of knowing. Criminals almost always used the same methods. They usually worked by day but occasionally by night. With saws, axes, and billhooks they cut down trees or removed branches, whereupon they hid the wood in brambles until it could be hauled away. They carried it on their shoulders or in sacks on their backs and tried to leave no trace of their activity. Contraband wood might be hidden under beds, stored in sheds, buried in fields, or submerged beneath the surface of a pond.

On March 29, 1836, Marin and Jacques Pôté, both brothers-in-law of Louis-François, hid ten sacks of both dry and green wood at a place roughly 250 paces "from the edge of the forest." At the time they were living in the village of La Croix. A warden discovered their stash.[30] On August 13, 1837, a warden arrested Jean Coiffé (or Coeffé), a long sawyer from Origny-le-Butin, along with two of his sons. Each of the offenders was carrying a "shoulder load" of wood from a beech they had just cut up.[31]

When a warden determined that an offense had been committed, he then proceeded to investigate it. If he failed to catch the criminal in the act, he might stake out the location. If no one turned up, he might search for tracks on the ground or in the snow. To trace the movements of thieves, he might also look for broken branches or wood stashed in the brambles. Once he was sure that the stolen wood was in a particular village, he would go with the mayor or deputy mayor to search houses, workshops, and nearby fields and ponds. The crucial part of his job was to ascertain "the identity of the wood."

The ease with which wardens could analyze and remember the color and identifying characteristics of trees and the grain patterns of wood is striking. The ultimate proof of a tree's identity was to match it with its stump. Pieces seized in a search could be compared with the stump to see if the grain matched. Most accused offenders refused to participate because they knew they would be found out. The procedures used for identifying trees should be of interest to anyone concerned with the history of identity. Methods for interpreting clues and signs that scholars have rather hastily imputed to the police of the late nineteenth century were already being used by the humble wardens of the forest of Bellême in the time of Louis-François Pinagot.[32]

To continue, I want to look at several cases that shed further light on these procedures. The first dates from 1822, a few years after Louis-François's marriage. On September 2, at ten in the morning, wardens determined that numerous offenses had been committed in a stand of 140-year-old trees in the canton of Le Coin à la Poule. Similar offenses had been noted during the previous three months. This time, three green beeches had been illegally cut down and removed, and their stumps had been covered with a mixture of earth, moss, and fallen leaves, on top of which the criminals had planted holly to hide their theft. But a woman was seen emerging from the brush "with a sackful of wood." It turned out to be Aunt Drouin's sister-in-law. "A couple of suspicious characters cut down a fine beech of ours, and this wood is from the top. This is my second trip. I took the kindling first, and now I'm taking the firewood. If you like, I'll show you where I found the top, and I'll also show you the stump. (We gladly agreed.)"[33] This statement is one of the few recorded utterances of a member of the Pinagot family (who was, to be sure, only a distant relative of Louis-François's).

The wardens had this to say about the encounter: "This woman, whom we know [as they knew almost everyone in the area] to be a Drouain married to Jean Coëfe (a Coefay) [*sic*] living with her mother and husband in proprietary community in the commune of Origny-le-Butin, village of La Fresnaye, did not enjoy a high reputation, nor did her family." At seven in the morning, on September 3, the authorities searched the home of Widow

Drouin, her son-in-law Coêfé, her eldest son, Augustin (Louis-François's uncle), and her daughter, Widow Biardeaux. Behind the house, in a "cultivated piece of land" belonging to Coêfé and Drouin (the son), they found the top of the beech; several more pieces were found in the house; "many others were being used as supports for apple trees heavily laden with fruit." The authorities also discovered a length of green birch almost three feet in circumference, which had been cut with a saw. "We recognized it by the bark" as the stolen tree, they affirmed. Nearby lay two tops of green oak. A shed had been built out of wood from the forest.

The wardens and the mayor then searched Augustin Drouin's house and asked his wife, Louis-François's aunt, to "open her apartments." In the barn they found a green aspen from the La Perrière section along with a sackful of green hornbeam that was to be used for a fence. In a nearby field belonging to the Drouin heirs (several brothers and a sister), the wardens found the rest of the wood taken from the canton of Le Coin à la Poule over the past three months. At the home of Widow Biardeaux, they noticed a newly built shed. On one of her "pieces of land" they also found two lengths of beech and, in her garden, a length of oak, along with two aspen joists that had been carefully buried. "The three women admitted taking part in the crimes." They were asked to "notify their husbands."

"Two of them told us in tears[:] it is unfortunate that we will pay for wood we do not have; we do not want to denounce anyone, but there are people in the commune who are making clogs with it." The warden thought it might be Gervais Duclos and went to his house. "We found Mathurin Guillin—the son-in-law of the Brodinne woman—a journeyman clog maker employed on an annual basis by the aforementioned Duclos.[34] He was working on clogs made from freshly cut beech, which we recognized from the bark, since they were not finished." Guillin claimed that the wood belonged to his master. But Duclos had a different story. He assured the wardens that "it was his worker who brought the wood this morning to make several pairs of clogs for him. The worker said, 'Yes, I brought it this morning in the hope of making some profit for myself. But I did not go into your forest to find it, I found it in the Gustins' field.' (He meant the Drouins, because they are not known by their proper name.)"

This case, which takes us inside a family that lived in Haute-Frêne and was related to Louis-François, also tells us a great deal about petty crime in the forest. Above all, it tells us what a bad reputation the Drouins had, and not just "the Gustins." We saw earlier that the Pinagots of Les Querrières had a disastrous reputation, and that the reputation of Louis-François's father, Jacques Pinagot, was not much better. But there is absolutely no evidence that Louis-François himself, despite his poverty, shared their bad name.

Several other vignettes will shed additional light on life among the poor people who worked in the forest. A woman by the name of Veillard, who lived in Haute-Roche, was cunning and cautious yet still managed to get herself into trouble. On August 29, 1835, the authorities searched her home and found three pieces of birch hidden in a straw mattress and "three other pieces hidden in a stack of firewood." Needless to say, this was wood taken illegally from the forest.[35] Much later, on July 12, 1843, a warden saw in the Vaugirard trench, in the heart of a thirty-five-year-old stand of trees, an "individual who was carrying a tree on his shoulder and a billhook in his hand. . . . [He was] wearing a rather old light blue smock and a white cotton cap, black trousers, and clogs on his feet." Note the description: Louis-François may well have dressed this way. On drawing nearer, the warden recognized the delinquent as the son of Widow Massot. When he saw the warden, the man threw down his tree, threw off his clogs, and took off. The warden called him by name and shouted out the charge against him in a loud, clear voice. The clogs that Massot "had been wearing on his feet were new and quite clean, with no blemishes of any kind."[36]

Warden Coquart was the most talented of the local investigators. On April 10, 1847, he questioned Louis Doguet, a farmer from Le Vieux-Hêtre, in a barn in which he had discovered "155 *douvelles de merin* [*sic*] of newly felled green oak," which the farmer's hired hands and domestic servants had removed from the forest by night. Coquart recognized the tree by the shade of the bark, the color, the sinuous outline, and the cut made with the same tool."[37]

On April 29, 1847, he followed the traces of a wagon hitched to a horse and loaded with two oak billets taken from a hundred-and-thirty-year-old stand of timber in the canton of the Chêne Sale. He passed through a charity work site: poverty at the time was intense.[38] "Working on repairs to the local road of the aforementioned commune [Origny-le-Butin] were Louis Pinagot [Louis-François's uncle], a woodcutter living in Haute-Croix, and his son Etienne Pinagot [his cousin], also a woodcutter, living in Les Querrières."[39] Both men accused the carter Charles Bouvet. The warden followed his trail. The cart had become mired in mud on the farm at La Croix and then had turned onto the Mamers road, where the wood was ultimately discovered. Thus the only surviving record of anything Uncle Pinagot or his son might have said during their lifetime is of an accusation made to an officer of the law. In a period of dire depression, these miserable woodsmen may not have taken kindly to the idea that a carter and the "wealthy" farmer who accompanied him might be able to enrich themselves and get away with it.

Forest wardens were a fixture of everyday life. Everybody knew them and no doubt tried to stay out of their way. Tangles with wardens were surely staples of conversation. As we have just seen, people did sometimes accuse their neighbors of crimes, but they may have done so to defend themselves. I have not turned up any trace of a lasting dispute stemming from a forest misdemeanor. Did such petty crimes really damage a person's reputation in the community? There is reason to doubt it. No doubt people had mixed feelings on this score.

Louis-François Pinagot lived in a rural society in which honor and reputation were primary concerns. It was a society organized around exchange and indebtedness, quarrels and arrangements. By *arrangement* I mean an agreement between two individuals or two groups as well as a way of resolving disputes if and when the initial agreement broke down.[40] In Origny-le-Butin during Louis-François's lifetime, every person's time was committed, regardless of whether that person was a servant, an artisan, a "worker," or a simple partner. There would be no point trying to find out whether barter, exchange of services, or monetary payments dominated in transactions between individuals. All three practices were intertwined in an ongoing system of compensation, which, when necessary, allowed for arbitration and conciliation. In this light, an arrangement was a mutual commitment by two individuals perpetually in each other's debt. The terms of the arrangement were carefully preserved in memory and sometimes even written down.

An arrangement was a carefully considered verbal commitment, sometimes made in the presence of a witness or, less frequently, preserved in writing.[41] It remained tacit when the practices involved were universally acknowledged. In the case of an order to an artisan, agreement was reached after bargaining over the price of the work to be done or the wage for a day's labor, with an additional sum for "drink." In 1836 Jacques Tertereau, a gelder, got into a disagreement with Louis Simon, a stonecutter from Origny-le-Butin. Tertereau claimed to have agreed on the price for a barn wall: "three francs per meter of height for labor plus drink for the workers." Simon insisted that he had not "agreed to a price based on height and intended to work by the day," as laborers of his sort usually did.[42]

We learn of the initial commitment through the court record of the subsequent dispute, that is, only after something has gone wrong. From this we learn about the variety of arrangements that existed in this society. During the first two-thirds of the century we find an almost endless range of agreements. We saw this earlier in the case of Riboux and Anne-Louise Pôté, the wife of Courville: two individuals could agree on a chore of some sort, a *corvée*, as compensation for the work of a hemp spinner. A chore could also be traded for a bushel of grain or a quantity of cider. We see this in an arrangement between Henri-Charles de Bloteau and his brother-in-law, the laborer Lehoux, in 1828. In fact, these two men were involved in a rather complex series of arrangements. Lehoux claimed that he was owed 19.80 francs for thirty-three days of labor plus a bushel of barley in payment for a barrel he had delivered. Charles de Bloteau countered that Lehoux owed him 4.10 francs for a "sackful of various items, including butter, bread, and other things," 8 francs for lodging, and 16 francs for "sixteen days' use of a horse for plowing and terracing."[43] Lehoux replied that he had used the horse for only twelve days.

Sometimes "chores" were performed to repair damages. On February 9, 1849, Louis-Jean Chartier, who owned land in La Mazaure, claimed that his neighbor Louis Cabaret owed him 5.25 francs for the cost of plowing land that Chartier rented to Cabaret and that Cabaret had failed to plow himself. The defendant argued "that it had been verbally agreed with Chartier that he would not do the plowing in question because Chartier, prior to ceding the right to use the land, had allowed his goat to graze in the field, and the exemption from the obligation to plow had been agreed on as compensation for the damage done by the goat." Chartier denied that any such arrangement existed. The upshot was an enduring feud between these two neighbors, who were now battling over the use of their common courtyard.[44]

Some deals amounted to nothing more than a simple barter. In 1837 Tertereau and René Faucon agreed to an exchange of grass for manure. Tertereau sold Faucon "a portion of the grass in his field for the sum of three francs together with Faucon's agreement to deliver to him all the manure produced by his cow while eating the grass." But Tertereau "gave part [of the grass] to his horse, claiming that he had reserved the right to do so." Faucon, who had already paid a franc, then refused to pay more than 1.25 francs. He meant to deduct the price of the grass eaten by Tertereau's horse, namely 1.75 francs, from the amount owed." Meanwhile, "he had delivered the manure produced by his cow."[45] He won his case.

Sometimes a day's labor, and not just plowing, was paid for in kind. In 1838 Marin Desile, a farmer from Suré, claimed that Jacques Hodent, a farmer and cartwright from Origny-le-Butin, owed him 6.40 francs for "a *quarteron* of firewood that he had sold and delivered to him." Hodent replied that he had done three full days and five half-days of work for Desile, "who had taken note of them." The plaintiff acknowledged that the defendant had worked for him but said that it amounted to at most four hours' work "to split a board and repair a support." Hodent stuck to his story, however, and proposed calling witnesses. He claimed to have done "various chores for 6.25 francs, not including the prices of cherries that he had sold" to Desile.[46]

Hauling was sometimes exchanged for food. In 1836 Marin Pôté, Louis-François's brother-in-law, transported building stones to Basse-Frêne in exchange for a *pipe*, or barrel, of apple cider.[47] On March 13, 1846, the carter René Clotet claimed that Jean Pôté, a clog maker from Saint-Martin, owed him five francs for transporting wood. Pôté replied that he had paid for the hauling with "hay for fodder, and that Sieur Clotet, having fed the hay [to his animals], was no longer owed anything." But was the hay actually consumed? This remained to be proven. Both parties produced witnesses at the next hearing. The question was whether Clotet's mule had or had not entered Pôté's meadow and whether or not the arrangement had been as the defendant described.[48] Foodstuffs could also be bartered directly. In September 1837 Louis Dutheil, a farmer, and Pierre Plessis, a clog maker, exchanged a barrel of cider for several pairs of clogs and forty francs in cash.[49] Every year, a clog maker's biggest purchase was his barrel of cider. The price of a *pipe* ranged from thirty to fifty francs, or a good month's wages.[50]

Some exchanges were more complex. On January 13, 1854, Louis Daubert, a tailor from Origny-le-Butin, claimed that he was owed twelve francs by Widow Trottier, a farmer from Chemilly, for labor and goods. The widow claimed that this debt was offset by "a lamb that he [Daubert] had bought at their place around seven years ago, which . . . was never mentioned in any account." "Daubert responded that the widow Trottier's late husband had been unwilling to take money" for the lamb and that "he, Daubert, had rendered the equivalent in service by supplying tailored goods." In addition, he had once brought the Trottiers potatoes, a fact that the widow acknowledged.[51]

Sometimes tools or implements were included in these agreements. On June 25, 1847, Germain Bourdon, a farmer from Origny-le-Butin, claimed that Fouchet, a blacksmith from the same commune, owed him two francs for money loaned together with a hoe and a sickle. But Fouchet replied that Bourdon owed him 3.70 francs "for miscellaneous work, in addition to which he had lent Bourdon a wheelbarrow, which Bourdon had damaged."[52]

In some cases, monetary payments, services rendered, and trade in kind were combined in ways that are impossible to sort out. In 1826 Simon Brodin's widow, who lived in Haute-Croix, sued Marin Guiot, a laborer residing in the same village, for 22.75 francs: 15 francs "for housing him and his family for the year ended on All Saints' Day last," 3.25 francs from an unpaid loan, "3.50 francs for a demi-hectoliter of barley," and 1 franc "for spun hemp." After repayment, the widow promised to return "a small box belonging to the aforementioned Guiot." The laborer challenged her figures. He had rented the house, he said, for 12 francs, not 15. His wife and Widow Brodin "had settled with respect" to the debt of 3.25 francs. Furthermore, the plaintiff "had without his knowledge taken the liberty of appropriating a small box containing a silver cross and ring, a pin, and three coins of 5.80 francs."

In fact, Mme Brodin had given the laborer and his wife lodging "in her own apartment." Mme Guiot had given her the box to store in a chest "along with her linen and clothing."[53] This dispute offers us a glimpse into how people shared space at the moment their arrangement reached the breaking point. Clearly, rents were low in this society of the very poor, who avoided cash transactions whenever possible. Yet we also see that a couple of laborers, no matter how poor, could still amass a modest collection of family heirlooms.

In 1832 Lesault, a farmer, claimed that Louis Foreau, a clog maker, owed him ten francs for a pig. Foreau pointed out, however, that more than a year earlier he had loaned his wagon to Lesault: "Most recently, he had sent his horse to Lesault's house to haul manure, and the plaintiff kept the animal for one day. Moreover, he had provided a pair of 50-centime shoes."[54] On July 8, 1831, Jacques Beaufils, a clog maker, sued Guedon, a lime burner, for 10.25 francs owed him for a quantity of peas and apples as well as a cash loan. Guedon, however, stated his belief that Beaufils owed him money because he had "broken a pot and drunk his cider . . . and for cooking his soup and feeding him for a week."[55]

Strictly speaking, an "arrangement" was an agreement that put an end to a conflict or, more precisely, a lawsuit. In 1850 Trouillard, a laborer from L'Hôtel-aux-Oiseaux, had ventured onto the "field of Origny," a piece of land belonging to Louis Doguet, an eighty-year-old farmer from Vieux-Hêtre.[56] Trouillard had come "with a litter to remove a large quantity of manure deposited on this plot as fertilizer." In his work as a mason, apparently, he needed horse dung. Bouillie, Trouillard's employer, told him that he could find some in Doguet's field and that "the old man would not say anything." Here we come to the heart of interpersonal relationships. In this milieu, when two individuals were in debt to each other or were certain of the nature of their relationship, there was no real need to ask for anything.

Nevertheless, Doguet in this instance filed suit. He notified the offending individual that he wished to discuss a settlement. Trouillard had gone "to see him to offer his excuses and *ask for an arrangement*." In the event, however, "there was no way to settle the matter." Nevertheless, Trouillard "offered in the presence of several witnesses to pay up to one franc," even though to his way of thinking the load of manure was not worth more than ten or fifteen centimes. Doguet explained his refusal to settle: "He did not want to enter into an arrangement because he wanted Trouillard to be punished for his dishonesty."[57] The judge found against him. Given the ridiculously small value of the manure, what this case shows is that the intended purpose was to blacken a man's reputation rather than to recover money owed.

When two people had dealings, it was possible, as we have seen, for money to change hands. Monetary debts fairly often figured in lawsuits and "arrangements" but rarely in isolation. Toward the middle of the century, usury became a serious problem in rural areas. Officials described its ravages in the Orne. Elsewhere, I have written about its crucial importance in Limousin during this period.[58] Money was lent at interest in Origny-le-Butin. Some loans were based on verbal agreements, but formal notes were more common than in Limousin. In Louis-François's milieu, however, cash loans do not seem to have played an important role (although this may simply be an artifact of the sources used).[59] Most loans were ridiculously small, usually less than five francs. Three or four days work was enough to pay them off.

In the course of my research I did not come upon any individuals reduced to servitude because of their debts, as was the case in Limousin. Nor did I find any "village capitalists" capable of imposing their will on debtors.[60] Lenders were generally in more or less the same position as borrowers. Money circulated among the poor: clog makers, laborers, and woodcutters. I found no cases in which a family's property was seized. My findings pertain, however, only to Origny-le-Butin, and in particular to the villages along the forest's edge. In these places there was little property to speak of: a few tools, some old clothes, a garden, a cottage, and at most a few acres of land. If usury existed, it may have been hidden as a result.

There were exceptions, however. On September 16, 1842, a farmer from Saint-Martin-du-Vieux-Bellême demanded that a clog maker by the name of Combe make good on a note for 170 francs payable on March 1. On October 14, a "keeper of baths" from Bellême tried to collect 52 francs on a loan to Jean-Baptiste Lesueur, a clog maker from the town of Origny. But on March 20, 1846, the same Lesueur demanded that Pierre Lesueur, known as Chantpy, a farmer from Chemilly, repay a note of 100 francs.[61]

When a debt became the subject of a lawsuit, it was usually because someone failed to pay for a delivered shipment of goods or because an employer failed to pay wages due to a worker. In such cases usury was not an issue. People owed money to the sacristan, the miller, the horse dealer, the baker, the workman, the farmhand, the gambling partner, or the tavern keeper because cash was scarce, the system of exchanges was complex, and compensations required continual adjustment.

On March 1, 1822, Etienne Rottier, the sacristan of the town of Origny, claimed that René Faucon, "landowner," owed him 7.95 francs "for candles given to him, wages for the digging of graves, and attendance at the burials of his wife and two children."[62] The justice of the peace decided to turn the case over to the mayor for an "arrangement." In another case, the same René Faucon, now identified as a "laborer in the town," was dunned for 8 francs by Denis Manthé, formerly a miller in Saint-Ouen-la-Cour, the remainder due "on a larger sum for wheat sold to him and delivered *several years ago* to the market of Bellesme."[63] Faucon claimed to have no recollection of owing that amount. On October 5, 1821, Pierre Epinette, a farmer from Chapelle-Souef, sued to recover 36 francs from Louis-François's father, Jacques Pinagot, this being the "remainder due on the price of a horse sold and delivered to him."[64] On May 19, 1820, Jean Fleury, a baker from La Perrière, asked Michel Loisnard, a laborer from Le Croix-Chemin (Origny-le-Butin), to pay 34.20 francs "for the price of bread."[65] This shows that among these very poor people indebtedness for food could mount up to a fairly substantial sum. Over the decades, the sums due to merchants in small nearby towns swelled. The broadening of the geographical range of legal claims is evidence for a slow evolution in modes of consumption. Little by little, merchants who sold novelties and hardware began to attract the poor of Origny.[66]

On July 9, 1820, Toussaint Coursier, a laborer and mason from the commune, sued to recover 23.50 francs from Jean Loitron, a mason from Les Querrières and, in fact, the "favorite" (lover) of Louis-François's scandalous aunt.[67] This was the balance due on a total of 36.30 francs "for wages for thirty-three days of work with him and on his behalf in various places at the rate of 1.10 francs per day." Thus we have precise information about how much a laborer earned in Origny-le-Butin at the height of the Restoration. On February 28, 1834, Jacques Lemarié, a tavern keeper from Le Gué-de-la-Chaîne, sued Jean Biardeau, also known as Billard, a long sawyer from Saint-Eloy (Origny), for nine francs to cover drinks for which he had gambled during an evening in the tavern. "Having lost, Biardeau must pay," Lemarié argued. The law unfortunately did not recognize gambling debts. Despite this, Biardeau was ordered to pay half the amount claimed.[68]

On July 15, 1853, Pierre Landier, Louis-François's first cousin and a weaver from the town of Origny, sued Clément Dagron, a resident of Vieux-Hêtre, for eighteen francs for having "shown" him his trade.[69] Dagron acknowledged that he had promised to pay thirty-six francs for three months of apprenticeship, but since he stayed with Landier only two months, he had withheld payment of eighteen francs of that total. The court nevertheless sentenced him to pay twelve francs on the grounds that the time spent in showing a trade to an apprentice was much more substantial in the first few months of the apprenticeship.[70] What is striking in all these cases is how long people remembered the details of their initial arrangements and, even more, the debts they were owed. Louatron's debt became an issue for the courts five years after it was incurred, while Faucon's "dated back several years."

Behind each of these lawsuits we catch a glimpse of the *brouille*, or dispute, arising out of the breakdown of an initial agreement or a failure to acknowledge a debt or a presumably serious affront to an individual's honor. If one party felt that a bargain had become unfair, or that the agreed compensation was no longer appropriate, or that the arrangement had become unworkable, a dispute might arise. People said that the parties to the arrangement *sont brouillés*, that they had become embroiled in a dispute. But this should not be taken to mean that they had become involved in a struggle for power.

These disputes were more a matter of animosity or hatred, and frequently they led to serious trouble between neighbors. Usually they grew out of a strong sense of property. Sometimes they were aggravated by lawsuits over boundaries, rights of way, or material damages.

Judicial archives are filled with cases concerning fences, ditches, and embankments. In this bocage region, the care with which people planted and maintained the thorn bushes that separated one field from another was rooted in the very depths of individual and family anxiety. This was no laughing matter. Any damage to a hedge, any encroachment, real or imagined, on a person's property, could lead to genuine suffering and loss of sleep. Bear in mind how difficult it was to acquire or rent land, how small most people's holdings were, and how detailed and specific the collective memory was when it came to matters of land ownership. This was as intimate a part of family life as the communal bell was of community life. A cut hedge, a moved boundary marker, the placement of a fence on a neighbor's property, even a mere opening in a hedgerow or a widening of a ditch or a cut in an embankment might signify an attempt to usurp someone else's property, an act of aggression. Against all these potential threats a man was obliged to defend his interests. To be sure, farmers who owned land were more sensitive to such threats than others, but even clog makers and laborers might share these fears if they had managed to acquire a garden, small plot, or cottage, or even so much as a hog.

Jean Bourdon, a farmer in the village of Le Plessis, owned a "piece of land" known as La Bretêche, which had once been a vineyard but was now "in cultivation." It adjoined a plot farmed by a man named Legars, who lived in Saint-Martin. In February 1819, however, Legars "filled in the channel that separated [the two properties], cut and damaged the thorn bushes that had grown there, and made a profit on the wood that he took."[71] Bourdon sued to force him to "reopen the channel."

Both parties produced witnesses who testified to what they remembered. Belanger had been a farmer in the vicinity for twenty-two years. Throughout that time, he said, there had been a hedge of thorns on the plaintiff's side and a channel "on Lejars's side." Louis Gouget had farmed the lower portion of Bourdon's plot for eighteen years, as far back as he could remember. Sieur Ripoux, the owner of Lejars's plot, had been trying to usurp Bourdon's land: "In doing his plowing, [he] would continue about four feet into Bourdon's side." He was obliged to return the land he had confiscated in this way. By arrangement, the two landowners had then agreed to dig a channel between their two plots. Above Bourdon's side, which remained uncultivated, brambles had grown, though no one was sure who had planted them. Ripoux, however, claimed that three or four years earlier, the farmer who had been using Bourdon's land at the time had also tried to take what was not his: "In turning the soil over with a shovel, he went beyond the limits of what was his." Witness after witness testified without really clarifying the matter. Jacques Trottier remembered having seen Lejars planting brambles, for example. In the end, the dispute had to be settled by arbitration.

On October 27, 1826, Jean Nugues, a farmer and landowner in Les Vieux-Aîtres (or Vieux-Hêtre) accused Jean Clinchamp of Saint-Martin of having filled in a ditch and leveled an embankment between their two properties.[72] In September 1846 Nicolas Bosse Sr., a minor notable from the town of Origny, complained that Jacques Tertereau, the gelder, had taken the liberty of digging up the hedge bordering his garden, which led to a lengthy dispute.[73] On the afternoon of January 22, 1847, Bosse Jr., a weaver, and Tertereau had hurled insults at each other in the middle of town. A dozen people were cited as witnesses, including Nicolas Filleul, the inn keeper and baker, a friend of Louis-François's.[74]

Let us turn now to a case involving people close to Louis-François. On May 23, 1849, the son of Jean-Baptiste Lorillon of Haute-Folie, one of a family of forest delinquents, took the liberty of planting a "dry hedge" (that is, a fence) along a piece of land owned by Julien Courville, a clog maker from Haute-Croix and Louis-François's brother-in-law.[75] He "ran over [the boundary] . . . by thirty-three centimeters on one end and thirty centimeters on the other." The justice of the peace went to inspect the scene of the alleged crime. He asked Lorillon to remove "the stakes or dry fence" within twenty-four hours.

Because of the patchwork of tiny plots, rights of way were extremely important. The loss of a right of way could make farming a piece of land impossible. It could block the use of a pond or trough for watering livestock or prevent a field from being harvested. Quarrels over rights of way could poison relations between neighbors. Take, for example, the long feud between Tertereau and the Dolléans, which lasted at least eighteen years. In December 1824 the gelder, who owned what had been the presbytery, dug a ditch and planted a hedge that prevented the widow Dolléans, a farmer from Hôtel-Gaulard, from gaining access to her property.[76] Two years later, the dispute reached a climax: on May 10 the widow caused "the wheels of her wheelbarrow to pass over a live young hedge and beyond into the wheat on the plot known as l'Ouchette," which was owned by Tertereau. She claimed a right of way, but her neighbor had dug up the road to "block the wheelbarrow."[77]

Tertereau and the widow's son, Michel Dolléans, a farmer from Renardière (Origny), each owned half of the garden of the former presbytery, which gave Michel a right of way to a shared pond. To annoy his neighbor, Tertereau dumped six wheelbarrows full of dirt into the pond, which was thereby "obstructed" and "dried out." The judge, after hearing a long procession of witnesses, found against him. The suit was settled in May 1838. The dispute was ended by an arrangement: Dolléans and his daughter were to be allowed right of way for their livestock, while "Sieur Tertereau, for his part, will erect a fence at the entrance to the pond . . . which shall roll on a pivot, open onto the pond, and close against Sieur Tertereau's hedge; it shall be two meters wide." Each of the parties would have a key and would ensure that the fence was kept closed. Maintenance expenses were to be shared.[78]

Another dispute illustrates the importance that common courtyards often had. Rights of way, boundaries, and damages were also at issue in this case. In August 1825 Jacques Tertereau closed off his portion of a common courtyard by building a wall one and a half meters high, backed by a hedge and rows of firewood. Etienne Rottier, a farmer from the town, lost his access to the well as a result. He insisted on his right of way but ran into opposition from Tertereau and the Dolléans, who in this case were on the same side.[79]

In 1829 the dispute took a turn for the worse. On Easter Sunday, two of Rottier's geese and their goslings "committed an infraction" against Tertereau's cabbage patch. Tertereau filed a complaint: "Sieur Rottier, by his own account, was present and watched the geese eat the cabbage." The gelder therefore decided to kill the gander. Only out of the goodness of his heart, he claimed, did he refrain from killing the goose. When Rottier asked for his gander back, Tertereau offered to sell it to him. Rottier was nevertheless sentenced to pay fifty centimes for the damage done by the geese.[80]

Like everyone in Origny-le-Butin, we know that Chartier and Cabaret, two farmers from La Mazure, quarreled in February 1849. They shared the village courtyard. Because of their argument, "they agreed on February 21 to share the courtyard equally . . . each man taking the portion adjoining his buildings." They decided to appoint several experts "to make the division" under the supervision of the justice of the peace, "who shall proceed to place boundary markers."[81]

The use of ponds could also be a source of trouble. A case in point took place in May 1849, when Louis-Charles Bailleul, who owned land in La Charpenterie, became embroiled in a dispute with Louis Bellanger, a farmer from La Trappe (both villages of Origny). Bailleul considered himself "the rightful owner of a pond situated at the lower end of the courtyard" of the second village. The previous September, however, Bellanger "had caught and removed the fish from the pond. [He} dredged the pond without notifying the petitioner and refused to give the petitioner his due portion of both fish and mud extracted therefrom."[82] We do not know how this case turned out.

Damage to property could also spark a feud. On November 16, 1838, René Cabaret, a clog maker from Chemilly, sued Pierre Landier, a farmer from Origny-le-Butin whose name we encountered previously, for twenty francs for damages done "at the end of last October by two of his cows, a calf, and a goat in one of his fields, which contained green peas, potatoes, and a pile of apples." (This case proves that some clog makers were also farmers, by the way.) In any case, Landier admitted that his animals had caused the damage. Sieur Trottier, Chemilly's deputy mayor, had gone out to estimate the amount, at which time Cabaret had asked Landier "to plow his small portion of the field" by way of compensation, but his request had been rebuffed. In the end, the plaintiff was obliged to accept the two francs the defendant was willing to pay to make good his losses.[83]

Often the mayor or his deputy became involved in the negotiation of an arrangement. The long feud between Tertereau and the Dolléans actually began in April 1820. According to the plaintiffs, Tertereau had chosen to use the land adjacent to a dividing wall as a place to store "manure, compost, and fecal material piled to the height of the wall, which causes damage and excess moisture in nearby buildings [pigsties] and makes them unhealthy for the animals that are kept in them." The judge referred both parties to the mayor of Origny-le-Butin.[84]

Disputes such as these will, of course, seem minuscule to most readers. But it would be pointless to try to get a sense of what evening conversations in the cottages of Basse-Frêne were like or to comprehend the main interests of villagers who lived nearby without overcoming this sentiment. If we are to avoid psychological anachronism, we must be alert to what people worried about, what made them suffer, and what embroiled them in disputes.

Everything hinged on the question of reputation. In this region honor was something a person earned rather than inherited. Once earned, it had to be protected against real or imagined assaults. Although ostentatious behavior was frowned upon, people were expected to demonstrate a capacity for autonomous action, an ability to maintain self-control in all circumstances.[85] An insult or even a mere allusion likely to diminish a person's standing in the eyes of his neighbors could be enough to spark violence. This was not, however, a society of challenges. The fear of being accused of cowardice does not appear to have been a strong motivating factor. Three values were sacrosanct: personal honesty, a woman's honor, and, to a lesser extent, professional competence. If any of these things were impugned, a person might have recourse to the courts to save his or her reputation. In villages such as Origny-le-Butin, where people were related by blood, culture, and social interdependence, honor reinforced the sense of group membership while, at the same time, allowing room for individuals to express themselves and stake a claim to social position.[86]

On July 14, 1820, the widow Maillard of Haute-Roche declared that from the time she lost her husband, the laborer Jean Massot and his wife "had continually harassed her with endless insults and annoying remarks of all kinds."[87] "The husband threatened to hit her and do damage," while the wife, "on the evening of the eleventh of this month," had publicly accused her "in the common courtyard of Haute-Roche of being a scoundrel and a thief" and claimed to have proof of these accusations. Mme Maillard had therefore gone to court.[88]

On November 4, 1822, the mole catcher François Maisonnier complained that the gelder Tertereau had accused him at eight in the morning in the courtyard of the former presbytery of being a bandit. This allegation was confirmed by a series of witnesses, including the Rottiers, who had, of course, had their own disputes with Tertereau on other occasions.[89]

Let us focus for a moment on Basse-Frêne, however. A quarrel erupted there in December 1837 between François-Marin Lebouc, a poor laborer whom we met earlier, and Julien Bouquet, a farmer from La Croix. Lebouc sued Bouquet for twenty-five francs in damages on the grounds that the latter had, on the eighteenth of the month "at about one o'clock," accused him in his own barn of being a thief. Two elderly witnesses testified, one of them seventy-two, the other seventy-five: François Cottin, Louis-François's uncle, was one of the two. The witnesses stated that Sieur Bouquet had insisted that Lebouc return two bales of hay that he had lent him. Lebouc refused on the grounds that Bouquet "had locked his mitten in his closet," whereupon Bouquet, vexed by this accusation, had called Lebouc a thief. The court dismissed Lebouc's complaint because the insult had been made "in the heat of an argument."[90]

Impugning the morals of a woman seems to have been an even graver offense. Here I will deal only with insults to the wives of clog makers so as to get a better grasp of what Louis-François Pinagot might have felt if his wife had been insulted. On September 29, 1837, François Brière, a clog maker from Saint-Ouen-la-Cour, accused the farmer François Deschamps of having, without provocation, assailed his wife with repeated insults the previous Friday "at three o'clock at night [sic]." This was confirmed by witnesses. Pierre Dagonneau, a twenty-six-year-old weaver, had seen "Deschamps heading for Sieur Brière's house" and "for reasons of curiosity, he had followed him." He heard him make "the most insulting and crude remarks about the Brière woman, saying that she led a disreputable life, in particular with a certain hemp weaver." Another weaver, Jacques-Louis Dagonneau, heard Deschamps say of Mme Brière "that he himself had had frequent relations with her." Both husband and wife had then called him a "bastard." Deschamps answered the charge by saying that the Brières had attacked his morals "by saying that he used women that cost him a lot of money."

Mme Brière, for her part, claimed that Deschamps had insulted her "by saying that she lived by prostitution, that she had had a child by a man whose name he did not mention, and that he himself was the father of another child."[91] It emerged in court that the Brières and Deschamps had traded insults on another occasion five months earlier. Deschamps was nevertheless ordered to pay a fine.

Now consider another case from Basse-Frêne. In 1850 another widow Maillard, a landowner, had herself "in front of several witnesses at various times, indeed almost daily, but in particular on Friday last . . . at nine o'clock in the morning, at the washhouse of Le Carouge, accused the woman Touchet of leading a morally disreputable life by comparing her to another woman said to be a disreputable individual and a thief." Mme Touchet was the wife of a clog maker from the village. She sued for fifty francs. Mme Maillard of course denied the charges: the women at the washhouse "did indeed speak of women with vices," but she had never said that Mme Touchet was one of them. Witnesses were called. Three of them testified that at the washhouse Mme Maillard had addressed the following words to the plaintiff: "You are just like the Brebi woman." This Brebi was a woman from Le Carouge "who had a bad reputation in the area." Mme Maillard was therefore ordered to pay the Touchets ten francs.[92] What this case proves, if proof were needed, is that washhouse gossip and widows played an important role in making and breaking reputations.[93] It also shows how comparisons were used to establish a hierarchy of esteem.

Another intolerable form of insult was to cast doubt on a person's honesty or professional competence, perhaps as a result of jealousy. There was a bitter feud between two gelders, Cornué of L'Hôtel-aux-Oiseaux and Tertereau of Origny. If Cornué is to be believed, Tertereau had been insulting him for years. In Bellême on Thursday, June 1, 1820, Tertereau publicly accused him of being "a thief, a scoundrel, and scum from the galleys."[94] A parade of witnesses appeared in court. Tertereau was ordered to pay damages of thirty-six francs, a very substantial sum.

Tavern arguments about matters of honor and reputation sometimes led to violence. We have already met the mole catcher François-Jean Maisonnier of Origny. On February 16, 1831, at nine in the evening, in a tavern kept by Filleul the baker, he called Etienne-François Rottier, a weaver whom we have also met before, a thief. Then he hurled himself at Rottier "in a rage, knocking him down, and he would have hit him if others present had not intervened." The defendant offered this explanation: "Rottier provked this brawl by insisting on having a drink at [Maisonnier's] table against [Maisonnier's] wishes." Rottier countered that it was Filleul, the tavern keeper, who had invited him to have a glass of cider at Maisonnier's table. Maisonnier was ordered to pay forty francs in damages.[95] In 1836 Simon, also known as Chatel, a mason from Origny-le-Butin, while drinking at Sieur Dolléans's place, had knocked down Tertereau the gelder, who was evidently disliked and probably feared by many people, although he was reputed to be an exorcist of sorts. To make matters worse, Simon had spit in Tertereau's face. Tertereau, his attacker explained, had allowed himself "to criticize [my] work."[96]

All in all, there does not seem to have been a great deal of violence in Origny-le-Butin, especially among the miserably poor forest workers. It may be, however, that what brutality there was remains largely hidden from view: many blows could have been exchanged in the depths of the forest.[97]

After exhaustive study of the judicial archives, several conclusions seem warranted. First, exchanges, agreements, and arrangements generally involved a very small circle of relations, mainly neighbors, occasionally extended to include a farmer or artisan from the town. Except for the occasional draper or baker with clients in Origny, the residents of the surrounding communes appear only when they rented a plot of land. A quick consultation of the archives of Bellême is enough to show that the people of Origny never dreamed of getting involved in the affairs of the cantonal capital or of airing their differences there. But if the horizon of local disputes was limited, this should not be taken to mean that all conflict revolved around the family. On the contrary, feuds among relatives were rare. The judicial archives suggest that, except in the most serious cases, disputes between two individuals or two families in Origny-le-Butin were generally resolved by arrangements concluded with the help of the mayor or his deputy, who served as arbitrators.[98]

These networks of relations seem fairly simple to decipher. In Origny-le-Butin we do not find the kinds of broad family strategies that are typical of the Gévaudan or the Baronies of the Pyrenees. Family structure is sufficient to account for this difference. The family here was a long way from conforming to the authoritarian model of the *ostal*. The collective duels and terrifying bar brawls so common elsewhere were unknown in Origny. The Perche also avoided the communal free-for-alls that bloodied the villages of the northeastern Lot.[99] It does not appear that lawsuits were used for purely instrumental purposes, as mere tactical maneuvers in a broader conflict, as was still the case in the southern Limousin at the dawn of the July Monarchy.[100] In Origny-le-Butin the purpose of going to court was much more limited. What accounts for this relative lack of zeal? The answer can be found in the isolation of households, the extreme fragmentation of property, the profound misery of the inhabitants, which restrained their ambitions, and above all the very shallowness of the local hierarchy.

What is more surprising is that it is difficult, even after reading many case histories, to make out networks of solidarity. I had expected to find that farmers supported one another and that clog makers did the same. This turns out not to have been the case. The depositions of witnesses show that in this homogeneous milieu, friendships were a matter of choice, with scant consideration given to marriage, neighborliness, or occupation. So far as we can tell, power does not seem to have been an issue. Priests in Origny were extremely discreet, and the nomination of mayors seems not to have involved power struggles between different families or clans.[101] Sporadically, however, we do find some evidence of short-lived tension between farmers and woodsmen.[102]

Of course, some of these findings may well be an artifact of the scale of analysis chosen. What is true for Origny-le-Butin may not be true for all the rural communes of the Haut-Perche. Conversely, however, the exclusive study of larger entities may well obscure what life was really like for the residents of these tiny communities, the elementary units of rural society at the time.

What the observer of Origny cannot fail to acknowledge is that many feuds were sparked by very simple things: boundary markings, hedges, rights of way, blockages, damages, a feeling of being robbed in an exchange, a fear of seeing one's reputation as an honest man, respected spouse, or good worker destroyed by a careless word. Strangely enough, jealousy and envy are rarely in evidence in these cases, where the predominant sentiment seems to be a desire to be left alone, safe at home from all forms of aggression. What people, regardless of their position in life, seem to have taken pride in was the sense that they had coped with life's difficulties "without asking anyone for anything."[103] Louis-François, who never became a subject of gossip, can be taken as typical of the majority of residents of Origny-le-Butin. Certain names appear repeatedly in these court documents: clever Brodinne and her son-in-law, Mathurin Guillin, a clog maker; Tertereau, the much-feared gelder; Maillard, the diligent widow; the disputatious Rottiers; the Ruffrays and Lorillons; and certain of Louis-François's less respectable relations among the Pinagots, Pôtés, and Drouins. These troublemakers were exceptions. By and large, this was a rather tranquil society, but one in which small antagonisms could smolder and occasionally erupt in flame. But just because these antagonisms were small, we should not make the mistake of thinking that they were foolish. In any case, it is moving to see these otherwise forgotten people emerge from obscurity simply because of their proximity to Louis-François Pinagot, the main subject of this book.

Let us not take an unduly pessimistic view, however, or allow our judgment to be clouded by our reliance on certain types of source documents. The bocage of Origny-le-Butin and the nearby forest were places of communal pleasures and joys and not just quarrels and disputes. The former are more difficult for us to see than the latter, however. Men, especially clog makers, enjoyed themselves at the tavern, where they drank hard cider. We know virtually nothing about what these taverns were like in the first three decades of the nineteenth century. Tavern keepers were not listed as such in census lists, so that we know who kept taverns only if they turn up in court records. Most were artisans as well as tavern keepers. In any case, men drank in their taverns every day, even on Sundays and even at night, despite regulations to the contrary.

During the Empire, the diocese of Séez was in the forefront of efforts to perpetuate the celebration of holidays that had been stricken from the official calendar. Later, residents of the Haut-Perche vigorously opposed measures to prohibit all commerce on Sundays and holidays.[104] In communes with fewer than five thousand inhabitants, the sale of cider, spirits, and coffee was prohibited, as was the playing of billiards, between eight in the morning and noon on Sundays, when services were held.[105] In October 1816 the innkeepers of Moulins-la-Marche petitioned against the severity of this regulation. In 1821 the mayor of Bazoches complained to the prefect that "services are endless . . . prolonged by interminable preaching and reading, [and] vespers begin at 3:30 and often end at sundown."[106] If the regulations were observed, the men of the town would no longer be able to drink. Ending the exemption that allowed drinking in taverns during services "would destroy commerce entirely and plunge the commune into misery." According to the mayor, what was crucial was the pace with which the priest celebrated the mass, and the curé of Bazoches was unbearably slow.

To tell the truth, although the prefect of the Orne occasionally chose to enforce the letter of the law, he generally showed himself to be tolerant: "In some villages it has always been the custom to sell only on Sundays," the prefect acknowledged in 1814.[107] In view of this tradition, he simply asked merchants to "move a short distance away from the church during services." In other words, the law very likely did not prevent the residents of Origny from sitting down and having a drink in a tavern on Sunday, even during church services.

A municipal regulation of April 29, 1834, made it illegal to serve drinks before five in the morning or after nine at night (ten on holidays).[108] This did not stop tavern keepers in Origny-le-Butin from serving outside the legal hours, for which they were often cited by officers of the law. The mayor and his deputy personally supervised enforcement of closing times.

On the night of March 19, 1843, François Filleul, a tavern keeper and baker, was fined for serving drinks.[109] On March 16, 1845, two drunks in Filleul's tavern carried on noisily throughout the night; they were habitués of the local establishments.[110] Both the tavern keeper and his clients were sentenced to three days in jail. In 1851 Nicolas Bosse, the deputy mayor, while making his nightly rounds at two in the morning, came upon "several people drinking and singing" at Widow Filleul's place.[111] The court proved unyielding, as the widow "had already committed the same crime several times before." Baptiste Lesueur's tavern was no less closely watched. On April 18, 1852, Nicolas Bosse reported that at around midnight he had heard a noise and caught in the act of drinking a gardener from Origny-le-Roux and three men from Chemilly.[112] In 1855 it was Mayor Herbelin who, while making "his regular rounds of the cafés," caught Modeste Bothereau, a twenty-three-year-old clog maker, sitting quietly "by the fireplace" in Lesueur's tavern.[113] And Louis Frenard, a friend of Louis-François's, was fined on June 6, 1855, for serving drinks to five individuals in his home.[114] It was "common knowledge" that he did this sort of thing regularly until eleven o'clock or midnight.

Clog makers liked to gather in taverns, especially in Saint-Martin, where many of them resided. On Sunday, February 14, 1836, Jean-François Maumy and Koenigsberg [*sic*] Brodin, both clog makers of that town, entered Jacques Lenôtre's tavern "at about nine o'clock at night to drink a bottle of cider." Maumy "threatened to smash everything in the house." His shouting attracted neighbors, who restored order by forcing Maumy and his companion to leave. "After being thrown out," however, Maumy returned and resumed his noisemaking. He was sentenced to five days in jail.[115] On June 27, 1852, in the tavern of François Lenôtre, Jacques's heir, four clog makers sat at a table with a shoemaker and a farmer. They were drinking cider after eleven at night. The tavern keeper pointed out that it was a holiday and that it was better for workmen to "chat" in his establishment than to "sleep in doorways" as others did.[116]

Youthful hijinks were not confined to the cabarets. On July 7, 1840, five youths, including a clog maker, "took turns knocking each other head over heels" outside a tavern in Origny at nine in the evening. Three of them were from Saint-Martin. People from the town testified that the youths had made a lot of noise, which had continued "into the night." Rigot complained that the "disturbers of the peace" had done "damage to his barley and broken his hedges by removing pickets." One of the troublemakers had forced young Rottier to retreat into his home "by throwing stones at him." Several of the accused were repeat offenders. Three of them were sentenced to five days in jail.[117] Twelve years later, Eugène Pinagot, a clog maker from Basse-Frêne and one of Louis-François's sons, joined the two Loinard boys, both long sawyers, and carpenter François Deschamp in "creating a disturbance on a public way at nine in the evening on a Sunday."[118] Each of the youths was ordered to pay a fine of one franc.

Hijinks such as these lead one to wonder what forms of traditional youthful behavior might have persisted in the Haut-Perche during Louis-François's long lifetime. Many traditional activities were outlawed early on in the name of public tranquillity, but enforcement remained lax until well into the July Monarchy. It is therefore reasonable to assume that Louis-François, unlike his sons and daughters, may have felt free to participate in various well-known forms of collective revelry. On March 7, 1824 (by which time Louis-François was no longer "young"), the mayor of La Chapelle-Montligeon reported that he was unable to enforce ordinances prohibiting carnival masquerades. Thirty individuals had strolled about the commune in disguise.[119]

Within a few years the authorities were taking a harder line. In 1835 the forest administration decided in no uncertain terms to put an end to certain traditional practices in Tourouvre. "For longer than anyone can remember, at least two hundred years, [the administration] had allowed local residents to take several young trees from the forest and plant them in town squares, where fires were lit in honor of the festivals of Saint John and Saint Peter [June 25 and 26]." Now, however, officials refused to grant the necessary authorization.[120] The young turned a deaf ear to the ban, however. One night they cut down three trees in the forest of the Perche. Six guards, armed with loaded rifles and sabers, tried to remove the trees "from the square on which they were planted." Their commander even took a burning brand from a bonfire and hurled it into the crowd, in the meantime ordering his men to draw their sabers.

After an hour of argument, the three hundred people in the crowd compelled the troops to withdraw. As they left the square, their commander addressed "several women in the crudest of terms, calling one a bi- - - and another a wh- - -" The mayor explained that it was traditional to plant a young birch or small aspen in the square and to attach a wreath of flowers to the tree. "For several days" the young people of the town customarily "dance around the tree and make merry. There is even something religious about the occasion, and no trouble has ever come of it."[121]

On an inspection tour, however, the conservator of the forests insisted that the forests would soon be devastated if all communes were authorized to stage celebrations of this sort. In ten or twelve villages of the region, "youths" had in fact asked the administration to authorize the removal of aspens from the forest. In Tourouvre, to the conservator's dismay, the mayor had lent support to the rebels "by dancing with [them] and serving them strong cider well into the night." Guards were officially stationed at the foot of the tree, and the same scenes were repeated on July 28 and 29 (national holidays). Some of the "rebels" had been imprisoned in Mortagne. According to the inspector, the mayor "lost no time in sending a thousand francs for their bail, then placed himself at their head and marched with them to the accompaniment of music and drums back to the village, where additional libations were served to the crowd."

Already, however, such unanimity in resisting the edicts of the forest administration seemed a thing of the past. If traditional celebrations were raucous, they were effectively shut down.[122] On February 21, 1845, a constable charged two youths from Igé with disturbing the peace after they paraded two effigies through the streets of the commune at two in the afternoon without the mayor's permission.[123] Even the charivari, a traditional and noisy mock serenade for newlyweds in which Louis-François must have taken part, was made a crime, as we learn from a case that took place not far from Basse-Frêne in November of 1851.

On November 25, at about nine in the evening, a substantial number of youths gathered in the village of Hôtel-Chapet, a commune of Saint-Martin. In fact, they had been gathering there for five evenings running for the purpose of mounting a charivari against "the aforementioned Couillet on the occasion of his marriage."[124] The deputy mayor came to put an end to the "noise and raucous insults that disturbed the town's peace." Among those present he noted four sons of clog makers, one laborer's son, a domestic, and two unemployed sons of widows. These young people ignored the deputy's orders and even went so far as to resume their merrymaking under his windows. They did so because they did not believe they were committing a crime: the charivari, according to them, was "something that is frequently practiced in the countryside." But the new sensitivity to noise[125] and touchiness about individual honor, coupled with a desire to preserve the public tranquillity, gradually led to the repression of what had once been a widespread custom.[126]

As noted earlier, it is likely that Louis-François Pinagot would have visited various fairs in the region. There was one rather unusual fair that took place quite near the villages he lived in at one time or another along the forest's edge. It would be surprising if he did not attend this event. From the time he was a young boy until at least 1848, a fair was held every year from July 2 to 4 on the elm-shaded square and streets of the village of La Bruyère.[127] It drew large crowds. Over the years, the fair grew so large that it spilled over into the forest itself, and the administration did nothing to stop it. Livestock were allowed to rest in the shade of hundred-and-fifty-year-old trees, and hundreds of horses were tied up. Two cider houses and three refreshment stands were set up under the trees, whose shade did much to account for the fair's success. People flocked to the village to have a look and while there sat down and drank cider. Of course, the horses trampled the ground and spoiled it. They also did damage to the trees. The trench marking the limits of the forest was destroyed by the large number of animals, and the huts set up among the trees presented a fire hazard. But people were very fond of this fair, and the forest administration was obliged to tolerate it until the middle of the century.

It is up to the reader to imagine how Louis-François might have enjoyed himself at a table beneath the oaks with a bottle of cider and surrounded by fellow clog makers from Saint-Martin. No document has survived, however, to attest to his presence at this joyful gathering, the closest to his home of all the fairs he might have attended.

the past decomposed

How can we imagine the way in which Louis-François Pinagot constructed his representation of the past?[1] We do not want to say that he possessed historical knowledge, because that would imply that he organized his thinking in terms of clearly differentiated periods. Of course, by "historical knowledge" one might also mean simply the variety of stories and oral commentaries committed to memory by our indigent illiterate and perhaps sharpened in the retelling. Indeed, the telling and retelling of stories during evening gatherings may have given him a sense that one era succeeded another, along with some notion of the distinctive flavor of each. But he still would have had no clear idea of chronology and no real ability to "historicize."

As chaotic as Louis-François's knowledge of history may have been, its geographical frame of reference was clear. The forest and bocage shaped the thinking of everyone in Origny. Illiteracy would also have been an important factor. Finally, Louis-François would have interpreted testimony about the past in terms of his social position, that of a poor laborer and clog maker related by marriage to farmers.

Any number of difficult questions remain, however, and we would do well to formulate them explicitly and consider how they might be resolved. In thinking about history, how did Louis-François conceive of temporal distance (or depth)? What chronological criteria ordered his thinking? Was it "ecological time" that mattered to him—the time of the forest and the bocage—or was he concerned with dates from his own family's history or the history of his village or region or nation? In his own mind, how did he link stories of the past to places he was familiar with? How much did he care about distinguishing between history and legend, and how capable was he of doing so, given the many cultivated observers who tell us that in the early nineteenth century legends continued to flourish among peasants even as scholarly histories were being written?

Through what channels was this composite knowledge of the past diffused? It has become customary to look for cultural mediations, but in this instance such a bias can be quite misleading, since it assumes that all historical knowledge trickled down from elite to masses. This preconceived notion obscures the fact that many mechanisms existed for the "horizontal" transmission of historical understanding and judgment, and that these obeyed a logic of their own.

Clearly, there are no hard and fast answers to questions such as these; we are reduced to conjecture. But let us not shrink from the challenge. All historians speculate in one way or another. Is it not speculation to assume that the denizens of the past would agree with historians about which events were major turning points, what the logic of their period was, and what categories ought to be used to interpret it? Of course, simplifying assumptions such as these make history easier to teach. Historians sometimes assume implicitly that people in the past shared their own hierarchy of interests and curiosities, or else they confine their attention to those they assume to have shared their interests. This leaves out huge numbers of people whose desires and feelings were different from their own and whose neglect was reserved for other things.

To take just one example, consider the familiar stages of the French Revolution as it is taught today: a constitutional monarchy with first a Constituent Assembly and later a Legislative Assembly, followed by a Republic that was by turns Girondin, Montagnard, Thermidorian, Directorial, and Consular. I doubt that this has anything to do with the way in which Louis-François Pinagot thought about the late eighteenth century, to the extent that he thought in terms of periods at all.[2] For him it was probably much simpler: an age of kings and lords followed by a period of revolution and then the reign of Napoleon.

Let us try to be more specific about what Louis-François might have known by taking a more comprehensive approach. What I propose to do is to review those historical events that *in my opinion*, based on what I have

learned about him, he would have been likely to have heard about repeatedly. I will consider these events in order of decreasing probability (of his
having talked about them) rather than chronologically.

In order to do this, I must try to identify with him, and in order to do
that, I must first make an effort to *deconstruct my own knowledge of history*. I
will ask the reader to do the same. Implicitly, therefore, we must forget, or
at any rate bracket, what we know in order to free ourselves from the habit
of interpreting in terms of broad conceptual categories and ideological
cleavages. Yet I cannot dispense totally with my own understanding of history, which I will need in order to extract from the past the ingredients that
Louis-François used to construct *his* understanding on the basis of a very
different logic.

Before getting to the heart of the subject, let us first consider how far
back in time his imagination might have been capable of traveling. Any
number of Louis-François's relatives lived very long lives. Some of the
people whom he saw frequently, including his father, uncles, and aunts (to
mention only those who lived in Origny), had memories that could be
traced back to the end of the Ancien Régime. Louis-François lived in close
proximity to a grandmother and great-aunt (on the Pinagot side) who had
known the middle years of the eighteenth century. In his village when he
was young lived many elderly people who could tell stories dating back to
the 1720s, and those people may well have heard in their own childhoods
eyewitness accounts of events of the 1640s. Among people living in Origny
in 1836, when Louis-François reached middle age, twenty-six (thirteen men
and thirteen women) had been twenty years old or more in 1789. In other
words, it is quite plausible to think that he would have heard many stories
about the period that we call the Ancien Régime, even though no document
exists to confirm this hypothesis. We have no idea, however, what the key
events of that period might have been for him.

What might he have heard about the age of kings and lords? This is a
question that has to be answered by anyone who wants to understand the
history of the two empires and the constitutional monarchy in Origny-le-
Butin. Unfortunately, we can't answer it. The *cahier de doléances*, or book of
grievances submitted by the parish to the Estates General at the beginning
of the Revolution, has been lost. Elsewhere in the *département*, however,
104 other *cahiers de doléances* have survived.[3] They contain grievances so
familiar to specialists that we can be almost certain of being on the right

track. Of course, the experiences of the Revolution, the Empire, and the Restoration led many to revise their judgment of what happened in 1789, but people are often comfortable with evolving judgments, more comfortable than is generally believed.[4] I remain convinced that many residents of Origny-le-Butin were quite capable of remembering how they felt in 1789, even if their views changed later on.

At the end of the Ancien Régime, the king still enjoyed the respect of people living in the region that would ultimately become the département of the Orne. This fact sheds light on the attitudes of people who lived through the Revolution and continued to live in the area in the nineteenth century. No genuine challenge was mounted at the beginning of the Revolution to the existence of the nobility and clergy as separate orders. By contrast, the authors of the *cahiers* were strongly critical of the privileges and abuses of their lords. The documents reveal unmistakable hostility toward the monastic orders, which wielded a great deal of power in the vicinity of Bellême. The *cahiers* also expressed opposition to the payment of the tithe but called for reform more often than for abolition.[5] They also criticized indirect taxes such as the *gabelle*, or salt tax: this was a major grievance. It seems a good bet that these complaints would have loomed large when people to whom Louis-François was close looked back on the age of kings and lords.

The decade that preceded his awakening to conscious life was the decade of the Revolution. We must therefore try to imagine what he might have heard about that event, starting with the probable and moving on to the possible.

During the first few months of Louis-François's life, and therefore prior to the period of which he could have had direct memories, a series of dramatic events took place in the Bellêmois. It is highly unlikely that these violent episodes would not have continued to be a topic of conversation throughout his childhood. If we are certain about any aspect of his historical understanding, it has to be this. The violent events I have in mind involved guerrilla fighters known as *chouans*, or, more hostilely, *brigands*, who were opposed to the Revolution. More precisely, we are looking at an episode of the second war against the *chouans* that took place between September 1799 and the execution of the Marquis de Frotté on February 18, 1800. The capture of Bellême and La Perrière by the legion of the Perche in January 1800 was the most striking of the dramatic events that unfolded around Origny-le-Butin.

At this point I must digress to give a brief explanation involving an interpretation of the facts that a person like Louis-François could not have supplied. In the Orne the events that took place in the period just before his birth and during his first two years belong to a second phase of revolutionary agitation. The period of enraged mobs was now over: it had lasted from 1789 to 1793. What followed was a period of "extreme weakening of popular movements. There was a *blurring of the boundary* between protest actions and popular discontent, between riots over the price of bread and theft of food, between *brigandage* and *chouannerie*."[6] Conflicts erupted one after another, and mixed up in them somehow, as either a real or imagined presence, were these so-called *brigands*. In official rhetoric this derogatory interpretative scheme was applied to every noteworthy event. What followed was a period of "banditry," agitation, and vague but permanent menace hovering over a series of events whose "idealized intellectual construction" was thereby rendered more difficult than ever.[7]

To be sure, the Haut-Perche became involved in *chouannerie*, the rebellion of the *chouans*, as early as July 1795 but in a rather cautious way.[8] It had little to do with the first war of the *chouans*, in which its participation did not go much beyond a few attempts to conscript partisans for the *chouan* cause. In 1796 and 1797 the Bellêmois remained calm, except for a few roving bands of former *chouans*. The real break came in September 1799. It was then that a group of *chouans*—or "bandits," as their enemies called them—from the forest of Bellême went after Dugué d'Assé, a former deputy of the Convention and, at the time, a member of the Council of Ancients. They ransacked his house and chased him into the woods before eight of them were killed and six others were taken prisoner by gendarmes and national guardsmen sent to deal with the situation. On September 7 the Directory proposed sending military units to reconnoiter the cantons of Le Mesle, Mortagne, and Bellême, where "brigands are operating in bands of three to four hundred well-armed men. They are robbing stage coaches and tax collectors, murdering republicans, burning their houses, chopping down liberty trees and telegraphs, and threatening public officials."[9]

A few weeks later, a second War of the Chouans began, with the Perche a crucial front. Until then the region had been at most a peripheral theater of operations. The *chouans* of Maine had communicated with those of Basse-Normandie by way of the forests of Perseigne, Bourse, and Ecouves. They had crossed the Paris-Brest highway via the woods of Ménil-Brout, a few miles west of the Haut-Perche. Now, however, the nature of the combat changed. From October until the end of the year, bands of *chouans* passed through the cantons of Tourouvre, Mauves, Nocé, and Longny. In January 1800 a so-called Legion of the Perche was organized with Chandelier in command. After forming up in Maine, the Legion moved back and forth between the Orne and Eure-et-Loir *départements*. Its partisan troops disarmed residents, burned administrative records and papers, chopped down liberty trees, whose wood the soldiers used for fuel, smashed any "altars of the nation" that remained intact, enlisted young men, and collected contributions. Soon, however, the legionnaires ran into organized military opposition led by Generals Guidal and Merle. Until then, terrorized municipal governments and national guard units had put up only weak resistance.

As a result, the Bellêmois was the scene of constant troop movements. For the first time, the region felt the "rumble of violence," which came from outside and was therefore very different from the violence that had sporadically erupted in rural communities in the past.[10] During the last days of December 1799 and the first three weeks of January 1800, the legion made the rounds of the cantonal seats of the Haut-Perche, pursued by republican troops who for a while seemed to be avoiding contact.

On January 19, at nine in the morning, four to five hundred legionnaires in two columns appeared on the outskirts of Bellême. They were dressed in "a uniform costume: a short *carmagnole* (jacket) and gray trousers, a round top hat, and a white cockade and plume."[11] Two to three hundred national guardsmen from the town set out to head them off but in the end decided to beat an orderly retreat. Fifty of them took up positions in the *maison commune*, prepared to endure a siege. They fired on the attackers, killing three *chouans* and wounding seven others. Exasperated, their adversaries "then grabbed a number of women and children and forced them to march in front of them. Carrying straw and kindling, they headed for the town hall," which they threatened to set on fire before killing everyone inside.[12] The guardsmen then surrendered.

By the time they withdrew at four in the afternoon, the *chouans* had destroyed vital records and other "public papers." They forced the terrified residents of the town to hand over not only silver but also ties, handkerchiefs, and shoes. All in all, however, their behavior was fairly restrained.

On January 21 the town was occupied again by eight or nine hundred men, who arrived early that morning. This time they were no longer so restrained. Bellême was defenseless. Republican patriots had fled for cover in the forest. After attending mass at the Church of Saint-Sauveur and smashing the national altar, whose fragments they scattered in the street, the *chouans* pillaged the homes of the most ardent republicans. They collected weapons and "taxes," for which they accepted payment in the form of watches, silver, and linen. That afternoon they turned back a column commanded by Guidal and chased it down the road to Mamers. The next day the legion left town at first light and headed toward La Ferté-Vidame, after which it turned back toward *le Perche ornais*, to Longny and Tourouvre. Before it could return to Bellême, it was destroyed in two battles, one near Le Mesle the other near Mortrée. During these episodes, in Nivôse of Year VIII (1800), the town of La Perrière, *chef-lieu* of the canton in which Origny-le-Butin was situated, was also occupied for three days by "brigands," whose number the mayor estimated at four hundred. According to the mayor, they "committed whatever crimes, thefts, and pillages they were capable of."[13]

Under such circumstances, what might a person living as the Pinagot family did in Haute-Frêne have felt? The Pinagots had been in the commune of Origny-le-Butin for ten years since leaving La Perrière, and the whole area was now engulfed in combat. They would surely have been quite anxious about the constant threat of fighting. Beyond that, however, it is quite difficult to decide where their sympathies might have lain. We know that rural people in the area did not much like the urban national guards, with whom peasants and, to an even greater extent, woodsmen sometimes clashed. It is doubtful that people in Origny-le-Butin, especially the poor living near the forest, were very happy to see either army in the area. The dominant feeling produced by these violent events, which swirled around rural communities in the vicinity without involving their inhabitants, was no doubt one of hostile anxiety. Subsequent complaints about Guidal's soldiers and even more about "brigands" tend to support this hypothesis. Still, it has to be borne in mind that it would have been tempting to play up the damage to one's property in the hope of extracting a few francs by way of compensation.

Origny-le-Butin is not mentioned in lists of estimated damages. Perhaps the commune, which was some distance from any of the main roads, was not actually occupied. It may have been spared from brief incursions by either camp. But the silence of the documents is not altogether convincing.

In order to collect indemnities, a dossier had to be compiled, but this was a difficult task for the poor administrators of such an insignificant commune. Evidence for this can be seen in the disappointment of the mayor of La Perrière, the cantonal seat, whose claim for damages was ultimately dismissed because he had failed to meet this prerequisite. It is unlikely that Origny-le-Butin emerged unscathed, since the adjacent commune of Chemilly suffered damages estimated at 1,860 francs.[14]

Subprefect Delestang noted "the frequent passage [of brigands] through the cantons of Bellesme, La Perrière [and others], the theft and pillage they committed against the inhabitants of these areas, and the wrongs that they did in forcing people to flee their homes and leave them vulnerable to being ransacked."[15] They were also guilty of "kidnapping citizens for ransom, especially those who had bought national properties," in addition to which they were responsible for "the constant passage of troops hunting for them everywhere, troops that local residents were obliged to feed and provide with linen and shoes, as well as for the many calamities attendant upon such a destructive kind of warfare."[16] Although these words were clearly chosen to have an effect on central government officials, they nevertheless bear out our contention. Note, moreover, that things did not settle down immediately. On August 2, 1800, "brigandage" was still being reported in the Mortagne region, and there was an attempted kidnapping in La Perrière.[17]

Louis-François Pinagot was two years old at the time. It is unlikely that, in stories that he might have heard subsequently, these events, which originated outside the commune, would have occasioned favorable comments about the urban national guard or the army, much less the invasion by the Legion of the Perche. Strong negative memories of these military episodes from the final stages of the Revolution may well have encouraged the wretchedly poor people of the region to approve of the First Consul's authoritarian moves.

Unrest stemming from poverty itself no doubt left a different kind of memory. These disturbances were less bloody and on a smaller scale than the clashes between organized armed forces discussed above, but they engaged the residents of these impoverished communes more profoundly. Shortages of food led to popular unrest, and this unrest would undoubtedly have been a frequent topic of conversation among the Pinagots and other forest workers in Origny-le-Butin and Saint-Martin-du-Vieux-Bellême simply because clog makers played a leading role in it.

This is not the place for yet another history of popular agitation and protest in the *département* of the Orne, which was one of the most turbulent *départements* in France from 1789 to 1795.[18] A rapid survey will have to do. At the very beginning of 1789, thus well before the outbreak of widespread rural unrest in the summer of that first year of the Revolution, and, indeed, well before the Great Fear, which deeply affected the Bellêmois, there were food riots in the Haut-Perche, and there would be periodic flare-ups over the next six years. Historians of the Revolution agree that such outbreaks were characteristic of autarchic rural societies, and there was a long history of peasant protest.[19] The first elections in rural Orne instituted a form of rural democracy that supplanted the earlier local assemblies.[20] At the end of the nineteenth century, Dr. Jousset of Bellême was able to trace the almost imperceptible transition from the old assembly of Saint-Martin-du-Vieux-Bellême to the new municipal council.[21] Festivals in the region were quite energetic affairs, and these, too, helped to cement communities whose poverty made them highly inflammable.

The workers of the forest of Bellême must have possessed vivid memories of any number of violent episodes: ransacking of castles, manhandling of "hoarders," disruption of markets, imposition of price controls under threat of violence. Such events had a direct impact on the lives of poor working people. Louis-François would probably have been brought up on stories of hardship and popular reaction, although it would not have been easy for him to reconstruct the chronology of events.

There were disturbances in February 1789 in the Laigle region of the Orne and the Ferté-Vidame region of the Eure-et-Loir. The trouble spread to the Bellêmois four months later. On June 17 forest workers, consumers of grain they did not produce themselves, armed themselves with axes, scythes, and a few rifles and moved on the town to support the poor workers there.[22] "The populace was supported by three to four hundred woodcutters, who came to *lay down the law in the town*."[23] The rioters were "led by a man on horseback wearing a yellow uniform with red lapels and armed with a saber." Before leaving the forest, he had spurred them to rebellion, telling them that "he was their father and would support them." This man, "assisted by an attorney from the town, issued passports to the carters, while on the following day officials were summoned from Bellême to apply the price set by consumers" to wheat from five merchants in the Mortagne area whom the rioters had forced to sell.[24]

On July 23 and 24, "mad Thursday and Friday," the Fear made its way through the Perche. Just five miles from Origny-le-Butin, Mamers cowered in terror. Emissaries from the town sowed panic throughout the area, telling people that "brigands" were moving down the road from Saint-Cosme to Bellême.[25] For the time being, however, the Perche avoided the chateau ransackings perpetrated during this same week by the peasants of the bocage of the western hills.

The day of reckoning was only postponed, however. In September 1792 aristocratic homes in the Mortagne district were sacked in a manner reminiscent of the pillaging that had taken place farther west three years earlier.[26] On September 16 roughly two hundred emissaries from a dozen communes converged on the château de la Grimonnière (La Ferrière-au-Doyen), some twenty-one miles from Origny-le-Butin. They were armed with pitchforks, muskets, halberds, axes, adzes, and drawknives.[27] When they failed to find the feudal titles they were after, they broke down doors and windows and smashed furniture. "Clog makers gave orders: 'Things must be smashed, men! Search everything and stick your bayonets in!' or 'Gentlemen, freedom is upon us. This house has to be gone over and sacked!'"[28] The ransacking continued for several days. The dovecote was burned and the mill destroyed. "They killed pigeons, drank wine, smashed bottles, chopped down trees."[29] Note that this episode once again reveals that forest workers played an important role in these popular movements and that clog makers, armed with the terrifying tools of their trade, were among the leaders.

In November, the Haut-Perche was inundated by a wave of violence unleashed by woodcutters from the forest of Vibraye and glassmakers from Montmirail (Sarthe). A "horde of brigands" turned up in Bellême and Rémalard. The national guard marched out to meet them and took several prisoners.[30] In August 1793 there were more disturbances, this time around the Mamers market. Several detachments of sansculottes visited grain storage facilities in the town and inventoried their contents. On November 28 Bellême again came under threat. An armed band from La Ferté-Bernard and Nogent set out to impose price controls in the town. The authorities, who had four companies of national guards at their disposal, nevertheless called for reinforcements to be sent from Mortagne in order "to proect the town against a *possible march by forest workers.*"[31]

During the winter of 1794–1795 and the subsequent planting season, the suffering was intense. The *procureur syndic* assigned to the Mortagne district wrote that he had seen "people eating grass . . . men like skeletons, a most distressing tableau."[32] From 23 to 25 Ventôse, Year II (1794), crowds of women gathered outside the district administrative headquarters and the *maison commune* of Mamers, shouting: "You scoundrels have been making us eat oatcakes at forty-five sols per twelve-pound lot. We're tired of it!" They persuaded officials to schedule a food distribution for the following day.[33] "Since the beginning of Germinal, the communes around the forest of the Perche have been in a state of insurrection. Armed with rifles, pistols, drawknives, and other tools, [the inhabitants] have been making the rounds of local farms looking for grain."[34] They broke down doors and requisitioned supplies. A roundup of ringleaders resulted in the indictment of a roofer, a clog maker, and a blacksmith, who had acted as spokesmen for the demonstrators.

Louis-François Pinagot grew up among people who either had or might have taken part in these disturbances. He no doubt heard many stories about the clog makers who inspired such fears not only in Bellême but also among the poor farmers who grew grain in the vicinity. Hostility toward the city and its authorities, a desire to dictate market prices, and hatred of grain dealers and hoarders formed a cluster of sentiments that remained firmly entrenched until well into the Second Empire. The misery of the revolutionary period continued to be invoked long thereafter, creating a long-term context for the numerous bread riots that marked Louis-François's lifetime.

It seems unlikely that Pinagot would have been unaware of the war waged by the *chouans* in the Haut-Perche and of the subsistence riots that occurred just prior to his birth and continued for some time thereafter. What we will look at next, however, is highly speculative. Elsewhere I have analyzed at some length the suffering that occurred in small rural parishes when sacred objects and other communal symbols and possessions were confiscated.[35] Such suffering appears to have been particularly intense in the Bellêmois. When the churches reopened in 1795, there were a number of tumultuous demonstrations by women determined to undo the patriotic generosity of municipal officials. Demonstrators pressured these officials—invariably men—and district authorities to secure the return of sacred vases, ornaments, and furnishings. This does not mean that the Haut-Perche was especially hostile to the civil constitution of the clergy.[36]

On the contrary, the percentage (58.3) of oath-swearing priests was particularly high there.

The intensity of this clash may seem surprising in a region that was initially favorable to the Revolution. But specialists in the subject have long since pointed out that it was in the most enthusiastically prorevolutionary regions that subsequent resistance was greatest, owing to the depths of the people's disappointment.[37] In the present case, the vigor of the outcry over the loss of sacred objects must be seen in the light of everything we know about the Percheron attachment to furniture, linen, and family silver: in the bocage, any threat to property, even a communal threat, was a cause for alarm. Bear in mind also that earlier, in November and December of 1792, the movement to defend "charities" expressed similar concerns, calling upon the authorities to permit public worship and protect local traditions.[38]

On 27 Ventôse, Year III (March 17, 1795), women from Saint-Martin-du-Vieux-Bellême gathered in the town square to express their outrage at the closure of their church, followed by the smashing of wooden cemetery crosses and church bells, and finally by the transfer of the contents of their parish crypt to Bellême. Their purpose, they said, was "to have the inside of the church restored."[39] They went to the home of Thoumelin, the former mayor, "to make him tell who had *ravaged* it. . . . Then they forced Sieur Thoumelin, along with Citizen Bourgis, the mayor, and the bailiff . . . to go with them to the district [headquarters] in Bellême to ask for the return of their church's ornaments." The authorities refused to grant their demand.

A group of *citoyennes* from Saint-Germain-de-la-Coudre had better luck.[40] On the same day they assembled at seven in the morning and headed for the *maison commune*, whose door they forced open. From 5:30 to 8:30 the tocsin sounded continuously. The women intended to go to Bellême to ask for the return of their church ornaments, which municipal officials had handed over to the authorities. In the meantime, they asked that an inventory be made of all the items that had been removed from the church and insisted that local officials sign it. The officials stalled for time but decided to order a halt to the sounding of the tocsin. A large number of women blocked the entrance to the belfry, however, and forced the officials to turn back.

Over the next two days there were similar but more serious incidents in Nocé. There, women gathered, and some of them climbed the bell tower and rang the bells over the protests of municipal officials. They, too, hoped to recover the "ornaments and silver and everything else that municipal officials confiscated and shipped off to Bellême." In a report of the incident written by a male hand, we read that they "rang the bell so hard that they broke the clapper, which will give us a little peace."[41]

On March 19 municipal officials in Saint-Martin-du-Douet resigned themselves to asking the district directorate to give back ornaments, linen, and furniture from the church so as "to spare us the pain of seeing women massed in the streets."[42] In Ceton on 1 Germinal, a crowd of women went to the *maison commune* and forced town officials to go with them to Bellême to ask for the return of their church ornaments. The mayor of L'Hermitière wrote that women there had been demonstrating for a week and that he felt threatened and no longer dared to visit the *maison commune*. "They refurnished the church with a large number of items," which they had seized by force, "saying that this furniture came from *their* church."[43] Women also chopped down liberty trees in the communes of Saint-Fulgent and Vaunoise near Origny-le-Butin.

In the end, groups of women from *most* of the communes in the district marched to Bellême, "shouting seditious slogans" as they went. The insurgents forced their way into warehouses and seized linen and ornaments that had been removed from churches.[44] On 7 Germinal, at a mass meeting in Bellême, women made their demands known but were careful to stress that until now they had always obeyed the law. Officials in the departmental capital feared that the movement might spread.

Origny-le-Butin does not appear to have been engulfed by the turmoil. This is not surprising because it was such a tiny commune, but what we know of Saint-Martin and Vaunoise suggests that many women in Origny probably shared the sentiments of women in these other towns. This hypothesis is reinforced by the fact that the residents of Origny later showed many signs of attachment to their church, which they carefully maintained, along with its bells, even after the commune was no longer recognized as a parish with its own branch church. In other words, there is no reason not to think that at evening gatherings the women around Louis-François might have told stories about this episode of female resistance to the authorities. This tells us more about feminine roles and gender relations in the Percheron bocage than do the standard accounts of traditional practices that are so often cited by historians.

We come now to the most terrifying incident of all: the "massacre" of the priest Louis François Charles du Portail de la Bénardière in Bellême on

August 19, 1792.[45] Although it was a striking episode, we cannot be sure that people in Haute-Frêne would have talked about it during Louis-François's childhood. Here we abandon the realm of the probable for that of the possible. During the summer of 1792, the Orne witnessed a series of episodes of extraordinary violence, as Pierre Caron pointed out long ago. Nine of the sixty-three murders that he catalogued throughout France took place in this one *département*.[46] Paul Nicolle has proposed a classic interpretation of these dramatic events: the murders committed in the Orne, which preceded the ones that took place in Paris in September, had similar psychological causes. Without prior concertation, young men, soon to be drafted into the army, set out to liquidate their "internal enemies" before leaving for the front. These youths were haunted by fears of an aristocratic conspiracy, of being attacked from the rear. Like the *patriotes*, they hoped to take advantage of their having been called together to settle old scores. Hatred, a thirst for vengeance, fear, and cumulative disappointments all conspired to direct their anger at certain scapegoats: nobles and refractory priests, a source of constant worry for most people, seemed tailor-made for the part.

Christine Peyrard offers a slightly different interpretation. In Bellême, citizens of the countryside, confronted with impotent local authorities, made up their mind to impose a popular, spontaneous, expeditious justice of their own. They modeled their efforts on those of the tiny commune of Ballon, which had resorted to practices reminiscent of the carnival. In the Perche, however, there were none of the rumors that circulated a month later in Paris, so that it is difficult to associate these episodes with the September Massacres.[47] To be frank, dramatic events such as these should not be interpreted within a narrow time frame: they were bloody acts that drew on a long tradition of similar crimes. The murders of 1792 cannot be understood without reference to this lengthy history, to a comparative history of murder and torture and the exhibition of pain and the advent of the "sensitive soul"—without reference, in other words, to a process of an anthropological order that was at work in the final years of the Ancien Régime. I have commented on this process elsewhere, drawing on the work of numerous other specialists.[48]

It is not my purpose here, however, to explore this scholarly debate. The question I want to raise is whether or not Louis-François Pinagot might have heard a discussion of the murder of Abbé du Portail and, if so, what people close to him might have thought about it. A brief review of the facts of the case may be useful at this point. The town of Bellême, the only district capital in the *département* without a club, had already witnessed a public demonstration on July 14. "Clog makers and woodcutters from the forest and members of the national guard of Vieux-Bellême[49] had insulted members of the district directorate, broken the windows of their houses, and pounded on their doors with sabers."[50] They did this because they felt humiliated at not having been invited that year to celebrate the taking of the Bastille and the anniversary of the Federation.

On August 19 the national guards of the canton assembled under the terms of the law of July 22, which provided for a "complement of public force" to be constituted in order to help with the effort of mass conscription.[51] The operation began at seven in the morning under the supervision of local authorities and *commissaires de la levée*, or conscription officers, and proceeded without a hitch until one o'clock.[52] They were then suspended until four, and everything was calm when the officials went off to eat lunch. At three o'clock a great ruckus was heard. A crowd had massed in the marketplace, and demonstrators were allowing only certain people to enter. The mob attacked the home of Abbé du Portail, a fifty-two-year-old priest who had retired to Bellême in 1787 and was not a public official, so that he had not been obliged to swear the loyalty oath stipulated by the civil constitution of the clergy. He had, however, made no bones about letting his hostility to the oath be known. In May 1791 he told the curé of Serigny, who had taken the oath, that he must retract on his death bed or risk being refused the last rites of the Church. Portail could not have been on worse terms with the curé of Saint-Sauveur of Bellême, who in the abbé's eyes was nothing but an "interloper."

After smashing the windows and doors of Portail's house, the mob attacked the furniture. Some of the rioters even slapped the priest's octogenarian mother. Ultimately, Portail was found hiding in the attic and was led away to the church of Saint-Sauveur. Members of the municipal administration and gendarmes tried to stand in the way, but the mob pushed them aside. The attackers insisted that their prisoner take the oath required by the civil constitution even though he did not come under its provisions. When he refused, his skull was shattered with clubs and pieces of wood, and then he was finished off with a saber. With shouts of *Vive la Nation!* the murderers urged onlookers to prove their civic spirit by striking the cadaver. Then the body was decapitated, and the head, stuck on the end of a pike, was paraded through the streets, followed by a crowd of children, who dragged the victim's headless body after them.

When the pike had been exhibited in all the windows of the town, it was stuck into a cart parked in front of an inn. Inside, the murderers sat down to drink a bottle of cider. They boasted of having done a "fine deed" and a good day's work. According to members of the district directorate, however, "the dismay on the sensitive man's face provoked as it were his own murder," and impotent sobs responded to the "barbarity of tigers." The rioters attacked the homes of twenty individuals whom they accused of sympathy for aristocrats and announced that "the destruction of the entire town" was imminent. The mayor was forced to visit the scene of the crime, while other local dignitaries fled.

Night put an end to the bloody uprising. The next day a few hotheads talked of resuming their campaign of justice, but the residents of nearby communes who had swelled the ranks of the rioters had returned home, and the authorities, having regained their composure, managed to restore order in the small town of Bellême.

Tongues did not begin to wag until after Thermidor. Of the thirty-two individuals denounced at that time, the grand jury indicted only fifteen. Nine of the accused were sent for trial in criminal court. Five were released. The rest were amnestied on 30 Frimaire, Year IV (December 21, 1795).

This chronological account of the event is based on the work of various historians. What a person living in Haute- or Basse-Frêne might have made of the episode would have been quite different. To begin with, one has to bear in mind the deficiency of revolutionary history at the local level. In 1878 the Bellêmois Jousset lamented the fact that the province of the Perche, "one of the least literary in France, has paid only meager tribute to history."[53]

Until the end of the nineteenth century, in the *département* that had been the birthplace of Hébert, Valazé, and Charlotte Corday, the memory of the Revolution was monopolized by adepts of the Counterrevolution, historians inspired by the spirit of Abbé Barruel.[54] As early as 1838, Abbé Fret set forth in his *Antiquités et chroniques percheronnes* a version of the facts that in all likelihood coincided with the version promulgated by the regional clergy during the Empire and Restoration. I shall return to this in a moment.

Given the evolution of sensibility with respect to the spilling of blood in public, it is hard to believe that the "cannibalistic" crime committed in Bellême could have been seen in a positive light in later decades, even by forest workers who might initially have given it their approval.[55] The spreading sense of horror no doubt condemned to silence anyone in Louis-François's milieu who might have witnessed or participated in the murder committed in August 1792.

By the same token, the clergy was free to present its own version of the facts, that is, to tell the tale in such a way as to make the victim out to have been a Christ-like martyr. Indeed, Abbé Fret did just that, and his account indicates the likely tenor of the edifying stories that must have been told about the event. "John the Baptist" Portail was a martyr who preferred to die an atrocious death rather than swear an oath in which he did not believe. The curé of Champs, who claimed to base his account on "eyewitness testimony," tells us that the priest was betrayed by one of his godsons, upon whom he had showered his blessings. This "new Judas," this "monster," a tailor in Bellême, was still alive when Abbé Fret took up his pen.[56] As the last survivor of the drama, "he leads a dismal life, mired in dreadful poverty and reviled by everyone in town."[57] Even his longevity is presented as part of God's plan to give publicity to his crime.

Fret reminds his readers that Portail was taken amid the "prayers, sobs, tears, and moans" of his octogenarian mother, dragged like Jesus [sic] into the public square, his humble Golgotha, bludgeoned, and decapitated. Then he describes a scene unknown to the historians Paul Nicolle and Joseph Grente: "Once the head was severed from its trunk, infamous M . . . and his epigones threatened to kill an unfortunate butcher from Pin-la-Garenne, by then intoxicated by fumes of wine, unless he plunged his arm into the victim's body and plucked out his heart."[58] The butcher did as he was told. "The organ" was then stuck on the end of a pike and paraded around town along with the head. Ultimately, the "dreadful trophy" was tossed "into the courtyard of the Auberge du Cheval-noir. The innkeeper—poor Joseph of Arimathea—gathered up the martyr's remains and gave them as suitable a burial as he could."[59] Meanwhile, the butcher came down with a terrible malady, of which he died a short time later.

This is not the place to interpret this incident of "cannibalism," as Paolo Viola has so ably done.[60] What matters to us is that this version, composed by an exact contemporary of Louis-François, is one that he may very well have heard from time to time.

These, then, are the main episodes from these ten tumultuous, violent, at times bloody years that could have left indelible traces on the memory of

Origny-le-Butin. Yet among the stories that may have allowed Louis-François to form his knowledge of the past, there is no reason to believe that there were not also narratives of another kind, recounting events less extraordinary, perhaps, but surely more joyful.

In Vieux-Bellême, the largest and liveliest of the forest communes, whose territory enclosed that of Origny-le-Butin and whose population consisted in large part of clog makers, the Festival of the Federation, July 14, 1790, seems to have been a day of revelry, as was February 6, 1791, the day on which three priests from the commune solemnly swore the oath of loyalty. Think, too, of the electoral assemblies, the bonfires to celebrate the capture of Toulon on 20 Nivôse, Year II (January 9, 1794), and the planting of a tree of fraternity on 30 Ventôse (March 20)—a sixty-one-foot poplar topped by a tricolor flag and planted on the town's parade ground.[61] More somber stories may also have been told during evening gatherings: about the conscription of local men, for example.

Thus far I have suggested any number of conjectures. The list is not exhaustive. It may be that a more intensely politicized Jacobin memory survived underground, as it were, during Louis-François's childhood and youth. Among the murderers of Abbé du Portail, for example, were three forest workers from Saint-Martin-du-Vieux-Bellême, including the terrifying carpenter Deschamps, also known as Bacanal (or Bacanard), who lived in the village of Carouge, not far from Haute-Frêne.[62]

This does not seem very likely, however, given the geographical distribution and social composition of *sociétés populaires* during the Revolution as well as the virtual disappearance of republicans during the Restoration.[63] It would fly in the face of nearly all the archival documents accumulated in the first few decades of the nineteenth century. We will have to consider the question, again, however, when we look at the spring of 1815.[64] Nevertheless, we cannot entirely rule out the idea that Louis-François might on occasion, in a chance encounter or a conversation with a coworker, have heard versions of the events of the Revolution other than those that he probably heard from the Church, his family, and his neighbors.

invasions

Louis-François Pinagot witnessed two invasions during his lifetime, one in his youth, the other when he was an old man.[1] On both occasions, the enemy's abrupt appearance expanded people's horizons to make them aware of history on a European scale. The presence of hostile, sometimes brutal, enemies, who would otherwise have remained invisible, forced people to adopt new criteria of judgment. The invasion of 1815, which came when Louis-François was seventeen, undoubtedly marked him for life. Later, as an elderly man of seventy-two, he endured some terrible weeks from September 1870 to March 1871. For many French people of his generation, these were the two great experiences of a lifetime. Not to grant them the attention they deserve would limit our grasp of the nineteenth century.

On two occasions, then, the inhabitants of the Bellêmois had dealings with Prussians: it is not difficult to understand why, here, "Prussian" was synonymous with "the enemy." There has been much discussion of French representations of Germany in the nineteenth century, and excellent works have been devoted to the attitudes of the elite.[2] In the rural Bellêmois, however, few people went in for subtle distinctions. In the early 1940s, after France and Germany had fought two more wars, I myself often heard very elderly women in the region talk about how the Prussians had suddenly turned up at the doors of their farmhouses seventy years earlier. Clearly, the experience left a deep impression.

Most of the documents (memoirs and letters) dealing with the invasion of 1815 pertain to groups other than Bellême's impoverished forest workers. They speak of nobles who took refuge in their country houses or of townspeople living in the region's small towns—all of whom the event marked profoundly. For instance, in 1887 Dr. Jousset wrote that he "was a child of twelve at the time and shared in all the anguish of my family, and even after seventy-two years the impression has not gone away."[3] The archives are full of incident reports and complaints about the behavior of occupying troops; we also have letters written by Marin Rousseau, a servant, to his master, Noël Périer de Villiers, who had left him to guard the château of La Gallardière.[4] From sources such as these we learn what Louis-François might have seen and above all what he *might have heard* about this dread occurrence.

The Prussians arrived in the Bellêmois on July 17, 1815, after crossing Eure-et-Loir.[5] They left the *département* of the Orne some two months later. The decision to withdraw was made on September 22, and the withdrawal was actually carried out between September 24 and 27, depending on the regiment. The Haut-Perche was hit harder than the *département*'s three other *arrondissements*. A list of military encampments dated August 1, 1815, allows us to estimate the density of occupation. On that date, there were 600 Prussians in Mortagne, 400 in Bellême, 250 in Tourouvre and Rémalard, and 350 in Longny.[6] In addition to those actually stationed in the area, some 40,000 men passed through the region. With these figures in mind, we can readily understand the reason for Subprefect La Morélie's desperate appeal to the vicomte de Riccé: "If you do not come to my assistance, . . . I can no longer hold out."[7]

Two of the three main storage magazines in the *département* were in Bellême and Mortagne. Supplies requisitioned by the occupation troops were kept in both.[8] The hospital of Bellême was full of sick and wounded Germans. The Prussians issued stern injunctions to local officials. On July 31, after the prefect tried to haggle over the tribute of 4,259,000 francs imposed on his *département*, Krüger insisted that inventories of all public treasuries be delivered to him within two hours. He demanded to see all departmental budgets and tax records forthwith.[9] Conditions of billeting, including quality of bedding and insistence on meat and vegetables for the troops, were spelled out in detail at Saint-Cloud on July 5. To complete the humiliation there was also a requirement that banquets be laid on for Prussian officers.

From all these documents we are able to form an idea of the local population's attitude toward the occupying forces. A minority had direct dealings with the Prussians. The rest learned whatever they knew second-hand, and we may assume that this was the case in Haute-Frêne. Of course, it is possible that, as carters, Jacques Pinagot and his son may have come into contact with the enemy. Nowhere do we see reports of serial rapes or murders committed by Prussian soldiers. Various types of "micro-events" were discussed.[10] First and foremost was the ransacking of private homes. Linen and wine seem to have tempted the Prussians the most.

Stories of ransacked castles made a particularly deep impression, especially since the Prussians forced tenant farmers to supply carts for hauling away their booty. On July 31 the chateau of Viantais (Bellou-sur-Huisne) was sacked, with losses totaling more than 20,000 francs. The Prussians carted off not just silver, jewels, and linen but books, engravings, and *objets d'art*. They smashed mirrors and instruments that they found on the premises.[11] The chateaux of La Pelleterie in Bivilliers and La Gallardière near Mortagne, owned by the Périers de Villiers, suffered the same fate.

Marin Rousseau reported to his master in French of rather uncertain spelling: "They did a lot of damage to the house, even though I welcomed them properly and sent for wine, poultry, and meat, which I gave them along with bread. It did no good. When they left, they took twenty-five bushels of oats." Fortunately, "they didn't drink any of your spirits or liqueur of any kind. They drank only ordinary wine, red and white. They did not drink the Burgundy or the Bordeaux." Marin also managed to save the peaches and pears in the orchard, which he had "picked up" rather than "allow them to be devoured." He assured his employer that "all the good houses were ransacked." The "Valdieu house was stripped of all its linen. They left the lady who is living there with nothing but the dress and blouse she had on."

The Prussians, according to the comtesse de Tredern, who was living at La Pelleterie, "took sheets, towels, and shirts." Those "who have been with me for the past two days have wagonloads." In no uncertain terms she added a judgment whose basis we do not know: "The Russians and English are behaving much better than the Germans."[12] The comte d'Orglandes was forced to feed a hundred horses in the stables of his chateau of Lonné in Igé, not far from Origny-le-Butin. The bad treatment meted out to local nobles was not without consequences: the sight of them being mistreated by the Prussians flew in the face of the allegation that the aristocrats were merely handmaidens of the enemy.

Locals may have been just as struck by Prussian gastronomic excesses as by their acts of larceny, particularly since the Haut-Perche was just emerging from a period of acute food shortages, not to say famine.[13] Indeed, the Prussians often sat down to feasts of Rabelaisian proportions. Blücher was billeted in Alençon from August 26 to September 10. The dinners he was served at the prefecture cost the *département* no less than 1,800 francs, not counting the banquets to which he was invited by the bishop of Séez. In Bellême, the mayor, hoping to win leniency from the conquerors, ordered that two banquets be held in their honor on August 3 and August 26. Eighty guests attended the first of these dinners.

And then there was the brutality of the occupier, to say nothing of his haughtiness. The Prussians did not like the fact that they had difficulty making their wishes understood. Their orders became all the more crude as a result and were sometimes followed by slaps or blows from the flat of a sword, a rifle butt, or a swagger stick. Some people had drinks thrown in their faces. Although German officers were said to have refined manners, ordinary soldiers liked to humiliate the French.[14] In the vicinity of La Gallardière, Marin Rousseau tells us, "they beat almost everyone with whom they stayed. Most people fled." In La Poterie, "everyone slept in the woods after being beaten." On August 27 he was making preparations to welcome 150 men and 180 horses to La Gallardière: "As you see, we do not look forward to a good week."

It is unlikely that Louis-François, living as he did in the shadow of the forest in Haute-Frêne, was personally obliged to serve the Prussians in these ways. In these trying times people counted themselves fortunate to live a good distance from any of the major roads. It is a good bet that Origny-le-Butin never suffered the misfortunes visited upon the inhabitants of Ménil-Brout, a small commune located on Royal Route No. 12.[15] It is probable, however, that ransackings, drunken revels, and brutality were prominent topics of conversation even in the villages along the edge of the forest of Bellême.

The withdrawal route chosen by the occupiers passed through the Haut-Perche. On September 25 the Prussian Fourteenth Brigade set up temporary headquarters in Bellême. On that day the First Regiment of the Pomeranian Landwehr withdrew via Saint-Martin, Saint-Ouen-la-Cour, and Eperrais. This route took it close to Origny-le-Butin. On the following day the Twelfth Regiment of the Silesian Landwehr passed through Saint-Martin-du-Vieux-Bellême on its way to Nocé. Thus we can be certain that Louis-François saw Prussians, and he may have been aware of this massive withdrawal.[16]

When the Prussians returned in the last years of his life, Louis-François was among those elderly people who had encountered them long before. No doubt this new invasion jogged his memory. It may have encouraged him to tell stories, and it is not difficult to imagine him recounting his souvenirs during evening gatherings of the clan in Basse-Frêne. In fact, he was more directly involved this time than in 1815. Bitter battles were fought in the Bellêmois between November 22, 1870, and January 16, 1871. The Prussians dug in nearby, and Origny-le-Butin was occupied. Louis-François would have been more impressed than he had been half a century earlier by the visual spectacle of the occupying troops, to say nothing of their auditory and even olfactory presence.[17]

The early summer of 1870 was a time of drought not only in the Orne but in many other regions as well. The prefect wrote on July 1 that Normandy, usually green, was now brown.[18] Livestock growers tried to sell or slaughter animals they could no longer feed. In order to avoid wholesale slaughter, the forest administration ordered that livestock be allowed to graze within designated sections of forest. Within a month, however, things were looking up: the grain harvest (except for oats and barley) promised to be good. Unfortunately, farmers where shorthanded, so that crops were "still standing" in the field on August 1. "Everyone set to work: old people, women, and children took up sickles, because there was not a moment to lose."[19] It is quite likely that in these difficult times Louis-François did not hesitate to come to the aid of Origny's farmers.

According to the prefect, hatred of the Prussians, which he characterized as "instinctive" and "traditional," was revived by old people's stories of "memories of the invasion," especially the stories of veterans who had fought under Napoleon.[20] People in the Orne expected the war to be short. They believed that it would also be bloody but hoped that the short duration would reduce the number of those "killed ingloriously by disease, which in extended campaigns is usually deadlier than enemy fire."[21] The Crimean and Mexican wars were still fresh in people's minds.

On August 1 the prefect wrote with confidence: "Never before has national and patriotic feeling manifested itself with such enthusiasm in all respects. Never before have men responded so eagerly to the call to arms."

When the troops were mobilized, crowds of well-wishers "accompanied our fine soldiers to the departure points." To be sure, he did add a few darker touches to this optimistic picture: "The call-up of the *garde mobile*" had been the cause of much anxiety; soldiers' families had been upset, because "they had become accustomed to viewing this institution as one whose intent was to produce a moral effect rather than a real one." The ban on paid substitutes for military service calmed things down somewhat, because it showed that the government was determined to treat all citizens as equals.

Furthermore, the prefect of the Orne reported what officials elsewhere were also saying in early August,[22] namely, that the people, "though not of very warlike disposition generally," had "joined in the general movement with uncommon enthusiasm."[23] The "parties are melting away" in response to the threat to the nation's safety. The bishop of Séez ordered his priests to say "public prayers for France and the army." "Everyone is avid for news," and dispatches were endlessly commented on.

Nevertheless, Origny-le-Butin seems to have been less enthusiastic than the *département* overall, at least to judge by the attitude of its youth. Only one young man from the commune volunteered during the course of the conflict.[24] Forty years later only eleven "veterans" of the Franco-Prussian War were listed, and only one of them had truly distinguished himself.[25] The commune did not build a monument to commemorate the conflict-this is actually not very surprising. In 1911 there was no grave in the cemetery of Origny to remind people of how bloody the war had been.[26]

Disenchantment quickly followed defeat.[27] The period between the fall of the Empire on September 4 and the signing of the preliminary peace treaty six months later was one of intense emotion marked by a series of highly visible events: the arrival and billeting of *gardes mobiles* and *francs-tireurs*, the enemy invasion, the endless troop movements characteristic of this war of maneuver, and, finally, the inevitable battles, occupations, incidents of looting, and requisitions that went along with it.

We have only a few memoirs and all-too-rare archival documents concerning this troubled period in the history of the Haut-Perche. As luck would have it, a young aristocrat, Marie de Semallé, aged nineteen, had been living since May with her mother and grandparents in the château des Feugerets, which stood on the territory of La Chapelle-Souef. She kept an extremely detailed journal, from which we can catch a glimpse of how the war was perceived by civilians living within a few miles of Origny-le-Butin.[28]

As one might expect, Marie de Semallé's world was quite different from the world of Basse-Frêne. At Les Feugerets people read as much as they could to get the best possible grasp on what was happening. Every day letters arrived from distant relatives. These aristocrats visited other aristocrats in nearby châteaux. Their servants also traveled back and forth as emissaries. The residents of Les Feugerets were in close contact with members of the bourgeoisie of Bellême, including Dr. Jousset, the notary Aunet, and various clergymen. Because of their religious convictions, they were charitable to the wounded and traveled to town regularly to attend religious services and say public prayers. When necessary, they took in refugees at the château and from them learned about the conduct of the enemy. On several occasions Prussian officers stayed at the château as well. In short, Marie de Semallé was in a position to see and hear many things that would have been beyond the ken of a man like Louis-François Pinagot.

She worried about the Paris neighborhood she loved, at that time under siege by the enemy. She consulted her maps. Several of her relatives were officers involved in the fighting. What's more, she knew German. She was excited by Klopstock's *Messias* and devoured Madame de Staël's *De l'Allemagne* in order to gain a better understanding of German culture. She took a comprehensive view of the conflict, no doubt far beyond anything a poor clog maker might have conceived. At several points she betrays a hawkish attitude born of her refusal to countenance the humiliation of France or to accept that the nation's sacrifices might have been in vain. The news of an armistice therefore plunges her into a deep depression. Of course, there is no evidence to suggest that such sentiments were shared by the inhabitants of Basse-Frêne.

Nevertheless, Marie de Semallé's journal is quite useful for our purposes. Surprisingly detailed, her text recounts many small events, together with hundreds of observations and rumors. It even tells us about the "sonic landscape." It allows us to imagine what Louis-François Pinagot might have seen, if not felt, and gives us some idea of the content of conversations he might have heard in various encounters or gatherings. Because episodes of this intensity induce a sense of acceleration in the pace of existence, precise chronology is quite important.

Between the news of the first defeats in early August and the end of November, the journal is dominated by information that Marie has gleaned from printed sources and by her comments on the preparations sparked in the area by the expectation of the enemy's imminent arrival. It is at this point that it becomes most difficult to imagine what an illiterate like Louis-François might have felt.

The residents of Les Feugerets received newspapers from all over: from Le Mans, from western France, and from the south. There were also local broadsheets and the occasional foreign or Parisian paper that arrived by balloon. The availability of printed sources of news did not prevent rumors from circulating, however.[29] On September 21 Marie noted that fear of Prussian spies had led people to look for signs they might have left on trees and fence posts.

On September 23, people began blocking roads and erecting barricades intended to halt the enemy advance (barricades that Octave Mirbeau would later mock).[30] For the first time, cannon fire could be heard from Les Feugerets. The date is important, because from this point forward people in the area felt directly threatened by the war.

What made the biggest impression at this time was the appearance of the *garde mobile* units. The Fourth Battalion of the Orne, which was hastily organized in Mortagne on August and declared operational on September 17, was sent to Bretoncelles on October 20.[31] It made contact with the enemy on November 20. It was ultimately dissolved on April 1, 1871, at Le Theil. By then only 700 of the 1,200 men enlisted in the unit remained. The battalion seems to have been poorly led and badly equipped.

On October 9 Marie de Semallé noted the presence of *gardes mobiles* in the area: they were camped everywhere, especially in the woods, where they lived in "birch barracks large enough to hold a hundred men." Indeed, in order to spare the inhabitants of the region, the administration chose to sacrifice the woods instead: log barracks were hastily erected. Some guardsmen were billeted in local homes, however.

On October 26 came the first announcements of the enemy's arrival, but no sign of enemy troops was actually seen. On November 20 the *mobiles* withdrew "in indescribable confusion" from Bretoncelles to Nocé and then Bellême, where they arrived at ten o'clock on the night of November 21.[32] They left the town at seven the next morning for Pervenchères and went from there to the forest of Perseigne before stopping in Sillé-le-Guillaume and Mayenne. The troops were demoralized by rumors that their commanders had betrayed or deserted them. It was said that some officers had actually gone home while their men camped in Bellême. In La Chapelle-Souef, Marie witnessed the disorderly state of the troops on November 22.

On the road she encountered "two hundred poor *mobiles*, fatigued and soaked and barely armed, surely coming from Nogent with their wagons, bread, and munitions." There were many others in Bellême, and they were "exhausted." Food was in short supply in the town.

That same day the Prussians entered Bellême by torchlight, singing as they marched, at around ten at night. They ordered people to open their doors and put lights in their windows. The next day they marched off in silence to meet the Army of the Loire. Marie's grandfather said that some of them had taken the Mamers road to reach Le Mans. If true, that means they would have passed within a few miles of Origny-le-Butin.

On November 22 and 23 a new phase of the conflict began. People told of seeing large numbers of Prussians in Bellême wearing black uniforms and spiked helmets, and these stories quickly spread around the region. "The streets were full of them," Marie's grandfather explained. "You couldn't pass without brushing up against Prussians, rubbing elbows with them." A huge stack of rifles in front of the town hall attested to the fact that the French populace had been disarmed; the rifles had been requisitioned and smashed. When the enemy's arrival was announced, a fair number of townspeople fled into the forest. Some hastily buried their most precious valuables. Louis-François might have had contact with frightened townspeople on either of these two days.

By now the Prussians were traveling freely along the roads of the Bellêmois. They were observed from Les Feugerets on November 25. Louis-François also might have seen them then. Marie wrote in her journal that five Prussian horseman rode down the road past the castle. "We saw them, and then ten minutes later we saw five more, and then a regiment of soldiers on foot and horseback with carts, meat wagons, and rifles. We all observed them through telescopes [which Louis-François most likely did not own]. . . . It was really a little frightening to be so close to those men. Some of them saluted, others were wounded, all had plump, pink faces, and many were young. Most of their empty four-wheeled wagons were covered with tarpaulins. Everything was filthy and miserable. They were moving fairly rapidly."

Conversation in the towns and villages of the region was animated. In La Chapelle-Souef and no doubt in Origny-le-Butin as well, all the talk was about Prussian pillaging and pilfering. In Bellême nothing was "coming in by post, telegraph, or letter." The war had arrived and could now be watched "live" as well as listened to in the form of eyewitness accounts. Those who had seen with their own eyes now had the floor to themselves, and class barriers broke down as people crowded in to hear and compare experiences. They discussed the news after mass and, even more often, after vespers. "In town we again fell into conversation," Marie wrote on November 28, "and people told stories about how they had escaped and what frightening moments they had experienced." Although the Prussians were in the habit of lighting large fires, which had aroused great fears, they "burned nothing."[33] There were no allegations of rape or murder either. To be sure, a poor fellow had turned up in La Chapelle-Souef on November 24 claiming that enemy soldiers had been "arresting able-bodied men and forcing them to march off with them." He had therefore "fled with a dozen others." But this rumor appears to have had a short life span.

By contrast, stories of plunder and pillage continued unabated. Marie nonchalantly listed victims from Bellême and La Chapelle. "They burned all of Malar's wood and left only his Kirsch." "They're finding oats and meat scattered about the streets [of Bellême]." About a man named Clinchamps, she writes that they took "his boots, his preserves, his oats, his butter, and his stockings." On November 27 she remarked that "they took Rhodeau's shirts" and "Mother Le Sueur's cow." The Prussians "drank three large glasses of *eau de vie* at Maître Guérin's" and "took three large loaves from Mother Charron." On December 3, during a visit to Bellême, Marie learned that Mlle Gislain's "coffee, chocolate, and bonnets all vanished." The Prussians also took sheets from Maître Morice. Only the "sisters," that is, nuns, were treated with respect, but of course they were the ones treating the wounded who filled the beds of the local hospital.

Dispatches from family members far from La Chapelle-Souef added to what residents of the castle saw with their own eyes and heard from friends and neighbors. On November 29 Marie learned that one of her uncles had billeted five officers, who had stolen "a fine wool cover, riding boots, many shoes, and liqueurs." In her diary the young girl added: "It's extraordinary, the amount of meat and wine these Germans pack away." Much the same thing had been said in 1815.

For a month and a half, from November 23, 1870, to January 8, 1871, when the Prussians made their second incursion into Bellême, confusion reigned supreme. An effort of imagination is required if we wish to have any idea at all of the detail of operations and of what people in the area might have seen. In the Haut-Perche, the blindness of Fabrice on the battlefield at Waterloo (in Stendhal's *The Red and the Black*) seems to have afflicted the entire society. The residents of Les Feugerets tried to follow the conflict. They consulted maps and devoured the few dispatches that came their way. In this way they learned on December 4 that the Parisians had attempted to break the siege, and on December 6 that the Prussians had recaptured Orléans. Yet they remained largely in the dark about what was going on in their own neighborhood. In Bellême fear of a return of the enemy imposed silence: the ringing of bells was prohibited.[34]

During these six weeks, Prussian as well as French infantry and artillery units were constantly on the move despite the intense cold and snow, which fell in abundant quantities on December 9. In Origny-le-Butin the municipality decided to open a charity workshop.[35] At the time, fifty able-bodied men, half of the total number residing in the commune, were out of work, while the rest found themselves reduced to conditions of extreme poverty. The misery was compounded by smallpox, which had recently broken out in the region.

Once again there was no shortage of stories. Comments on the behavior of the enemy continued. "There was more talk of the Prussians' visit to Bellême. There will always be talk about it," Marie de Semallé noted on December 22. Occasionally, someone actually saw enemy soldiers, either in camp or on the road. On December 8: "We enjoyed the trip to Le Theil with mama. . . . All day long there were Prussians marching along the road asking for food and drink, and six hundred of them set up camp at the castle, where they dragged animals right up to the entrance and carried still bloody meat up to the pretty bedrooms, where they did their cooking." On December 23 Prussian cavalry galloped past Les Feugerets, and twenty uhlans were seen in La Chapelle-Souef. On Christmas Day twelve Prussian soldiers came looking for straw. They threatened to burn down the town within three days if they didn't get what they wanted.

These incursions did not prevent the deployment of French infantry units or the transit of recently mobilized soldiers. On December 14 a hundred soldiers from Le Theil passed through La Chapelle-Souef with no superior in charge. Two days later the *mobiles* of Le Perche mounted guard around Les Feugerets. On December 23 Marie ran into two other guardsmen and a *francs-tireur* in town. Remember that Prussian cavalrymen were seen in the commune twice that same day. On December 26 the town of

Bellême was full of French soldiers. "Nothing but *mobiles* in the streets," Marie recorded the next day. "You see them everywhere, along with *francs-tireurs* from the south, who speak badly and wear Tyrolian hats with feathers." On January 1 mobilized troops from Alençon and La Ferrière camped at Les Feugerets. "In the evening we gave them fruit, bread, and cider, and Maria took fourteen of them with her to chapel."

The real novelty resulted from the massive influx of *francs-tireurs*. According to P. Pitard, a *mobile* of the Fourth Battalion, the *francs-tireurs* were shameless foragers. As strangers to the *pays*, or region, they did not feel the same scruples toward the local population as did the Ornais. They were also better equipped. Marie de Semallé confirms this information in her diary entry for January 8, 1871: "Amilly is devastated, ruined, destroyed by Lepuski [*sic*], isn't it dreadful, by the French. There are two hundred *francs-tireurs* in La Chapelle [Souef]." The next day they requisitioned a hundred and fifty loaves of bread. On those two days, of course, they were in headlong retreat. "In La Chapelle," Marie continued, "we saw a line of three hundred men with knapsacks and wearing uniforms of every sort: green *francs-tireurs*, Bordeaux *francs-tireurs* with gray trousers and red stripes, . . . ʒouaves, soldiers of the line." Meanwhile, the curé offered shelter to five Garibaldians and the chaplain, who was American. The captain apologized for his troops. Two men had been shot the previous Saturday.[36]

This time there was genuine war in the canton, and the occupation was for real. On January 8 the noise of battle could be heard from Les Feugerets. "We heard cannon fire," Marie noted, "as I have never heard it before." The aptitude of these civilians for analyzing battle sounds is worth noting: "We heard Prussian cannon, French cannon, machine guns, and then rifle fire. There was fighting at the barricade and on the road to Nogent, and at La Renardière, La Bulardière, La Barre, and Couasme." Two officers and seven soldiers asked for shelter in the castle. They had just left the battlefield and were exhausted.

On January 8, in fact, after intense fighting around La Bulardière and La Barre, Prussians again entered Bellême.[37] They took up positions on the squares and inside the town hall and post office, took over the telegraph office, and invaded many homes. According to Dr. Jousset, "it would have been impossible to pull off a more precise, complex, or total occupation."[38] The epidemic of "confluent smallpox" or "black pox" spread with the influx of enemy soldiers.

In the area around Bellême, all the towns and larger "villages" filled with Prussians.[39] In Sérigny, where a small number of *francs-tireurs* had put up resistance, the Prussians destroyed religious ornaments, smashed furniture, and converted several houses into stables. After a Prussian soldier was killed, the frightened residents of Gué-de-la-Chaîne took refuge in the forest. Prussians occupied Origny-le-Butin on January 13 and 15.[40] On the fifteenth the Prussians who had been camped in Bellême left for Mamers by way of Igé, but others arrived to relieve them on January 18. On January 31 Marie reported that her grandfather had seen fifty "tall, proud, insolent" hussars in Bellême. With few exceptions, the French always referred to "*the* Prussians" as though they were all the same. The fighting continued until the night of January 16, and sporadic artillery fire could be heard. "On our way to vespers," Marie noted on Monday the sixteenth, writing of the night before, "we were frightened by very intense cannon fire from the direction of Mamers and less intense fire from Nogent." Never forget that for civilians the war was above all a panorama of sound.

By late January rumors were rife in the marketplace of Bellême. Reports that strike us as extravagant were repeated endlessly, but even in the midst of the enemy people did not know what they could believe and what they could not. Ignorance of what was happening outside of the Haut-Perche acted as a spur to the imagination, as did the wait for decisive news and the hope of unexpected victories. As early as January 17 there were reassuring rumors: "The Prussians are losing more people than we are," Marie noted that day. And on the morning of the twenty-fourth: "Oh, what a good way to wake up!" The dispatch had been full of good news: "Prince Albert wounded, Bourbaki in Mulhouse, Versailles surrounded, P. Charles in retreat, victory of Garibaldi, Vinay, and Ducrot at Melun; victory below Meudon. Forty thousand Prussians out of action." But that night Marie added a sad note: "The good news was false." Indications such as this suggest that here, people expected that the war would end happily right up to the bitter end.

Meanwhile, there were more reports of ransacked castles, which circulated at the very least among the nobility. In Boissy a former coachman was supposed to have revealed to the Prussians places where precious items were believed to have been stored. He had pointed out locations of silver, linen, and wine. The château de Viantais, already sacked by the Prussians in 1815, had allegedly suffered damages estimated at forty thousand francs.

Voré had been ransacked: silver, linen, and wine—the same trio recurs in all the reports—were taken, along with cigars, sugar, and medications. In the Dordogne in August 1870, peasants suspected nobles of complicity with the Prussians. The peasants were afraid that the enemy would spare the castles and burn only their villages. In the Orne, however, such rumors seem to have been scotched by the experience of 1815 as well as the behavior of Prussian troops in 1870 and 1871.

News of the armistice did not reach Les Feugerets until the evening of February 3. Until then the residents of the castle had appeared to be better informed than the peasants of the region. Earlier that day there had been "talk of an armistice." That night Marie wrote that "the forts have surrendered, a twenty-one-day armistice has been signed, and the army and the Paris security force have been disarmed. A constituent assembly will be elected on the eighth and will meet on the fifteenth in Bordeaux." This time the details and prognostications were correct. The news had been passed on by Maître Aunet, the notary of Bellême, in a letter he gave to Louis, a servant at Les Feugerets who frequently made the rounds of the area's aristocratic homes to gather information. The length of time it took for this news to arrive at the castle is rather surprising: according to Dr. Jousset, the announcement of the halt in the fighting reached the capital of the canton on January 30.[41]

Incredulity persisted at Les Feugerets, however. The next day, a Saturday, Marie's grandfather returned from Bellême with the report that "nobody in town knows if the news of the armistice is to be believed or not." What was true of the townspeople was even more true of the peasants. On Wednesday, February 8, the day set for elections, Marie reported that "people in the canton of Le Theil were not aware of the armistice or the elections." This is hard to believe, but what matters is that it seemed plausible to Marie. In this "southern" canton, the rumors were no longer reassuring as they had been in the past; in fact, the reports were now darker than the reality, and along with the facts there were many tall tales: "They say that Jules Favre and Trochu are dead and that Bourbaki has committed suicide." Not much news reached Les Feugerets from besieged Paris until February 13.

What about the predictions of an imminent end to the war? "People are always talking about peace," Marie noted on February 24, "but nobody believes in it." Sixteen days after the elections, uncertainty persisted in the

Bellêmois. It was not dispelled in Marie's mind until March 4. On her way back from the château de Dorceau that day, she saw "large numbers of Prussians shouting, singing, and screaming in Bellême, which made us believe in peace."

In Marie's diary, and probably in conversations at the castle, there were two ways of describing the Prussians. The soldiers were ugly, dirty, and brutal. On Sunday, February 19, Marie was riding back from Dorceau with her grandmother in a small carriage. The road was clogged with artillery, infantry, and cavalry. "They had their helmets, their flags, and their cannon, and the road was covered with newspaper, rubbish, and leftover food." In the town of La Chapelle-Souef on March 6, "they are smoking their long pipes, brushing themselves, drinking cider straight from the pitcher, and talking." At mass a Prussian sat "between mama and me. He was very ugly, very dirty."

The only thing Marie appreciated about the Prussians was their military music. "We still hear the bugle call from Appenay," she wrote on March 7, "and the truly admirable music of which we caught a few harmonious notes on the road to Igé in Bellême." But the next day she saw thirteen soldiers from the train, totally drunk. The road to Bellême was thick with Prussians: "This morning we saw only black, tonight only white. These soldiers of the Landwere [sic] in very dirty black (with blue hands) sang, but badly." Louis-François Pinagot may have seen similar sights and heard similar sounds for months on end, but there is no reason to believe that he would have judged them according to the same criteria.

In Marie's eyes, officers were far more approachable than soldiers. Of course, she was able to observe the former more closely than the latter. On Sunday, February 26, Prussians occupied Les Feugerets. "Dinner at seven. We talked music, literature, Wagner, whom they adore, the cathedral of Magdeburg [where they were from], Cologne. . . . They looked at the German books and albums, and at nine they retired. They were surprised and delighted to hear us speak their language. Because of that, they asked for nothing and took nothing . . . the fruit earned their admiration. They wore black and, of course, the familiar pointed helmets." On Tuesday, March 7, five Prussian officers were staying at Les Feugerets. "My God, they're tall," Marie observed. "They speak French wonderfully." Like their comrades before them, they looked at German books and engravings after dinner, and they admired the fruit. "They talked literature and music and looked at

books." The next day, the postman delivered a packet of seventy-eight letters. Epistolary relations with the capital had finally been reestablished.

Origny-le-Butin was occupied again on February 24 and 25 and then
again on February 27 and 28. After that it was time to total up the damages.[42] The occupation of the Bellêmois had been harsh: possession of
weapons had been prohibited, supplies had been requisitioned, mail had
been placed under surveillance, and the flow of traffic had been impeded.
Medicine had run short, commerce had been disrupted, and cash had grown
scarce.[43] Some rural people feared the return of *assignats*.[44]

When the canton's mayors met in Bellême on February 24, 1871, they
tried unsuccessfully to forestall the assessment of special taxes. Here and
there, municipal councilors and leading taxpayers also tried to oppose the
demands of the occupation authorities. In Origny-le-Butin they gave in on
March 1.[45] Damages in the commune were estimated on November 27,
1871, as follows: requisitions in kind, 1,268 francs; cash tribute, 632 francs;
occupation fees (billeting and transport, theft and pillage), 2,456 francs—or
a grand total of 4,356 francs.[46] This was a considerable sum, given that the
annual receipts of the commune amounted to 988 francs in 1860 and would
rise as high as 2,401 francs in 1873.[47] Comparison with the figures submitted by other municipalities in the canton also suggests that the officials of
Origny-le-Butin were once again incompetent and failed to list all the damages that the commune sustained.

According to the final report of damages, dated January 25, 1872, the
commune billeted 1,439 men and 537 horses.[48] It provided nineteen days of
transport. On the list of individuals who suffered from the presence of the
Prussians, we find several of Louis-François's relatives: Louis Pinagot of
La Croix (his son), Julien Courville of La Haute-Folie (his brother-in-law),
Léon Renaud, a clogmaker from Basse-Frêne (one of his sons-in-law), and
Etienne Pinagot, a farmer from La Rigorière (a first cousin).

Louis-François, by now an elderly man of seventy-two, had thus lived
through eighteen terrible months of drought, intense cold, and epidemic. A
dark cloud had been cast over his old age by the work stoppage, the presence of the Prussians, the anxiety of the war, the cost of the occupation, and
no doubt the defeat of French forces. At least he did not have to mourn the
death of any of his offspring. His son Louis, elected a municipal councilor
in 1817, had achieved a certain status, at least in the eyes of his fellow citizens. Despite the depressing circumstances, Louis-François may well have

felt protected from the worst of the misery and misfortune. We cannot gauge his moral suffering, however. Ten years after the war, in 1880, Dr. Jousset, though a stranger to the revanchist sentiments of some of his countrymen, acknowledged that "the horror of the Prussian is still fresh in everyone's mind and will be passed on from generation to generation."[49] What might that horror have been like for a man who, twice in his lifetime, had seen these foreigners, perhaps the only foreigners he knew, invade his living space?

CHAPTER 9

"the audacity of the poor"

Now that we have tried to imagine how Louis-François Pinagot might have conceived of the history of his time, it might be a good idea to ask about the other events that defined his temporal framework. Obviously, in addition to his marriage, there were births and deaths in his family, and so on. Unfortunately, it is impossible for us to gauge the effect that such events may have had on his personality. In the course of trying to understand him, I came to believe that what mattered most in shaping his perception of time was the need to survive. He suffered through a series of intense crises during which meeting basic biological needs must have required his full attention. Of course, this is only conjecture on my part, but I feel on firmer ground in proposing the calendar of famines as a chronological framework for Louis-François's existence than I would in, say, ticking off a series of political regimes.[1]

By chance I chose to study a poor clog maker who spent his entire life in the most wretched part of one of the poorest *départements* in France. One prefect after another stressed the region's extraordinary poverty. Between the time when Louis-François first went to work in late 1810, when he was about twelve, and the spring of 1856, when he was fifty-eight, famine struck the Bellêmois nineteen times. During nine of those famine years (1828–1832,

The chapter title is from a statement made by the subprefect for the Mortagne district on January 24, 1847.

1839, and 1846–1848), Louis-François was officially listed as an "indigent" with a family to support. Coping with the shortage of food would therefore have been his primary concern.

In a sense, it is unfortunate that this was the case I drew at random, because I have elsewhere repeatedly called attention to the danger of taking too pessimistic a view of the nineteenth century. Misery is loquacious; it leaves traces, whereas prosperity does not. The officials behind most of our source documents (mayors, gendarmes, prefects, prosecutors, and so on—all men, by the way) had their eyes riveted on misery, which they did their best to control and alleviate. If we look exclusively at such sources, we run the risk of overestimating the difficulty of life and overlooking its happier moments. But the fact has to be faced: Louis-François Pinagot had to deal repeatedly with poverty or the prospect of poverty, not to say starvation.

We know a lot about cycles of misery. A generation of historians devoted themselves to the study of price and income fluctuations. This is not the place to delve into the mechanisms they uncovered. Let us concentrate instead on the poor inhabitants of Origny-le-Butin and other nearby communes. Some two thousand people who worked in the forest of Bellême had to use their meager income to procure grain because, unlike the farmers who lived in the vicinity, they produced none of their own. This situation fostered anxiety among property owners and government officials, who feared that bands of woodcutters, sawyers, and clog makers would resort to begging, sometimes accompanied by threats of violence. Occasionally, there were even outbreaks of bread riots of the kind that had once been so frequent in the region,[2] or at any rate of a somewhat modified kind that developed in the nineteenth century.[3]

Because of this periodic threat of violence, officials were forced to develop policies to deal with poverty. We will need to look at the main lines of that development and at certain doubts that arose in connection with it. The people of the region preferred the sort of charity that is sometimes characterized as "spontaneous," that is, assistance offered directly by one person to others in need—others with whom the donor was personally acquainted. By contrast, organized philanthropy (made available through local offices or committees) encountered numerous obstacles. Over time, however, philanthropic methods gradually became more sophisticated. Public relief policy relied on increasingly detailed survey data. The identification, registration, and enumeration of the poor gave rise to a mass of documents (passports, certificates of indigence and mendicancy, communal and cantonal questionnaires and statistical summaries) that are a historian's delight. The authorities sought to confine the indigent within a particular *département*, canton, or even commune, depending on the severity of the crisis. To that end, they relied on a series of coercive procedures ranging from arrest of individuals "without papers" to physical expulsion. This system reached its logical culmination in 1865, when mendicancy was prohibited within the *département* of the Orne.[4]

The administration also worked to set up a network of charity committees and bureaus. These were responsible for distributing aid and shifting resources from commune to commune within a canton. One remedy in particular became quite popular: the charity workshop, which local officials began to see as a sort of panacea. When times were especially hard, sending in the troops was sometimes seen as, if not the ultimate remedy, then at least the only way of keeping the peace. At this point exclusion was not considered. The goal of charity efforts was above all to preserve the bond between the indigent individual and his family, neighbors, priest, local government officials, and other members of the community. Confinement of the indigent was of course a way of maintaining order and defending property, but it also reflected a desire to foster a sense of responsibility among the "haves" so as to avoid uprooting the "have-nots." It was assumed that local people with property had no need of surveys and inspections to understand the needs of the poor.

Administrators believed that the communes along the southern edge of the forest of Bellême had a long tradition of bread riots. One prefect, La Magedelaine, wrote that in 1788 forest workers "had driven back a squadron of cavalry sent to force them" to allow food shipments to move unimpeded.[5]

The advent of the Consulate did not stem the disturbances. On 22 Floréal, Year X (May 12, 1802), when Louis-François was not quite four years old, a group of women from Saint-Martin, accompanied by men armed with pitchforks and muskets, stopped a merchant's "cart" and forced him to sell thirty loaves of bread at a price they set. Next, the troublemakers seized a wagonload of wheat and "drove it to the town hall," where they intended to distribute its contents.[6] This appeal to municipal authorities showed that the people involved believed that they were acting legitimately: the authorities were expected to give official sanction to the actions of the crowd according to the principles of a kind of moral economy. On this occasion, brigades of gendarmes from Mortagne and Bellême were sent in to restore order, backed by a detachment of cavalry. The prefect ordered that the wheat be taken to Mortagne and called for fifty dragoons to be sent to Saint-Martin. The inhabitants of the "commune as a body" were required to indemnify the victims.[7] On 1 Prairial (May 21), the "guilty parties" were arrested.[8] If we are to understand this firmness, we must bear in mind that the Second War of the Chouans had only recently ended.

The Orne did not produce all the grain it consumed. Its neighboring *départements*, especially the Eure-et-Loir, made up the deficit. In 1811, however, the Parisian market proved more attractive. By the spring of 1812, when stored grain supplies had been exhausted, a five-month period of "alarm, privation, and suffering" began. Over the course of the summer, La Magdelaine sent a series of distressing reports to the ministry: "A considerable number of indigents have been forced to eat bran and some rather disgusting herbs, and they felt happy when they were lucky enough to add a little butter or cheese to this not very nutritious mixture."[9] "They mixed . . . wheat, rye, and buckwheat with barley, oats, beans, peas, and vetch. In some cases, the bran and ground beans combined to form a mixture that could not be baked into bread. In some cantons, they made porridge out of bean flour or mixed bran with greens or cheese with herbs."[10] The situation became less tense by August 1812, but the next winter proved difficult as well.

Despite an obvious "fermentation of the populace," there were no outbreaks of violence.[11] The prefect feared "events" and attributed the calm to resignation. The nature of the regime and the international situation explain this apathy. But the number of gangs of beggars continued to grow. In the Mortagne district, groups of fifteen, twenty, or even twenty-five individuals begged "insolently for alms."[12]

The crisis raised urgent questions in the bureaus of the prefecture. La Magdelaine blamed price controls, which had been reestablished in May 1811.[13] He lamented the excessive amount of land devoted to forest and pasture in a *département* that failed to produce enough grain to meet its needs. He examined the mechanisms for assisting the poor, emphasizing the primacy of "spontaneous charity," the only form of charity available in rural villages. During the summer crisis, he wrote, "the farmer felt considerable commiseration for the poor." "In the countryside, the poor are more scattered" than in the city, and "the hearts of farmers and landlords who harvest what they eat have not been hardened by wealth." These individuals "are closer to nature . . . the sight of misery touches them more profoundly, and they do not count every piece of bread." With the help of neighbors, the pauper "comes peacefully to the end of his distress with help from various quarters."[14] By contrast, the people of the region displayed "insurmountable reluctance" when it came to giving to the *bureaux de bienfaisance*, or charity offices.

"Every person is governed by private affections and considerations of kinship, neighborliness, public opinion, and perhaps even self-esteem. They will give alms when and how they please, and they will stubbornly refuse to allow any intermediary whatsoever to participate in their distribution. Indeed, I am aware of cases where donors seeking to evade administrative rules intended to eliminate public begging have asked paupers into their homes to receive the assistance set aside for them. I am also aware that curés and priests take such a dim view of the system that they think the administration ought to be kept out of this type of transaction."[15] "Some well-to-do and wealthy landowners have distributed bread, flour, vegetables, and cash *in their homes* on certain days of the week."[16] Most of them were nobles, as was the case in Igé and La Chapelle-Souef.

The people who were involved in charitable giving hated the administration's surveys. To be sure, La Magdelaine wrote, "the first research into the private distribution of alms was welcomed enthusiastically. Everyone was quick to respond to our questions." Subsequent official surveys aroused anxiety, however. People "regretted answering the original questions" because they feared that "a tax for the poor" might be in the works. The prefect concluded his report with a word about the danger of surveys, which in his view did "more harm than good when carried too far. In this respect, it is prudent to rely entirely on the decisions of individuals."[17]

Still, "organized," as opposed to "spontaneous," charity did exist, though still in rudimentary form. In the *département's* small towns, supplies were handed out and Rumford-style soup was served. As of April 16, 1812, there were four charity kitchens in operation in the canton of Bellême, one of them in Saint-Martin. These provided free rations to 1,146 people each day, not including additional meals delivered to the hospice for free or sold at prices ranging from seven to sixteen centimes.[18]

The Rumford-style soup kitchen offended the alimentary sensibilities of rural residents as well as their sense of individual dignity. "People say that the poor don't want soup," the prefect reported, "and that they prefer bread," so that they were more inclined to beg than to visit soup kitchens.[19] According to the prefect, the crisis of 1812 changed attitudes somewhat, because people were forced temporarily to substitute vegetables, potatoes, and dairy products for bread.[20]

Although it is true that administrative officials tended to interpret rural social relations in an idyllic manner, which may have influenced their reports, there is every reason to believe that Louis-François and his father could have obtained bread when they needed it from relatives and others who lived nearby. It is unlikely that they resorted to this option often, however. A carter with a small plot of his own would have been expected to provide for his own needs, especially since the public works undertaken in response to the crisis proved to be a windfall primarily to entrepreneurs and carters.[21]

The same was probably true for Louis-François during the severe crisis of 1817 and 1818. The harvest of 1816 had been sufficient in quantity, but the grain, "ripened with difficulty," had been "stored for the most part before the sheaves were sufficiently dry." The grain had "gone bad before it was even threshed."[22] It yielded less flour than usual. When prices began to rise in the spring of 1817, "farmers gave all available work to family members and *dismissed the hired help.*" From that point on, the prefect wrote, "the indigent class began to die of starvation." In early May gangs of paupers "crisscrossed" the countryside. "Farmers sought to ward off violence by giving them all the bread they asked for. Many gave alms with their own hands."[23]

At this point farmers began refusing to sell to anyone but a middleman. In the neighborhood of the forest of Bellême they turned away woodcutters and clog makers who came to them with "cash in hand."[24] On May 5, a group of laborers from Igé, "men with very impoverished families," stopped a wagon laden with grain and forced it to go the town hall.[25] The wagon's owner had no license, its driver had no passport or "wagon letter," and no registration plate was attached to the vehicle. The wheat belonged to an innkeeper from Saint-Cosme (Sarthe), who had long been accused of "battening on the people." Despite the disapproval of the mayor, who opposed distributing the grain, another attempt to interfere with the transport of foodstuffs occurred that evening.

Three days later disturbances of a far more serious kind occurred on the marketplace in Bellême. At about one in the afternoon, "a large number of forest workers marched into" town. "They were lined up in ranks and armed with large clubs. A *command* was issued [emphasis in original], and without insulting the authorities or making any seditious remarks they marched toward the marketplace, which nothing could prevent them from taking over. They set price controls on wheat, and terrified merchants did their bidding. They carried off a considerable quantity of grain, halted all transportation, and beat a man who dealt in wheat. . . . We have been assured that during the disturbance no insults were uttered against the government. '*When there is no bread,*' they said, '*we are not afraid of prison. Do with us what you will.*' . . . The need to remove the grain they had taken caused them to disperse at the end of the day."[26] That night six of the demonstrators, including one woman, were arrested and taken to jail in the district capital. The national guard refused to intervene. The prefect expressed his fear that the trouble would spread to the woodcutters in the forest of Tourouvre and to the blacksmiths of Randonnay.

In Mortagne it was rumored that forest workers were on their way to free their comrades held in jail there. Witnesses claimed to have heard the insurgent workers "beating barrel staves and other curved pieces of wood in such a way as to create a loud noise, which echoed throughout the forest . . . but lumber dealers went into the woods and threatened them, telling them they would never work again, and with wise counsel" managed to nip the uprising in the bud.[27] Thereafter the administration sought to place the workers under constant surveillance. The vicomte de Riccé asked the subprefect for the Mortagne district to order "the sales agents for the forest of Bellême . . . to examine the workers' records, to ask for an evaluation of each man's morals, to insist that they account for any transfers of personnel, and to make them responsible for any insurrectional assemblies the workers might mount in the future."[28]

The prefect also ordered justices of the peace, mayors, and curés to compile a census of the indigent within three days.[29] He considered new procedures for public assistance. One of Riccé's ideas was to "assign the poor to the homes of the wealthy in proportion to their wealth."[30] He finally decided that charity should be organized at the cantonal level. Mayors were supposed to aid the paupers of their canton, with the burden distributed among the municipalities of the canton according to their resources.

Leaving one's commune to go begging was strictly prohibited. Mayors were supposed to issue mendicancy cards authorizing the bearer to beg "from individuals who did not give to the charity office."[31] Upon presentation of a certificate, able-bodied men could apply for work at charity work-shops. Any able-bodied indigent who refused to work was considered to be a "vagabond," which was a criminal offense. Mayors were supposed to warn people under their jurisdiction that it was illegal for them to leave the Orne. Beggars from outside the *département* were arrested and punished. The prefect made it clear that he was determined to prevent "any invasion of paupers" in his *département*.[32] In particular, he asked mayors to "reject all beggars from the Eure-et-Loir."

At the end of June prices decreased and the crisis eased. According to the mayor of Saint-Martin, workers from the forest of Bellême were still beg-ging in August and September. In an unusual departure, "groups of people are going to the fields where the harvest is under way to gather kernels after the sheaves have been formed. It is very difficult to hold them back or to prevent them from stealing unbound sheaves before the farmer has com-pleted his task."[33]

In January 1818 the results of the census came out.[34] There were 1,709 able-bodied indigents in the canton of Bellême and 39 in Origny-le-Butin, including eleven heads of family, eighteen women, four boys, and six girls above the age of twelve. Disabled indigents (defined as those unable to work) numbered 2,053 in the canton and 53 in Origny-le-Butin, including seven heads of family, four women, sixteen boys, and twenty-six girls. All in all, indigents represented 22 percent of the commune's population. In Saint-Martin-du-Vieux-Bellême the proportion was even higher.

In a letter to the prefect, Germain Bourdon, the mayor of Origny-le-Butin, listed "eighty-six paupers," "thirty able-bodied men," forty-two children, seven "stretcher cases," and seven widows. He issued a cry of dis-tress: "I have made every possible appeal for charity, and I have found in subscriptions and voluntary alms only a third of what we would need to put a stop to mendicancy in our commune. . . . It is an impossibility for us to feed all our poor."[35] In 1817 the municipality distributed twenty-two kilo-grams of bread per day to its indigents. Bourdon added that the municipal-ity "of Vaunoise has supplied us with ten kilograms of bread per day by order of the prefect, according to the distribution fixed by the cantonal committee."[36] As to the number of "paupers, . . . there may be seven or eight able-bodied men this winter who will have no work."

The mayor of Bellême, meanwhile, offered his opinion that five of the canton's communes were "taken care of."[37] Voluntary gifts of bread had made it possible "to adequately support the non-able-bodied poor," and residents employed the rest where there were no public jobs to be had. In four other communes, including Origny-le-Butin, "similar arrangements" were being worked out. Of course, all of these municipalities asked for assistance. The only optimistic note was that the mayor of Saint-Martin reported that "relatively well-to-do residents and farmers" were giving "bread . . . and even soup to their closest neighbors" in addition to the official distributions of aid.[38]

The period 1828–1832 also proved quite difficult. Times must have been hard for Louis-François, who was now married to a spinner and still had young children at home. The crisis was particularly severe for the forest workers of Bellême. In December 1828 the prefect reported that the forest region was the part of the *département* that caused him the most worry. "There is a mob of women with no source of income other than begging. They surround every wagon that enters" the town. Most were from Saint-Martin. "Entire families [from the commune] come and rent a wretched room in Bellême in order to gain the right to assail residents and travelers with their importunate and often arrogant demands." "These gangs have already gone out into the countryside and nearby villages and threatened to return with even more people if they weren't given bread."[39]

In May 1829, as a new season was beginning and the previous year's supplies were running low, the situation grew worse. Gangs of beggars no longer hesitated to resort to threats and violence. For that reason alone, this year would remain engraved in memory. In Courcerault a landlord and his wife were "cruelly bludgeoned . . . with clubs."[40] In Ceton, a gang of three male and three female beggars and a twelve-year-old child from the Eure-et-Loir and Sarthe were arrested by local residents. The gang had molested a "small farmer" who had offered them only cider and refused to give them bread. In self-defense, "the master" had fired a shot into the thigh of a beggar who had punched him.[41] On April 27 the royal prosecutor informed the justice minister that dangerous gangs were on the move throughout the district. He said that he was quite worried, because the forest workers of Bellême, "though not without work, seem bent on abandoning their workshops to join gangs and roam the countryside."[42]

The winter that followed the revolution of July 1830 proved to be just as difficult, this time because of the lack of work. In January 1831 the prefect emphasized the desperateness of the situation in the cantons of Mortagne and Bellême.[43] A year later forest workers again felt the sting of hard times. The prefect, Clogenson, pleaded with the ministry on behalf of the commune of Saint-Martin, "the most wretched in the *département* of the Orne." "Mendicancy is the regular resource of at least a quarter of its inhabitants, and the high price of food, compounded by the stagnant state of business, has deepened their misery over the past several years." The same was true of "all the surrounding communes, where the beggars of Saint-Martin are forced to go to seek the commiseration of the public."[44]

The prosecutor deemed this situation explosive as early as 1829, and in order to deal with it he ordered the gendarmes to "break up all meetings of beggars and people calling themselves beggars" and "to arrest anyone who enters a house without the permission of its owner."[45] In November 1830 the prefect called upon mayors to see to it that "vagabonds and beggars *foreign to [their] communes* [are] sent back to their place of residence if they have passports and arrested and handed over to the royal prosecutor if they are without papers."[46] Mendicants were supposed to carry certificates from their mayor and were once again forbidden to leave the commune in which they resided.

What was new this time around was the increased reliance on charity workshops, whose nature Prefect Clogenson spelled out clearly on November 3, 1830: "By [charity work] I mean digging by hand, transport of soil by wagon, and demolition, these being the only tasks that can be continued during the winter season. These kinds of jobs are particularly suitable for the charity workshop system."[47] It is a very good bet that Louis-François Pinagot worked on one of these projects during one of the many periods of crisis that his region endured.

In September of 1839 Bellême witnessed the Affair of the Barricades, the only violent episode in the region that did not involve outsiders. It was mainly an urban affair. Forest workers were less directly involved than in the events we have described thus far. But it occurred at one of the most difficult moments of Louis-François's life. For us it is an excellent indicator of the climate that prevailed at the time on the outskirts of a small town that Louis-François probably had frequent occasion to visit.

The economic and political crisis that marked the end of the first decade of the July Monarchy did not spare the Orne. On September 18 and 19, 1839, disturbances broke out in the capital of the *département*. More than a hundred people commandeered a wagon on rue Saint-Blaise. There were similar incidents in Mortagne and, shortly thereafter, in Rémalard. In Bel-lême the trouble was far more serious, however.[48] On September 19 a mob halted a grain cart in the heart of the *faubourg* de Sainte-Lorette. The sub-prefect decided to call in gendarmes from Mortagne, Le Theil, and Rémalard and to go to Bellême personally. He arrived the next day, accom-panied by the prosecutor. The commandant of the national guard told him that his troops could not be relied upon. Some of the officers had gathered at the town hall and were refusing to take action against the poor. But the gendarmes were able to disperse the crowds that had assembled outside the building.

At about two in the afternoon, the subprefect, who had been too quick to celebrate the fact that calm had returned to the *faubourg*, learned that the grain cart had been halted once again. He hastened to the scene, accompa-nied by gendarmes on foot. "When we reached to fork where the Rémalard road splits off from the road to Nogent-le-Rotrou, I found a barricade con-structed out of a large number of carts. . . . Fearing that another barricade would be built behind us with carts parked in the crossroads, . . . I had the gendarmes clear the barricade. . . . At that moment, an angry mob, armed with crowbars roughly five and a half feet in length, charged us to prevent us from moving further down the road." The royal prosecutor was "attacked by three individuals. . . . I ran over to help and managed to free him."[49] A gendarme was hit in the head and slumped to the ground. The subprefect picked him up and sat him down but received a hard punch to the stomach. Mounted gendarmes then galloped in and rescued the besieged officials. The cart that had been stopped was allowed to proceed on its way.

Upon returning to the scene, the subprefect continued, "we found another barricade where the previous one had been. I gave orders to remove it, . . . and it was destroyed without opposition." Beyond the crossroad, however, the subprefect and prosecutor were "attacked with a hail of gravel from the roadway." Only a few gendarmes were hit. After the officials returned to the center of Bellême, several more substantial barricades were built "out of carts turned on their side and linked together with ropes and chains." The roads to Nogent and Rémalard were thus effectively blocked.

Throughout these events, groups of women had egged the rioters on. The prosecutor heard one of them say that "she would have to kill her chil-dren because some people wanted them to die of starvation." A young phi-losophy student was struck most of all by the presence of these women. In his view the "altercation" was mainly between the prosecutor and the mothers. One of the women said that he ought to be "strung up by his feet." "Some of the men said that he ought to be bludgeoned first, and it wouldn't be long. Other men and women cried out, 'Kill him! Kill him! Let's get rid of that b- -! He's the one who ordered the release of the wheat wagons.'"[50]

On September 21 things were still in turmoil. People in Bellême deliberated about whether to march on Mortagne to seek the release of the men who had been arrested the night before and to prevent the departure of the grain that had been sent to the market there. During the night there had been a discussion of ways to resist further arrests: warrants were "not to be honored."[51] Patrols were organized for the purpose of halting any wheat wagons that might attempt to pass through the town under cover of darkness. On the following day the crowd's spirits were dashed, however, when twenty people were arrested by a company of infantry. In October a trial was held, but the jury proved to be lenient to a degree the prosecutor deemed criminal.[52] The accused—seven women and thirteen men—were all acquitted except for the man who had struck the gendarme and one of the men who had attacked the magistrate.[53] All were artisans from the outskirts of Bellême.

Late in my research I discovered this surprising fact: in the year 1839, Louis-François Pinagot and his wife owned a cow. I learned this from the parish register kept by Father Pigeard. This mysterious cow complicates the question of the Pinagot family's status. In the parish register they are included among the parish's "second class," comprising families that owned one or more animals, but they were the only members of this class listed as "poor." This confirms they did indeed belong on the list of indigents. The cow seems to have been anomalous.

It is unlikely that Louis-François bought the heifer with cash. More likely he obtained her through some arrangement with a farmer. He probably could not afford to rent the pasture necessary to feed the cow either. She was probably allowed to graze along certain paths and in pasture belonging to neighbors, who must have had some sort of arrangement with Pinagot. In any case, the 365 gallons of milk that the animal would have produced in a year could have been used to supply Louis-François, his wife, and their five children with butter and cheese when food was scarce. In good years the family may have sold a calf for extra cash, since its regular income was below the subsistence level.

The years 1846, 1847, and 1848 were among the worst that Louis-François Pinagot experienced. His wife died on January 1, 1846. The fact that several of his children still lived at home but were now of working age helped him surmount these hard times. The economic crisis of the middle of the century has been studied often, and this work has given rise to lively debate. We shall concentrate in what follows on the impact of the crisis on the residents of Basse-Frêne. In late October 1846 the subprefect informed his superiors of the urgent need for charity workshops in the Bellême region.[54] In the following month the mayors of La Perrière and Origny-le-Roux complained about the influx of beggars. On November 7 there were disturbances in Ménil-Brout. In January 1847 there were rumblings of rebellion in the Buzançais and bread riots throughout the nation, but nowhere was the misery more intense than in the Bellêmois.[55] Once again, this was the region of the *département* hardest hit by the crisis. According to the prefect, 20 percent of the inhabitants of the canton were indigent, and in Saint-Martin-du-Vieux-Bellême the proportion was even higher.

On January 24 the subprefect of the Mortagne district complained of the "audacity of the poor." In La Perrière and Bellavilliers, "gangs of twelve to fifteen workers, who earned one franc per day in the charity workshops and whose wives and children received weekly assistance from the charity committees, abandoned their workshops and armed themselves with heavy clubs" and for two days went about from commune to commune in search of alms.[56] On January 27 the prefect, quite worried about the situation, ordered two companies of infantry and a detachment of cavalry into Mortagne and Bellême.[57] The poor began roaming the countryside as they had done in 1829. The only way to stop them was to send in the cavalry. According to the prefect, the crisis arose not because there was a shortage of work but because the workers realized that they could make more by begging than they could by working. There were only 400 unemployed in the Mortagne district, he said, but 1,500 additional workers chose to join gangs of beggars rather than work.[58]

This time Louis-François was directly affected by the economic crisis and its consequences, along with other residents of Basse-Frêne. The commune of Origny-le-Butin was required to assist 86 indigents (18 percent of the population).[59] According to one record of municipal council deliberations, the number of people receiving assistance was as high as 107 (24 percent of the population).[60] Thus the commune was one of the worst off in the canton. It was unable "to maintain its poor," the subprefect complained. "I have good reason to believe that those who are not receiving enough aid are begging in nearby communes."[61] And bear in mind that Basse-Frêne, where Louis-François lived, was this tiny commune's epicenter of misery.

Origny-le-Butin "is populated half by indigents attracted by the proximity of the forest of Bellême, to whom bread must be given. The commune is assisting 107 paupers. It has only 58 kilograms of bread to give them each week."[62] The amount needed was 321 kilograms. The municipality was given permission to make up the deficit by drawing on funds set aside for the schoolhouse. The mayor asked that a charity workshop be opened. This time it was apparently difficult for the commune of Vaunoise to help its neighbor because 15 percent of its own population was indigent.[63] The high mortality rate among children placed with wet nurses is another indicator of the severity of poverty in Origny-le-Butin. Between 1840 and 1848, thirty-one *petits-Paris* were buried in the parish cemetery.

In the spring of the following year, the industrial crisis triggered renewed misery, especially among clog makers. Master craftsmen were obliged to fire their workers "because they cannot borrow enough to sustain manufacturing and cannot sell their wares."[64] In Saint-Martin-du-Vieux-Bellême 150 people had no work, including 130 woodworkers. In Origny-le-Butin 15 woodworkers were unemployed. It is reasonable to assume that Louis-François was among them, given the number of clog makers in the commune.

Despite this, the municipal council steadfastly refused to allow the creation of a charity office, which the prefecture had ordered on December 9, 1847. Origny lacked the necessary resources, and, to make matters worse, "our priest, the man most to be relied on in these matters, has been sick for more than a year" and "three-quarters of the time he does not transact business, . . . which limits the church's income."[65] What's more, the commune had already spent four thousand francs to build a small bell tower to replace "the tower that caused the church to shake."[66] For these reasons, the municipal council rejected any thought of establishing a compulsory subscription for the benefit of the poor. On the other hand, it asked that the contractor hired to repair the road be compelled to hire only workers from the commune.[67]

Hard times struck again in 1853, 1854, and 1855. High food prices kept anxiety high among forest workers. In October 1853 beggars began roaming the countryside once again in defiance of the law.[68] In Saint-Martin-du-Vieux-Bellême the number of paupers was between 800 and 1,000, or more than a third of the population. The winter of 1853–1854 was very harsh, moreover. The municipal council of Origny-le-Butin, which spoke in February of "the most abject poverty," stuck to its guns. It continued to refuse to provide funds to set up a charity workshop. It once again sought permission to use funds set aside for the rental or construction of a schoolhouse, and it asked for aid to help with the purchase of food.[69]

According to the subprefect, charitable donors were much "less active" than they had been in 1847. Their generosity was dampened by difficulties stemming from the crisis that followed the establishment of the Republic, by the assessment of the "forty-five centime tax," by "the depreciation of all securities," and by resentment following threats of pillage in the first half of 1848.[70] But according to a census in the Mortagne district in 1854, the number of indigents had apparently declined somewhat from its peak.[71]

During the winter of 1854–1855, mendicancy once more reared its head in Origny-le-Butin, and the municipal council renewed its request for aid.[72] There was grumbling about the unusual length of time that food prices had remained high. In October 1855 fifty-seven people were still listed as indigents (12 percent of the population). Two months later severe winter weather forced an interruption of work in the forest of Bellême.[73] The prefect asked the minister of the interior to provide special aid to this very poor region, but his request was ignored. The situation did not improve until the spring of 1856.

Louis-François Pinagot was then fifty-seven. He would never experience intense poverty again. The modernization of agriculture, the increased fluidity of the economy, and the expansion of the market to national scale fundamentally changed the nature of the economy. The sudden and paradoxical increase in the income of clog makers, coupled with the substitution of glove making for spinning (followed shortly thereafter by an exodus of workers from the region), reduced the degree of misery in Basse-Frêne.

Here, the Second Empire marked the end of a world. As begging decreased, policy shifted. In 1865 the prefect decided that the time had come to outlaw begging in the *département*. This was done by decree on February 3. The prefect expressed his certainty that "true paupers" were now receiving public assistance and that "habitual beggars have returned to work."[74] The ministry of the interior approved the ban on begging, which was coupled with a reorganization of charity committees, an order requiring every commune to draw up lists of indigents, and an appeal to priests to devote more of their attention to the distribution of public assistance.

The war of 1870 inaugurated a new period of difficulties, but of a different type. If Louis-François suffered from the war, his suffering was no doubt less persistent and painful than that caused by the prolonged famines he endured so often during his life. Still, we must not let his suffering distract us from the fact that he was a parishioner and a citizen as well as a poor clog maker. In the next chapter we will turn our attention to these other aspects of his existence.

the parishioner, the guardsman, and the voter

The construction of citizenship has tended to capture the attention of nineteenth-century political historians.[1] What can such a concept mean when applied to a man like Louis-François Pinagot, an obscure, illiterate indigent residing in a tiny hamlet such as Basse-Frêne? Properly interpreted, the concept of citizenship may not be totally irrelevant to understanding his life. He lived at a time when people were just beginning to understand one of the fundamental rights of democratic politics: universal male suffrage. Even though he lived virtually in the woods, political debate was not necessarily foreign to him. In the Cher, only a few hundred miles from Origny-le-Butin, woodcutters were able over the years to express various forms of collective opinion that we might think of as political.[2]

What can we find out, though, about Louis-François's convictions? Can we penetrate his understanding of power and his relation to the people who wielded it? How did he conceive of politics? Did he take an interest in issues beyond the local level, issues involving people outside his own little world, in which everyone knew everyone else? Can we answer even this simple question? When it comes right down to it, can we even say whether Louis-François followed political debates at the local level? We have little to go on, not only in his case but also in the case of most of his contemporaries. Analyses of political debates and strategies and election results can never shed much light on the attitudes of people who never expressed their opinions, which is to say, most of the population, other than a small number of

political advocates and the few individuals who have been rather preten-
tiously described as "cultural mediators."

Detecting political opinions confronted nineteenth-century administrators with delicate problems. They were forced to make surveys that we
might characterize as unscientific and to draft peremptory reports that we
might say were without solid foundation if it weren't for the fact that the
most scholarly history is based on these dubious underpinnings.[3]

In any case, if we hope to gain any feel whatsoever for the political real-
ities of the time, we must begin by looking into how political opinion was
ascertained. A great deal of historical scholarship relies on this rudimentary
"political science." Two things will be clear at once to anyone who looks
into the matter: the methods used were ad hoc, and the results were dis-
torted by all sorts of regional, social, and political prejudices. Administrators instinctively relied on a vague "theory of temperaments" derived from
neo-Hippocratic philosophizing. Their "scientific methods" are worth
examining in some detail, and I do not intend this statement ironically. My
purpose in looking into the ways in which knowledge of public opinion was
constructed is not to discredit the methods on which government officials
relied. What this rudimentary political science provided was a mold into
which shrewd observers poured abundant data derived from minute observation and keen intuition. Their "regional" reports give us insight into
noteworthy continuities. More than that, the very same categories of the
imagination that shaped the vision and writing of contemporary social
observers also influenced the people they were observing, those at the base
of the social pyramid, whose behavior is what we are investigating.

Let us therefore turn our attention now to the way in which the prefects
of the Orne, the subprefects for the Mortagne district, and their various
informants—gendarmes, policemen, and local notables—looked at "the
populations" for which they were responsible. What we find when we do
this is surprising. Among the most lucid observers, there were some who
already shared our feelings of helplessness, who conceded that they found
themselves up against something impenetrable, and who expressed to
higher authorities their regret at the lack of reliable sources of information
and instruments of measurement. To be sure, they were in the minority, but
it was a courageous minority.

On June 12, 1828, the prefect, Séguier, threw up his hands in despair. He
refused to obey the ministry's orders to prepare a report "on the people's

state of mind." This is how he explained his refusal to the minister of the interior: "Your Excellency is aware that I have no funds at my disposal with which to pay secret police agents to penetrate the various classes of society and report to me on the opinions expressed by this or that individual and on the myriad circumstances that shape public opinion. My only sources of information besides myself are thus other administrative officials. Hence there can be no doubt that our information about the thinking of individuals whose principles may be contrary to those of the government is highly imperfect. It is therefore my opinion that periodic reports would not be of great interest to Your Excellency, since each such report would perforce simply repeat the contents of preceding ones."[4]

For this honest expression of his view, the prefect was severely reprimanded. On October 22 he therefore threw in the towel and submitted a standard report of the type requested by the ministry. People in the region were calm, he wrote; the "public spirit" was moderate and apathetic. We know, however, that in 1792 the Orne was the theater of the most violent massacres; one of the bloodiest *chouanneries* of the whole revolutionary period was born in the bocage. To be sure, the two statements are not necessarily contradictory: the physical violence of the rebellion can be interpreted as a kind of declaration by people who otherwise lacked the rhetorical means to take part in the kind of political debate suggested by the minister's wish to know the public's "state of mind" (*état des esprits*).[5]

"Differences of opinion exist here as they do elsewhere," Séguier wrote of his *département*, "but with the characteristic moderation of the region's inhabitants. Everyone has his newspaper and reasons in more or less the same way as his political mentor, but it is all done so quietly that difference exists without debate. In social circles one hears almost no political discussion, and where differences of opinion do manifest themselves, people listen to one another and discuss their differences without heat or passion."[6]

On December 20 the prefect offered the minister further assurance that all was well: "The [*département* of the] Orne is in this respect one of least fickle in France. Many things in addition to the phlegmatic character of its inhabitants conspire to maintain it in this state, which is highly desirable for the administration."[7]

The same reasoning was applied at the local level: Mortagne was a "changeless, lifeless town" inhabited by rentiers.[8] Here we see the Balzacian model of the provincial city, mired in the past and permeated by the odor of mildew—a place where time passed slowly if at all.[9] Séguier, having made up his mind to comply with his minister's wishes and supply the information requested, nevertheless remained skeptical as to its value: "This information, which I have gathered from various sources, is so deeply imbued with their prejudices, and their reports are so discordant, that I am constantly torn between hope and fear."[10]

At the wellspring of political intelligence, then, disagreement and bias were so evident that any attempt to synthesize the information gathered inevitably seemed misleading.[11] Still, the very effort to gather such intelligence remains interesting because it represents a systematic effort on the part of shrewd observers and attentive listeners to write down what they saw and heard.

Let us now zoom in for analysis on a still smaller scale: the subprefecture of Mortagne was one step closer to the "source" of public opinion, or so it might seem. Indeed, the Mortagne district was the part of the *département* that lay within the historic limits of the Perche region, so it is tempting to look at these reports as evidence of the way in which Percherons, the people whose difficult history we have been examining, saw themselves.[12] Images of the Perche as a geographical, social, and historical unit were invoked to explain political attitudes. Because of the diversity of the Orne as a whole, it was more difficult to give this sort of explanation at the departmental level. The reliance on regional steretotypes is apparent even without a formal quantitative analysis: in reading a substantial number of subprefectural reports, I did not come across a single one that questioned basic stereotypes about the region.[13] "The inhabitants of the former Perche are cold and imperturbable," wrote Subprefect Chartier-Desrieux on September 30, 1834. "They readily submit to being led as long as their interests are respected. They love liberty, but not to abuse it. They desire political rights more as something to have than as something to use." "They are not capable of enthusiasm of any kind. Hence party politicians (*hommes de parti*) will very likely find little here to fuel their passions."[14]

Much later, on April 24, 1853, one of his successors wrote:

> The population of the Mortagne district is generally speaking cold, indifferent, and lacking in political initiative. Honest, sober, and sensible but self-centered and shiftless, the people are difficult to move in any direction, whether for good or ill. Consumed by love

of home and concern for their own private interests, they pay little attention to politics and the public interest. Departmental and communal interests are the only ones they worry about. In this region, therefore, good administration is the best way to ensure the continued popularity of the government and to influence public opinion.

Fairly well educated and blessed with a slow but tenacious intelligence, the Percheron is too down-to-earth (*positif*) to have elevated thoughts, but he makes up for it by his wonderful grasp of business. He can be criticized for lack of candor. He does not say everything he thinks and avoids overt conflict with the authorities, but if he is ill disposed, his inertia can be such as to weary even the most resolute of wills. He can also be criticized for being a hairsplitter, for taking undue pleasure in walking a fine line between what is legal and what is not, and, finally, for exhibiting instinctive hostility to innovation of any kind.

In politics, the Percheron is prudent to excess and always afraid of compromising himself, so that he never anticipates events. In grave situations, he waits until France makes up her mind, until some outside impetus forces him to abandon neutrality and take sides.[15]

A noteworthy feature of this report is the emphasis on the work of the administration, on the tightened link between, on the one hand, listening and measuring and, on the other hand, the desire to "influence public opinion" and "actively combat extraneous influences." Here we see the gap that divided the July Monarchy from the Second Empire. In other respects, both reports harped on the same basic themes, namely, that Percherons are slow-witted, tenacious, mundane, cautious, and stuck in their ways.

We know how these kinds of reports were constructed and how persistent this "geography of temperaments" was. Nowadays it is easy to make fun of this kind of thinking, but to do so is to forget that it was not only widespread but strongly internalized. Indeed, we cannot be sure whether the kinds of judgment contained in these reports reflected behavior or shaped it.[16]

This political-geographical rhetoric was further complicated by a rhetoric of "class" analysis. On December 30, 1817, Blondel d'Aubers, the subprefect for the Mortagne district, peremptorily asserted that "only the *rea-*

soning class of society is public-spirited. Here, no fixed opinion dominates. Opinion fluctuates, like the stock exchange. For two-thirds of the year, it orients itself to the events of the day. Right now, parliamentary debates have captured the public's attention. In the assembly and in the salons, the debates are the same, and so are the anxieties, but this is incontrovertible proof of the independence of public opinion. This is the inevitable consequence of constitutional government, which cannot fail to improve the nation's mind.[17]

"I come now to the class of farmers, the class of the people. . . . They will submit to guidance and in general see the public interest only through the eyes of others. All this changes, however, when the matter at issue touches their own interests. Out of selfishness, they will then abandon their habitual indifference and concern themselves greatly with such questions as whether taxes will be the same this year as last or how many of their children or workers conscription will claim. Nevertheless, the opinion of this class must be regarded as good. It is tranquil, obedient, and not agitated."[18]

Here we find a conviction often expressed by Norman administrators: that the public opinion to be measured and analyzed was exclusively that of the "reasoning class," which kept abreast of events and was avid for news and information. People of this class, it was said, were capable of perceiving the public interest. Each one was an individual, unlike the undifferentiated masses, which were inert and potentially violent, untouched by the fluctuations of politics, and essentially changeless. Between this preponderant mass and the "minds" on whom the politics of the constitutional regime depended stood "the extreme classes," which were "habitually discontented."[19] Unmoved by the public interest, the *people* were nevertheless paradoxically subject to the influence of rumor, that is, to unpredictable, incoherent forces not directly linked to parliamentary debate.[20] Because of this, it was impossible to analyze their thinking and foolish even to attempt to do so.

On April 18, 1835, the subprefect wrote that "any attempt to observe changes in the opinion of the masses occupied with the slow and sometimes arduous work of agriculture is unlikely to yield much of a result even to the most practiced eye. Industrial and manufacturing populations are more mobile, owing to the variety of their products."[21] This association between, on the one hand, the slow pace of work and limited variety of its product and, on the other hand, the slow pace and limited range of political opinion reinforced the traditional opposition between brain and brawn, as did the association of immobile workers with unchanging ideas.[22] Summing up this view in the same year, the prefect Derville remarked that the masses were "little concerned with political theories and systems."[23] In the absence of other evidence, we would do well to take these remarks seriously. The attitudes that underlie them also shaped people's ability to form opinions, take in information, and participate in public debate.

What does all this tell us about Louis-François Pinagot, however? Stereotypes are powerful, but we know that our sources' means of gathering information were limited and that they were hamstrung by preexisting systems of representation and fundamentally uninterested in the attitudes of the masses. Hence their views may tell us little about the man we are most interested in.

Since this is what we have to work with, however, we have no choice but to proceed by induction, deduction, and intuition. Let us assume, therefore, that Louis-François shared the traits that were attributed to the Percheron masses. We have no idea what his personal political views may have been. The best we can do is say a word or two about the conditions under which his opinions, if any, would have been formed. We can also ask whether he did or did not vote in the few elections in which he was eligible to take part. There is no evidence of his having participated in any riots or demonstrations. Such participation would have constituted a form of political expression, but its absence tells us nothing. All we can say is what his probable sympathies would have been given his place in society, thereby applying the fundamental axiom of political sociology, which in all honesty may not be very accurate. Finally, we can look to see if there is any record of his having participated in local debates.

So let us begin the hunt for Louis-François Pinagot, citizen. If voting were all there was to it, our story would have to begin in 1848, by which time he was already middle aged. He did not participate in any election of any kind before that year, unless we count elections of officers and noncoms of local national guard units from 1830 on. But citizenship is a matter of duties as well as rights, and those who possess and exercise certain rights help to influence its development. With this in mind, let us begin our story in 1815, when Louis-François was only sixteen or seventeen. In the normal course of things, he would have begun to take an interest in things outside his family and beyond the narrow circle of his neighbors at about this time.

The future in those days must have seemed uncertain, and we may assume that this was a source of unspoken anxiety. During the Hundred Days, Louis-François would very likely have been afraid of conscription, which would have been hard to avoid if the war had gone on for very long. He may have thought about evading the draft. To be sure, the Orne was not a center of draft resistance.[24] Year after year the prefect, La Magdelaine, congratulated himself (a little more than he deserved) on the smoothness of the recruitment process in his *département*. In 1811, however, he was obliged to dispatch troops to arrest 474 deserters, although admittedly only 71 of these were from the Mortagne district.[25]

In 1815 Louis-François had a chance to observe universal male suffrage in action.[26] Sixteen years later he may have been reminded of that occasion by what he saw in April 1831.

Was he old enough in 1815 to have been aware of the echoes of national politics, to have followed the political scene in all its considerable vagaries, and to have grasped the most important issues? These questions force us to look at the local political situation in that terrible year and to consider the "state of mind" of people in the region. The *département* of the Orne had remained calm throughout the early years of the Restoration, but for a few antitax demonstrations stirred up by hostility to *les droits réunis*.[27] This is not surprising in a region so sensitive to the connections between drinking and politics. By contrast, the end of the Hundred Days was greeted here by some fairly vigorous royalist movements, although these admittedly had little impact on the rural communes of the Perche.

On June 24, after vespers, an angry mob forced the mayor of Gacé to take the tricolor flag down from the bell tower. Between seven and eight o'clock the next morning, a group of fourteen- and fifteen-year-old youths marched through the streets of the town with a white flag. At about nine that night, three hundred people gathered then ran through the streets until two in the morning shouting, "Vive le Roi! Vive la fleur de lys!"[28] According to La Magdelaine, many of these people "came from taverns and were drunk." This was a standard pejorative characterization of the adversary's attitude, one that would be repeated again and again over the course of the nineteenth century. The movement subsequently spread to neighboring communes.

The next day, a crowd of seven or eight hundred attacked emblems of the Empire in the town of Vimoutiers.[29] There, too, the tricolor flag was taken down and ripped to shreds. The crowd carried a white flag through the streets and then flew it from the top of the church steeple. This absolutely standard reversion to tradition also affected nearby communes. Fighting broke out in Séez, while tension mounted in the bocage country. A white flag was attached to the steeple of the church of Sérigny, not far from Origny-le-Butin.[30] It is thus possible that young Louis-François Pinagot witnessed something of all this turmoil.

But that is not all. At the end of the year, the marquis de Puisaye, a member of the *chambre des représentants* [*sic*], tried to put together a "royal and Catholic army" in the region of Bellême and Rémalard. The effort came to naught, but according to the prefect, it was enough to foster in the minds of the local populace a sense of "the imminence of civil war": "Some say they are against the king and the authorities, others that they are against the Jacobins."[31] Thus the ultras' "scheming" had managed to awaken the ghost of *chouannerie*. People in the Bellêmois were "distraught" and anxious, while elsewhere the "White Terror" was unleashed. Although we now know that these fears were groundless, that is no reason to underestimate them.

Between that terrible year and the fall of the Bourbons, it is a good bet that the subsistence riots of 1817,[32] which undermined confidence in the stability of the regime and of the dynasty and led people around Origny-le-Butin to believe the rumor that France had been sold out to foreign powers, were the national events that seemed most important to Louis-François Pinagot.[33] During these fifteen years, what other political developments might have had an impact on him?

Now that he was directly concerned by military recruitment, he would have had to pay close attention to this danger. How did things stand in the region? According to the prefect's self-congratulatory reports, the call-up (on September 10, 1818) of 80,000 men who became eligible for service in 1816 and 1817 went off without a hitch. When lots were drawn, there were no disturbances anywhere, and obedience was "exemplary." The cantons around Mortagne were especially docile.[34] The levy of 40,000 men from Louis-François's group (the class of 1818), which was ordered on April 28, 1819, also proceeded without problems. The youths of the *département* answered the call "without a murmur."[35] The subprefect for the Mortagne district seems to have been particularly pleased. The prefect even remarked on "the noticeable improvement in public opinion concerning the law of recruitment [of March 10, 1818] compared with last year," an improvement that might seem to defy credulity since things could hardly have gone better the year before, to hear the prefect tell it.[36] The law was well received, he assures us, and young people were convinced that everyone was being treated equally.

It is easy to imagine how Louis-François would have reacted to a note written by the prefect, La Morélie, on August 7, 1819: "The young men expressed joy at the announcement of the provisional closing of the list for the contingent, and shouts of 'Vive le Roi!' could be heard, accompanied by cheers."[37] Louis-François might have been among those who were cheering, because he either drew a lucky number (55) or was exempted for some other reason.[38]

Still, we would do well to be take the prefect's self-congratulatory pronouncements with a grain of salt. From a report dated September 23, 1819, for example, we learn that 220 of the young men drafted from the classes of 1816 and 1817 eventually deserted.[39] Although mayors were ordered to track deserters down, they were often indulgent toward youths. Some pretended to be unaware of deserters in their communes, while others did not hesitate to issue them passports. Only a small number were arrested. Very few rejoined their units on their own.

Royal festivals were held at designated times throughout the kingdom. These were a good way of telling people about the monarchy and keeping them informed of events of national significance.[40] Even in the most remote villages the birthday of Louis XVI was celebrated every year. Priests read the martyred king's last will and testament from the pulpit. Every town was also required to celebrate the day of the royal namesake: Saint-Louis on August 25 and, later, Saint-Charles on November 4. Twenty-one communes of the Mortagne district also decided to celebrate the baptism of the duc de Bordeaux in June 1821. Three years later the death knell was sounded for Louis XVIII. The coronation of Charles X was also observed throughout the country.[41]

Unfortunately, there is no record of the ceremonies held in Origny-le-Butin on these occasions. Let us try to imagine the scene by examining a report on the night of Saint-Charles (November 4, 1825) by the mayor of Origny-le-Roux. A high mass was celebrated "*avec le tedeom* [as the mayor spelled Te Deum]." "We rang the bells on the eve of the holiday, and during the day we attended mass along with a substantial number of other residents. We witnessed nothing but joy and love for our monarch and shouts of 'Vive Charles X.'"[42] On the death of Louis XVIII, the curé of Origny-le-Butin "rang the death knell." The commune had previously celebrated the baptism of the duc de Bordeaux.

This festive celebration began in the last years of Louis-François's "youth," the brief period between communion and marriage. During that time it was permissible to dance, court girls, and indulge in a variety of traditional practices[43] that were likely to have been particularly intense on the edge of the forest.[44]

In those years Louis-François's awareness of politics, or, to put it less grandly, interest in public affairs, would have been limited at best to local issues. What, if anything, did he think about the mayor and the municipal council? At first sight, it might seem likely that the apparatus of municipal government would have been beyond his ken. Under the Restoration, the "council" was not elected.[45] Its members were appointed. In Origny-le-Butin it consisted entirely of very minor notables, most of them farmers with land of their own. Forest workers were excluded.

As it happens, however, Louis-François's father-in-law, Louis Pôté, was if not a member of the municipal council, then at least one of the commune's leading taxpayers. He was therefore consulted about certain decisions. What's more, he held a power of attorney for Maître de Villereau of Bellême, who owned nearly twenty-five acres in Origny-le-Butin. In that capacity he was present, for instance, along with his friend César Buat, at the council meeting of October 5, 1824, when the communal cadaster was prepared. Pôté was one of a small number of landowners responsible for assessing the commune's various properties. He was among those "familiar with the different parts of the territory."[46] Thus there is every reason to believe that Louis-François would have heard through the family grapevine at least some report of these debates, which dealt with a burning local issue of the day.

At the end of 1815 the mayor of Origny-le-Butin was Fidèle Armand de Bloteau. Jacques Pinagot, Louis-François's father, knew the Bloteau family quite well and later acted as its proxy. As it happens, Fidèle de Bloteau was the central figure in the only local political "affair" ever to attract the attention of authorities at the national level, an "émigré drama" with Balzacian overtones. Since it affected people to whom Louis-François was quite close, it is worth looking at in some detail.[47]

In September 1815 Fidèle de Bloteau, a former captain in the Aunis regiment and staff officer in the Sixth Division of the Vendean Catholic and
Royal Army, was named mayor of Origny-le-Butin, replacing Sieur Morel,
whom the prefect, the vicomte de Riccé, had found to be a "poor servant of
the king."[48] Clearly, this former émigré, who boasted of "belonging" to the
duchesse de Duras, enjoyed the support of people in high places.[49]

In any event, it soon became apparent that he was also somewhat
deranged. "One day a criminal was being sought in his commune," and
because the mayor thought the gendarmes were not doing their job, he
"ordered that the tocsin be sounded and made everyone in town stand guard
around the man's house." The fugitive evaded capture, however, whereupon the mayor "had his wife incarcerated, evicted his young children from
their home, and sent the key to the subprefecture."[50] As a result of this
episode, the vicomte de Riccé decided to reinstate Morel, who was now
somewhat belatedly seen to "profess correct principles and enjoy the esteem
of respectable people."

This reinstatement was maintained despite howls of protest from the
ultras, who continued to back a man they considered to be "steeped in
honor and feeling." He had "never abandoned the party of his legitimate
sovereign."[51] The marquis de Puisaye, the prince de Broglie, the marquis
de Frotté, all deputies, along with the vicomte de Chabot, mayor of La Perrière, and officials of several other nearby towns all pleaded strongly in
favor of the unfortunate Fidèle de Bloteau. In 1816 the dismissed mayor
himself wrote to the minister: "The cruel revolution stripped me of my
estate and my fortune. Honor is all I have left." He asked to be allowed "an
honorable end to my career."[52] But his plea fell on deaf ears.

As the years went by, the erstwhile émigré succumbed to nostalgia and
looniness. He began to make statements against the aristocracy, the clergy,
and the government that were denounced as seditious. On September 15,
1819, shortly after he appeared as a witness at Louis-François's marriage, a
warrant was issued for his arrest. Gendarmes turned up at La Brumancière
at three-thirty in the morning. But Bloteau had "somehow fortified himself
in his castle, where he had amassed a quantity of arms and munitions" after
taking the trouble to crenelate the walls and create defensive loopholes.[53]

The new mayor of Origny was called in to help, but soon Bloteau was
threatening to shoot him if he dared set foot in the courtyard of his "castle."
At five o'clock Morel resorted to a subterfuge: he sent his son, a mere child,

to Bloteau's home, where a servant admitted him. The gendarmes, who had concealed themselves nearby, then rushed in. But Bloteau had prepared a fallback position. He barricaded himself in a bedroom, where he had previously stashed "three large loaves of bread." From this room it was also possible to reach the cellar, so that the besieged lunatic was unlikely to run short of food. He had armed himself with a rifle and saber and prepared holes in the door through which he could shoot at anyone who came after him.

A lengthy negotiation ensued. The former mayor hurled insults at the gendarmes. Then, for nearly an hour, he delivered himself of "a sort of general confession," in which he admitted among other things that he had been unfaithful to his wife and impregnated a young woman, for which he begged God's forgiveness. He accused the gendarmes of doing the bidding of his enemies, the nobles, and of being "under the spell of the devil's magic." He also claimed to have had a recent encounter with the devil in the cathedral of Séez. Satan had red eyebrows and was disguised as a priest. Bloteau's ranting was interspersed with "seditious outbursts": "Vive Louis XVII!" "Vive les Bourbons!" "Vive l'Ancien Régime!" "Down with the government!"[54] At one point the madman opened a window and fired into the courtyard to repeated shouts of "Vive Louis XVII!"

He then put on the uniform of the Aunis regiment and, with much ceremonious posturing, opened the door. The gendarmes found themselves face to face with a man wearing "crape on his arm and on his hunting knife," with "a large club dangling from one arm, and armed with a rifle." Hand-to-hand combat ensued, and in the subsequent melee the gendarmes' lieutenant was slightly wounded, whereupon Bloteau extended his hand and declared himself to be the man's prisoner.

He was taken to the prison in Mortagne. Along the way, especially while passing through the streets of the town, Bloteau had screamed like a lunatic, "Vive Louis XVII!" "When we reached the square," the lieutenant wrote, "he again begged us to shoot him." In the end he was released on grounds of insanity.

The misfortunes of the former émigré, whose ravings, steeped in history, made his tragedy somehow emblematic, undoubtedly became a part of Origny's local lore. The incident was of the sort that people would have talked about and commented on, perhaps even taken positions on, and in so doing they would, of course, have had to think about the past.[55] Obviously, the Pinagots would have discussed it when they gathered in the evening.

We come now to the question of Louis-François's participation in the public life of his community. I see only one public activity in which he would have taken part at this stage of his life: road work. This chore was still referred to as a *corvée*, or obligatory labor, just as it was called in the Ancien Régime. It was compulsory for "anyone listed on any of the direct tax rolls as well as sons living with [such persons] and able-bodied male servants above the age of twenty." The law also applied to "every draft animal or beast of burden, every saddle or harness horse, and every wagon."[56] Jacques Pinagot would have been particularly affected by these requirements.

In Origny-le-Butin every taxpayer was required to provide one or two days of work per year, depending on the year. One could, of course, "buy one's way out with cash." The price of this exemption ranged from 1 to 1.2 francs per day, which was prohibitive. We know for certain that the Pinagots "freed themselves in labor" (for five francs), because this is recorded in the record of municipal deliberations. So did Louis Pôté, Louis-François's father-in-law, who was obliged to pay eleven francs in 1828 on account of his livestock, and Jacques-Augustin Drouin, Louis-François's uncle. On compulsory work days the church bells were rung to summon the workers. This public announcement of a communal obligation placed the common interest on everyone's agenda.

Still, there is no denying the fact that the labor obligation was quite minimal, and all signs are that, during the first quarter of the nineteenth century, the inhabitants of Origny-le-Butin thought of themselves more as parishioners than as citizens. Evidence of this can be seen in the numerous signs of suffering caused by the elimination of religious services. The banning of bell-ringing, the disruption of church services, the neglect of the local cemetery, and above all the absence of a priest were experienced as deprivations, as affronts to the communal identity of Origny's residents. For nearly twenty years, the impediments raised to attending religious services and catechism classes in Origny fostered animosity against the nearby town of Vaunoise, whose good fortune contrasted all too sharply with Origny's degradation. This irritation never led to violence, however. Louis-François no doubt shared the collective bitterness. We know for a fact that his father-in-law, Louis Pôté, did.

Why was Origny penalized as it was? Clearly because it lacked a sufficiently powerful patron. Without a prominent person to back its claims, the community had a hard time getting anyone to listen to its grievances. It was difficult for the residents of the commune to understand the reasoning behind the Concordat, and no one bothered to explain it to them. The issue was finally resolved between 1820 and 1827 thanks to the intervention of the comte d'Orglandes, the castellan of Lonné.

On 10 Fructidor, year XII (August 28, 1804), when the threat to the local parish first arose, the municipal council asked that Vaunoise and Origny be joined together. It submitted its arguments in a document that tells us how the aldermen saw the situation.[57] "The church of Origny-le-Butin is nicely decorated and situated in a healthy and pleasant setting in the center of the commune." By contrast, the church in Vaunoise was "difficult to access." It was situated "far from any dwellings" and could be reached only by trails that were almost impassable.

Inside the church of Origny "there are ornaments for the divine service." In addition, it was "easy to find nearby housing suitable for the priest." The church of Vaunoise was too small to benefit from the union. It was "located in an isolated spot." Ornaments could not be left there for fear that they would be stolen. There was no house nearby suitable for a priest. The residents of Origny were prepared, moreover, to "supply anything that might be necessary" to a priest. Fees charged for pews would help to defray expenses. At first the commune's arguments carried the day, but for reasons we do not know, the original decision was reversed, and Origny was made a part of the parish of Vaunoise.[58]

On 14 Thermidor, Year XIII (August 2, 1805), the municipal council protested the injustice of this decision and expressed its pain at being forced to "abandon so beautiful a church."[59] A short stay was granted. On November 20, 1806, an imperial decision bestowed on the church of Origny the status of annex or oratory of Vaunoise by an imperial decision.[60] Two years later, however, came the final blow, in application of the decree of September 30, 1807, which ordered that the parish map be redrawn. The subsidiary church at Origny-le-Butin was eliminated, the commune became part of the parish of Vaunoise, and Origny's church was deconsecrated. At the time, it was equipped with two bells, one of which weighed more than 400 pounds, and boasted of a crypt containing, among other items, a massive silver chalice, a silver container for holy oils, a silver-plated custodial, and a beautiful copper censer.[61]

For the next twelve years, the municipal council and residents of Origny-le-Butin repeatedly complained to the prefect about this decision.

They did what they could to keep their options open.[62] On December 3, 1808, not long after the church was closed, the council unanimously voted to request that it be designated as a chapel. The aldermen promised to pay the chaplain under the terms of an agreement not unlike other customary "arrangements" in the commune. If a chaplain agreed to serve in Origny, they would offer him an annual salary of four hundred francs plus a housing bonus of a hundred and twenty francs. In 1809 and 1810 they offered five hundred francs plus a housing bonus of a hundred fifty francs. The municipal council also proposed to assume the full cost of maintaining the church and presbytery. But nothing came of these gestures.

A royal order dated August 25, 1819, rekindled hope. On October 5, thirty-three residents of Origny-le-Butin sent a petition to the vicars-general of the diocese of Séez.[63] The signers included all the minor notables of the commune. This time they based their case on the piety of the inhabitants, who had kept up both the deconsecrated church and the cemetery, for which they had raised the sum of two hundred francs. They argued that the need for lengthy travel would discourage religious practice. "No union [of churches] was ever more painful than this one." The distance between the two communes constituted "an insurmountable obstacle to attending religious services," since roads were "impassable for eight months of the year." The church in Vaunoise was too small, moreover, and "not just by a little but by half." All these statements suggest that Louis-François's religious observance must have been somewhat negligent. To further their case, the residents of Origny even offered to solicit "voluntary contributions" to purchase a presbytery.

On November 7 the municipal council voted unanimously to request that Origny-le-Butin be designated a parish branch.[64] The subprefect said that he, too, favored the proposal, and in 1820 the request was granted. It then became necessary to purchase a presbytery, since the old one had been sold during the Revolution. From 1822 to 1827, this project claimed the lion's share of the council's attention.[65] The expense was more than the commune could afford. In October 1823 the prefecture granted permission to borrow 4,799 francs in order to purchase a house adjacent to the church.[66] For the commune of Origny, this was a colossal sum. Hearings were held, and twenty-eight people testified. Among them was Louis Pôté, who shared the opinion of the commune, and no doubt of his son-in-law, "that the purchase was indeed necessary."[67]

The next order of business was to make the house worthy of a priest. Everyone gladly pitched in because they wanted to "keep the priest," "Father" Pigeard, who had come to the church in 1826 and was willing to live in a humble abode comprising a bedroom, a study, and a kitchen.[68] In the following year, the comte d'Orglandes begged the minister of cults to "take pity on the unfortunate inhabitants of Origny."[69] He obtained a subsidy of five hundred francs. The priest, meanwhile, decided to demonstrate humility through self-denial. He announced that he was prepared to do without curtains, bed canopies, and "other objects he needs."[70] To ease his burden, his parishioners promised to transport anything he needed free of charge. In 1828 the council noted that "Monsieur le curé has no place to store his firewood or to stable the horses of his visitors" and therefore decided to build him a woodshed and a stable.[71]

The people of Origny thus managed, at great expense, to regain religious control of their community and to restore its religious identity, which had for a time been threatened by the preaching of two apostles of the "Petite Eglise." Church bells once again enlivened the sonic environment. But this success weighed heavily on the finances of the impoverished commune. During the difficult middle years of the century, as we have seen, repairs to the church and steeple, renewal of the bells, and maintenance of the presbytery all took precedence over the construction of a schoolhouse, as well as over relief for the poor.

The years 1830 and 1831 would prove important in the process of constructing citizenship. As it happens, these were also the years in which Louis-François's indigence was first officially recognized, although it may have begun earlier. This must have had a profound effect on the way he saw himself and others. On May 13, 1831, Louis-François was listed among the sixteen individuals whom the municipal council believed it "must exempt from the tax on movable property in view of their limited resources."[72] He was also exempted from the corvée, or compulsory labor. This was the result of a secret ballot held by the council. Louis-François's name appeared on the list alongside those of Louis-Sébastien Pinagot, his uncle from Les Querrières, who had lost his way in life, and Marin Pôté, his brother-in-law, a victim, like his sister Anne, of a tragic decline of status. Fortune had not smiled on the family. Yet it was at this time that certain aspects of citizenship became accessible for the first time. Let us return, therefore, to political events.

On August 9, 1830, the day Louis-Philippe I was enthroned (at that time only as lieutenant-general of the kingdom), the Mortagne district expressed its support for the new regime in a predictable administrative style. "I have acquired the certainty," the subprefect wrote, "that the tricolor was generally flown in the communes of the district with unimaginable enthusiasm. Everything was calm, and patriotism, formerly held in check, leapt from its hiding place with the alacrity of an electric spark."[73] Once again, the state of public opinion was gauged in terms of the number of flags flown.

We may assume, therefore, that in Origny-le-Butin the change of regime went without a hitch. For Louis-François, the chief result was his enlistment in the national guard. The institution is worth dwelling on for a moment. On August 5, 1830, the provisional prefect ordered that national guard units be established in all the communes of the *département*. They were to be "made up of all citizens between the ages of eighteen and sixty."[74] This measure, an application of the laws of October 14, 1791, was promulgated in the Mortagne district on August 9, 1830.[75] Its application proved quite slow. By the end of October, none of the rural communes in the canton of Bellême had yet put it into effect.[76]

The government asked the prefect to do what he could to "persuade the national guards to adopt the *rural uniform*," that is, the *blouse gauloise*, or, better still, a more sophisticated outfit consisting of the *blouse*, a knapsack, a saber, and, if possible, a shako with pompom.[77] This was the uniform awarded on May 1, 1831, to the winner of a contest held in the tiny commune of La Mesnière on the king's birthday.[78] The winner was a twenty-two-year-old weaver who was a soldier in the guard. The fact that the government tried to make this uniform obligatory shows that it wanted to establish the new regime on the basis of a specific set of social and historical images. Unfortunately, the cost of a *blouse gauloise*, some fifteen to eighteen francs, put it beyond the reach of a man like Louis-François.

According to a series of prefects, however, the national guardsmen of the rural Orne would have been prepared to bear this expense if they had been supplied with arms. Not unreasonably, the men declared that "the uniform without a rifle is nothing but a fancy costume."[79] As of November 10, only seven hundred rifles had been distributed to national guard units in the *département*.[80] A number of historians have seen this reluctance to arm the masses as a missed opportunity for the regime to establish itself on a firm footing and for Louis-Philippe to establish himself as a "Napoleon of the people."[81] Although the prefect asked for rifles for the twenty-four largest communes, his request went unanswered. So did the petitions submitted by various communes asking that arms be issued to their units, including Tourouvre and Le Theil (to confine our attention to communes in the Perche).

A company of infantry of the national guard did exist in Origny-le-Butin, but I was not able to ascertain the exact date when it was organized. In April 1831 it comprised a hundred men: four officers, six noncommissioned officers, and ninety soldiers, including Louis-François Pinagot.[82] On that date none of these men was armed with so much as a borrowed rifle. None wore the *blouse gauloise*. None was properly equipped. In 1855, when the guard's weapons were returned to the armories of the war ministry, the Origny-le-Butin unit declared that it had none.[83] For these peasants, as for us, however, the military nature of the institution was not its essential characteristic. Enlistment in the guard was connected with the elaboration of the concept of citizenship. For the majority of guardsmen (other than those who had been old enough to vote in 1815 or even 1793), membership in the guard provided the first opportunity to participate in an election. For Louis-François, the experience was new, and we know that he did take part in the first election.[84]

Until the end of the July Monarchy, officers and noncoms were elected in Origny-le-Butin as they were in other communes. At noon on June 29, 1831, the guardsmen of the "ordinary service" were summoned to "the hall of the communal house," probably the mayor's residence. The sixty-five electors present chose the man who was to be their captain.[85] On May 31, 1834, there were eighty-five guardsmen and sixty-four electors.[86] On April 25, 1848, two months after the establishment of the Second Republic, seventy-two guardsmen were inscribed on the books and fifty-seven of those electors were present, which suggests a participation rate almost identical to that of the July Monarchy. None of the Pinagots received any votes in any of these elections, a fact that is probably indicative of their status.

As limited as the activities of the guard companies may have been, they were not limited to the election of leaders. In 1831 and 1832 the rural national guard demonstrated a certain zeal despite its lack of arms. There were numerous reviews that brought thousands of soldiers to the cantonal capitals. One has to try to imagine what such opportunities for self-presentation, not to say showing off, were like for rural people who never went to town except for fairs and markets, at which time they had to endure the mocking, scornful, or overly familiar looks of pretentious townspeople. In 1831, when the king went to Normandy, national guardsmen lined up along his route, especially where administrative boundaries were crossed.[87]

Of course, there was a "geography" of attitudes: small cleavages fragmented the institution. On June 21, 1831, 1,100 men from ten nearby communes gathered in Le Mêle.[88] Among them were the seventy guardsmen of Essay, all wearing the *blouse gauloise*, no doubt thanks to the generosity, or the exertions, of Roederer, the new mayor. The former senator from Normandy staged numerous reviews of the guard, which gave him an opportunity to offer the troops political instruction. He taught the men from Essay about the Constitution and about their rights.[89] In Origny-le-Butin, however, there was nothing of the kind, even though the two communes were only fifteen miles apart. Here, there was no prominent person of wealth, birth, or talent, no one to transmit the liberal ideology. Origny did not even have one of the minor mediators often found in other rural communes. In short, Louis-François had no opportunity to enjoy, let alone comprehend, the political eloquence of a *grand notable*.

The national guard never really took root in the communes of the canton of Bellême. Of the 2,833 guardsmen registered in the district on December 14, 1831, only 327 wore uniforms, while 157 others said that they intended to buy them; 259 were armed and 245 fully equipped. To be sure, 187 were veterans of the military.[90] The Pinagots had neither arms nor uniforms nor equipment. In Origny-le-Butin it would have been ridiculous to go to such expense. "This fine institution is threatened with ridicule," the prefect of the Orne noted in 1835. People made fun of anyone who spent money on uniforms and equipment.[91]

The activity of the guard thus amounted to a few cantonal battalion reviews, triennial elections followed by oath-taking ceremonies (solemn occasions whose importance needs to be appreciated), and participation in national holidays, banquets, and occasional Sunday drills. The frequency and size of drills and parades varied from commune to commune. In Origny-le-Butin, enthusiasm seems to have waned quickly. By the end of 1832, the guard unit refused to convene a disciplinary board. In that year the municipal council allocated a total of just fifteen francs to the guard. On paper, the Origny guard unit was a company of the battalion headquartered in Saint-Martin-du-Vieux-Bellême. In fact, to be a soldier in this unit once it ceased to march in ragged weekly drills and forlorn Sunday reviews meant little more than to turn out on local and national holidays for celebrations and parades. The same was true in many other rural communes. For our purposes, therefore, what matters is the guard's association with holiday celebrations and official pomp and circumstance.

In the Orne as elsewhere in France, disaffection with the guard grew worse after 1834. In that year the guards of the Mortagne district rarely performed the prescribed maneuvers. Within months the prefect was complaining about the low turnout. Apart from Alençon and one or two other towns in the district, guardsmen were ordered to report "only for special occasions such as patronal holidays and fairs meetings for parades, and maneuvers have become increasingly rare and draw few men in a *département* where the *military spirit has never existed* [emphasis in original] and where most national guardsmen are armed only with clubs." In short, "enthusiasm is nearly spent." "Military instruction, which was never very advanced, has been totally abandoned. Nearly everywhere there has been no progress toward improving uniforms and equipment but rather the reverse."

"In this essentially peaceful region, it is very difficult, not to say impossible, to maintain a regular and permanent organization of the national guard, which has so little in common with the not especially militaristic habits and customs of the inhabitants. Indeed, how can one explain to peasants the need to travel some distance without weapons or uniforms, which many of them cannot afford to buy, in order to participate in assemblies whose only consequence is often to waste their time and cost them money."[92] When the subprefect of the Mortagne district blamed the refusal to arm the guards for this lack of enthusiasm, someone at the prefecture added an ironic note to his report: the argument was not valid, this official observed, because in the rural national guard units, "nobody wants weapons."[93]

Our task is to gauge the role that these pathetic demonstrations of virility and civic spirit, soon threatened by ridicule and disaffection, might have played in the development of Louis-François Pinagot's political consciousness. I am inclined to believe that the guard took on a certain importance in his eyes during the first few months after it was revived but that later it came to be identified more and more with the celebration of national holidays.

At the time, these national holidays were numerous, and they generated real enthusiasm, even in the countryside. They included the July holidays, which were sometimes celebrated from July 27 to 29 but more commonly postponed until the following Sunday, as well as the king's birthday on May 1.[94] Unfortunately, we have no document containing information about how these holidays were celebrated in Origny-le-Butin. One again, therefore, we have to look at nearby communes and then try to imagine what the kinds of ceremonies we find there might have meant to Louis-François.

On July 28, 1833, Origny-le-Roux honored the heroes of July. In the morning a drummer summoned the forty-five-man national guard unit to assemble. "When the municipal council gathered, the commander of the guard had the national guards maneuver for an hour and a half. Then there was a race, and the man who came in first was awarded three francs, and another three francs went to the man who fired closest to a target. After that, liquids were dispensed to everyone present at the ceremony. Things did not break up until nine at night, and the crowd escorted the winners of the games to their homes with drums beating and everyone singing similar songs (*chanson analogue*) and oft-repeated shouts of 'Vive Louis Philippe!' Our priest spent a brief but very joyous moment with us at our ceremony."[95]

On July 24 of the following year, the municipal council of Bellavilliers decided to pay for powder and shot to be used in celebrating the national holiday with a target shooting contest: "The person who wins will not pay his share of the expense of the banquet to be held in the evening, for which the price of admission will be sixty centimes."[96]

In 1831 Damemarie, some seven miles from Origny-le-Butin, celebrated the king's birthday on May 1, as usual. The mayor ordered that the national guardsmen, or at any rate "those who could afford it," should come armed. He then reviewed the troops at ten in the morning. The priest celebrated a high mass for Saint Philip and Saint James. When the ceremony was over, there was a "grand parade," which was greeted "with enthusiasm." After a *Te Deum* was sung at vespers in the presence of the guard, the mayor and councilors received the oaths of the officers. The day ended with a "shooting contest" and a "public dance." "Every man and woman in the commune, young and old alike, attended this celebration dressed in holiday garb. This was even more brilliant than the so-called patronal holidays, and when the day was over everyone returned home in total calm and with evidence of great contentment. The mayor, his deputy, all the members of the municipal council, and the captain of the national guard all dined together for the greater union."[97]

Although religious ceremonies in rural areas during the July Monarchy were less impressive in scope than they had been earlier under the Restoration or would be again under the Second Empire, celebrations of national holidays were by no means secular occasions at this time. The reader will already have noticed the mayor's careful distinction between the national holiday and the traditional patronal holiday (or assembly) that marked the locality, although the agendas for the two occasions were not very different. The national holiday was the best opportunity for those who did not have the right to vote to pick up echoes, however muffled, of what all the talk about "the nation" meant.

Nevertheless, we should be careful not to underestimate the importance of the law of March 21, 1831, providing for the election of municipal council members. The law stipulated that, in the largest communes, no more than 10 percent of the population could participate in the voting, but it also allowed for broader participation in the smaller communes.[98] At this level, then, the significance of the law was far reaching. To be sure, Louis-François did not acquire the right to vote at this time, but two members of his family did participate in the electoral ceremony, as did numerous other people among his acquaintances. He may have listened to them as they made up their minds, and he would have been even more likely to have witnessed the solemn oath of loyalty to the king and the charter as they handed in their ballots. Hence in communes of this size, contrary to what many historians say, the exercise of the right to vote on April 23, 1848, did not come as a complete novelty.

In the Orne *département* the number of electors instituted by the law of 1831 equaled the national average. This was also true for the 517 communes of fewer than 3,000 inhabitants.[99] In Origny-le-Butin there were fifty-three voters in 1831, or 14 percent of the population (45 percent of men of voting age).[100] Among those to enjoy the newly-granted right were Louis Pôté, Louis-François's father-in-law. In that year he participated in both rounds of the voting. In 1834 he was even granted two votes. In their first experience with broad-based voting, people tended to spread their votes around: they voted either for themselves or for their most respected neighbors. The results therefore reveal the relative prestige of the various members of the community.

No Pinagot appeared on the list of electors. The entire family belonged to the half of the population excluded from suffrage. Most of the voters were farmers who owned their own land. Among those who acquired the right to vote we also find Tertereau the gelder, whom we have met before, the cartwright, and three other woodworkers (two clog makers and one long sawyer). In other words, these first municipal elections deepened the existing gap between two groups of Origny residents. In the first council election, thirty-one of the fifty-three electors voted in the first round (58 percent) and twenty-five in the second round (47 percent). Louis-François's uncle Jacques Drouin, a clog maker, abstained, as he would do again in 1837 and 1840. The other clog maker who voted, François Courville, voted in the first round but not the second. Apparently, even in 1831, woodworkers were less eager to exercise their new right than were farmers. Over the years the participation rate declined slightly. In 1840 and 1843 it was 45 percent in the first round.

If Louis-François took any interest in these elections, his reaction was probably mixed. He was no doubt aware of the campaign, since his father-in-law, one of his uncles, several of his neighbors, and a couple of fellow woodworkers were prospective voters. There were voters in every clan in Origny, and these clans were intimately intertwined, so word-of-mouth must have been important in shaping people's attitudes. Louis-François probably listened to debates and witnessed the officers' oath-taking, as was mentioned earlier. Yet he was probably also painfully aware of being excluded from the ceremony. When half of a commune's population enjoyed the right to vote, it is natural for us to think that it must have felt humiliating to belong to the other half. But would our poor clog maker have shared our feelings? In any case, the fact that he could not vote in the 1830s must have made the acquisition of the right to vote in March of 1848 seem all that much more valuable. But did any of this mean anything to Louis-François?

The right to vote that was granted in 1848 differed in significant ways from the right granted to the fifty-three electors of Origny-le-Butin in 1831. This time it was not limited to municipal elections. Every man twenty-one years of age or older could now vote for *conseillers généraux* and representatives to the Constituent Assembly. The same voters would later be called upon to elect a president of the Republic and members of the Legislative Assembly.

For Louis-François this form of participation in the political life of the nation posed problems of two kinds. Exercising the new right to vote required knowledge of affairs outside the group, indeed of society as a whole, insofar as the word "society" had any meaning. It took a certain level of general knowledge to follow debates at the national level.[101] As to the mundane practical matter of voting itself, the illiterate voter had to trust the people who helped him mark his ballot and who tallied his vote. Voting must have been a daunting business: after the long trek to the cantonal capital (or section), the newly enfranchised rural voter would have been expected to cast his ballot under the mocking eye of local luminaries.

There is no getting around the fact that we will never know what Louis-François's political sentiments actually were, what he truly believed and felt about politics. An event that took place within two miles of Basse-Frêne does give us a hint of what he might have felt about the Second Republic, or so we are tempted to assume because of the status of the people involved: on April 3, 1848, "workers," no doubt clog makers, from Gué-de-la-Chaîne, at that time a section of the commune of Saint-Martin, planted a liberty tree in the center of the village. This was a tree they had cut down in the domanial forest, an act of "vandalism" that elicited the same kind of protest from the administration as when youths cut down trees for traditional ceremonial purposes. When a forest warden asked if they had obtained the mayor's authorization, the workers "answered that there was no longer any master now that the Republic had been proclaimed."[102] In periods of transition it was common to believe that power was up for grabs.

The electoral list for Origny-le-Butin was posted at the beginning of April, in case anyone wished to file a complaint. The name of Louis-François Pinagot appeared on it, as well as on the list of March 31, 1850.[103] At that time he was listed as Louis-François Pinagot, *also known as Pôté*, so as to distinguish him from his uncle from Les Querrières and his older son. Unfortunately, we do not know if he participated in the April 1848 election of representatives to the Constituent Assembly. All we know is that people from the rural Bellêmois complained about having to travel to the cantonal capital in order to vote. We do, however, have information about the June by-elections. Of the 123 potential voters in Origny-le-Butin, only forty-five participated in the election. Only one Pinagot voted. His first name was Louis, but we do not know whether it was Louis-François, his uncle, or his son. Etienne Pinagot, a clog maker and first cousin of Louis-François, abstained, as did his son, a woodcutter, as well as Jacques-Augustin Drouin and his son. In general, the participation of clog makers and long sawyers was below average.

On July 30, 1848, 51 of 124 registered voters took part in the municipal council election.[104] "Louis-François Pinagot, also known as Pôté," did not vote. Neither did his son. Only Uncle Louis Pinagot, a laborer, bestirred himself to cast a ballot. It seems likely that it would have been the same in the June election. Jacques Drouin abstained, but his son, also a clog maker, voted. None of the four Courvilles cast a ballot. Out of a group of seventeen clog makers and seven long sawyers, only eight voted (six of the former and two of the latter). This participation rate was distinctly below average.

To sum up, then, there is no evidence that Louis-François availed himself of his right to vote. He abstained in July and probably in June as well. The voting lists for April have been lost, as have those for August, when general and district councilors were elected. Nevertheless, one thing is clear: forest and woodworkers, most of them illiterate, were hesitant to exercise their newly won right to vote.

Louis-Napoléon Bonaparte seems not to have had much of a reputation in the region at first. In the June 1848 elections, he received only five votes in the canton of Bellême. The prince's candidacy for the presidency remained a secret in the Mortagne district until September 17. On that day, or, rather, that night, posters announcing it went up under cover of darkness, and the subprefect, who backed the official candidacy of Cavaignac, hastened to have them torn down, although he never managed to find out who had put them up. He called them "troublemakers."[105]

On November 11, however, he was forced to recognize that support for the prince in his district had swelled to overwhelming proportions. "As for the rural areas," he wrote:

> they seem to want to nominate Louis-Napoléon Bonaparte. The peasants, full of ignorance, prejudice, and foolish illusions, will vote not for a man but for a *name*, a *memory*. So widespread is Napoleon's renown in the countryside, and so great his popularity, that his name alone will suffice to win over the ignorant masses. I have no idea what prestige, what miraculous powers, they ascribe to the man who bears that name. According to them, Napoleon will lower taxes, revive credit, and bring them higher prices for their horses and cattle. *We need a master, we will elect an emperor, he will make himself emperor like his uncle.* He will take care of our business.

This is what they say. Still, some of the older peasants remember how they suffered under Napoleon, but they cannot fight against the verve and enthusiasm of the old veterans, who recount the great man's exploits in the taverns. [emphasis in original][106]

This text gathers together a number of common assumptions about peasant attitudes, which were usually portrayed in broader strokes. The subprefect was remarkably specific in his analysis of the public's state of mind. Note, in particular, the link he sees between ignorance and the power of memory, between renown and enforced illusion, as structural elements of the peasant's system of representation. The connection between the restoration of empire and the restoration of credit and rise in livestock prices made the peasants better prophets than the learned subprefect with his contempt for "foolish illusions."

In the Bellêmois, however, doubts about the prince were not uncommon. Unlike many communes in the *département*, Origny-le-Butin was by no means unanimous in its support. A major turning point came when universal male suffrage was abolished on May 31, 1850. In Origny-le-Butin the new law proved disastrous: the number of voters was reduced by 53, from 127 to 74 (a 43 percent reduction). The number of people still entitled to vote was only slightly greater than the number of municipal electors under the July Monarchy.[107] Basse-Frêne was all but deprived of representation. The entire Pinagot family lost the right to vote, with the exception of Eugène, one of Louis-François's sons, who was at the time a soldier in the Sixty-Second Regiment, stationed in Versailles. It would be going too far to say that this upset them. The loss of this basic right of citizenship may not have been such a bitter pill for them to swallow, given the fact that most of them had abstained from voting when they had it.

The restoration of universal male suffrage on the night of December 2, 1851, put all the Pinagots back on the rolls. We find the names of Louis-François, his father, his uncle, and his cousins. Only the eldest son was left out, and there is an indication on the voter list that this was because he had left the commune.

The inhabitants of the Orne did not take part in the insurrection that followed the coup d'état.[108] To judge by the results of the plebiscite and, more convincingly, the number of celebrations, the Bellêmois at this point overwhelmingly supported Bonaparte. The *Echo de Mortagne* recorded the adherence of the local authorities to the new regime with praise whose intensity betrayed the depth of its earlier anguish. On January 11, 1852, Mortagne joined in the celebration that was being held throughout France.[109] And when the restoration of the Empire was celebrated on December 5, 1852, Bellême similarly joined in.[110]

In Origny-le-Butin, however, the doubts expressed on December 10, 1848, did not vanish when it came time for the plebiscite. Of 117 voters, 16 voted no and another cast a blank ballot. In other words, a total of 15 percent of the electorate refused to vote "yes," a considerable percentage given the circumstances in which the election was held. Much later, when another plebiscite was held on May 8, 1870, 19 of 119 voters expressed their opposition. But let us turn now from electoral analysis to the matter of Louis-François's participation, as well as that of his relatives and fellow workers, in the various elections that were held between 1852 and 1871, and of which records have survived.[111]

One fact stands out: slowly but surely, forest workers learned about the electoral process. Of the fifteen clog makers on the voter rolls, only three voted in the municipal elections of 1855. Louis-François abstained, as did his relative by marriage Renaud and all the Pinagots. The only family member who voted was Jacques Drouin. At the dawn of the Empire, the residents of Basse-Frêne were thus quite stingy with their votes. In the municipal elections of 1859, Louis-François did exercise his right to vote, but few people in his milieu followed suit. Only three clog makers, one woodcutter, and one long sawyer voted, for a total of five forest workers out of twenty-four registered to vote. Similarly, only six laborers voted out of a total of twenty-four.

By 1868 things had changed. In that year eleven clog makers and seven long sawyers exercised their right to vote, for a total of eighteen voters out of twenty-nine registered. Nine of twelve laborers also voted. Louis-François's family was only moderately involved in the process, however. Pierre-Théodore, Victor-Constant, cousin Jacques Drouin, and son-in-law Bourdin abstained, but Louis-François himself voted in both rounds of the election.

In 1869 he participated in the legislative elections, as did Pierre-Théodore, the clog maker who lived with him, and his son Louis, a farmer. Fifteen of twenty registered clog makers and long sawyers voted, for a turnout of 75 percent. This, however, was still below the turnout of farmers, 86 percent of whom cast ballots.

During the eighteen years of the restored Empire, Louis-François's status improved, and so, probably, did the esteem in which he was held in the community. We saw earlier how he rose from poverty. The paradoxical improvement in the clog trade, the replacement of spinning by glove making, the relative prosperity of agriculture, the persistent exploitation of the forest, and the fact that all his children were now of working age had all worked in his favor. A first indication of the modest improvement in his status came in 1856, when, at the age of fifty-eight, he bought a cottage from Jean Trouillet in the heart of the village of Basse-Frêne. The house was small, just over 900 square meters, and had only two openings. Its fiscal revenue was estimated at seven francs, which put it in the lowest tax category. Adjacent to the cottage was a plot of 2,500 square feet.[112] The scope of the acquisition should therefore not be overestimated. It is worth noting, moreover, that the Leboucs, a couple we know to have been deeply mired in poverty, made a similar purchase at about the same time.

In any case, Louis-François Pinagot, the former indigent who had long been exempt from the usual excise taxes, now figured on the lists of the commune's landowners. He had long been a friend of César Buat, a farmer typical of the minor nobles on whom the Second Empire liked to rely to administer the needs of the smallest rural communes. It is a safe bet that Louis-François's friendship with the mayor helped to increase his prestige in the commune, particularly since Louis-François was a decent fellow: he had never been caught poaching or committing a violent act. He had raised his children properly and managed to marry two of his daughters off to respectable young men from the commune despite his family's mediocre reputation.

The most significant change, however, involved his eldest son, Louis-François, whose status had improved markedly. When he returned to Origny-le-Butin in 1866, he had settled in La Croix, where he built a house.[113] Early in the war with Prussia, on August 7, 1870, Origny-le-Butin elected ten municipal councilors. Sixteen "citizens" received votes, forty-seven of which were needed to get elected.[114] Louis-François Pinagot Jr. came in thirteenth among the candidates receiving votes. Thirty-six of his fellow citizens had voted for him. Thus he was now a public personage.

On April 30, 1871, a few weeks after the departure of the Prussians, the people of Origny-le-Butin again voted to elect ten new councilors. César Buat, who presided over the election, opened the polls at eight-thirty in the morning. The ballot box was equipped with two locks, with the mayor holding the key to one and the former mayor, Mathurin Guillin, the eldest of the election overseers, holding the other. Voters were called to cast their ballots in alphabetical order. They handed their ballots to the mayor, who then placed them in the ballot box. Of the 124 registered votes, 109 voted, which shows what considerable interest there was in these municipal elections. Louis-François Jr. received fifty-two votes, which put him in eleventh place among the candidates, but only nine citizens obtained absolute majorities, so that a second round of voting was needed to choose the tenth councilor.

The second round took place on May 7, 1871. The polls opened at eight in the morning and closed at "two in the evening." One hundred and eight ballots were cast. Louis-François Jr. received the support of fifty-two of his fellow citizens and beat his opponent by one vote. He was the only newly elected member of the council. The fact that the second-round votes were not scattered among many candidates proves that there had been a campaign and that the voters had split into two camps, each united behind its candidate. When the outcome was decided, the ballots were publicly burned. It is not difficult to imagine the emotion of the winner's father, Louis-François Pinagot Sr., now seventy-three years old. The former indigent and illiterate clog maker had lived long enough to see his eldest son become a personage in his hometown. Through him, Louis-François would henceforth be able to keep abreast of local affairs and participate in them as he saw fit.

Louis-François Jr. proved to be a very energetic councilor. He was prominent in every debate. Along with the farmer Michel Virlouvet and his friend Sichou, he represented the forest workers, or, rather, the people who lived along the forest's edge, as opposed to the townspeople and the wealthier farmers. For the first time in his life, Louis-François Sr. was called upon to take sides in the conflicts that pitted one faction of the community against another. At this stage, moreover, enough documents have survived in the municipal archives to give us a glimpse of the passions that held sway in the administration of communal affairs.

The matter of the forest trail was by no means a new issue. It had come before the council earlier, on February 10, 1840.[115] Because of the considerable tonnage of wood taken from the forest, the commune was obliged to make frequent repairs to the trail that ran along its edge to La Perrière. Inevitably, this created a certain amount of acrimony directed against the forest administration. On October 13, 1854, the council had asked that the trail be classified as a "district road" (*chemin vicinal*), but its request was rejected, only to be resubmitted on May 10, 1856. Now the petition called for "opening up" the forest and "the area" (*contrée*), which "contains twenty-eight dwellings within an area of eighty hectares of poor land owned by a number of people, most of them forest workers without substantial resources." The only trail providing even indirect access to this "area" became an impassable bog for at least six months out of the year, because its width was too narrow to allow for drainage ditches.

The council deplored "the difficulty experienced by citizens of this area, who cannot travel by wagon along this trail without considerable effort, especially the workers who have a hard time finding anyone to haul the wood and other things they need to their private homes." If we hope to understand the difficulties that Louis-François had to put up with all his life, this affair is worthy of our close attention.

A government road agent inspected the forest trail and refused to classify it as a "district road" on the grounds that it was "of no interest to anyone but a few local residents." The council then invited citizens to submit their views on the matter between March 23 and April 23, 1856. The mayor hoped that by appealing to public opinion, he might be able to overcome the administration's opposition. The results may have surprised him, however: ninety-one residents expressed opposition to the reclassification and only thirty-seven supported it. Clearly, the majority who felt that they would derive no benefit from the work to be done were opposed to spending any money on it. The issue divided the commune, and the resulting division would endure for more than twenty years. Despite this outcome, and despite the opposition of nine councilors, who felt that the trail "comes to a dead end at the forest's edge," César Buat resubmitted the petition for reclassification and was rebuffed yet again. Nothing more happened until the final two weeks of the Empire.

In the spring of 1870, the issue was raised again. By a vote of seven to two, the municipal council asked for a trail from the town of Origny to the forest by way of Basse- and Haute-Frêne to be classified as a "rural road," provided that there would be no additional tax burden as a result. On

November 14, 1871, the municipal council came to the conclusion that there were two trails in need of reclassification: the one leading to the forest and another from the town of Origny to the limits of Saint-Martin-du-Vieux-Bellême. Since it was impossible to pursue both projects at once, the council opted for the second by a vote of seven to three. The farmers had defeated the forest workers. Toward the end of April of the following year, a book was placed in the town hall in which voters and taxpayers "interested in the commune" could record their opinions. Thirty-nine of them opted for the forest trail, which "will open the way to thirty-odd homes." Logically enough, they received the backing of the forest administrator. But seventy-two voters and/or taxpayers favored the other trail.

The first petition mentioned in the record of deliberations for May 5 bore the signatures (or marks) of three lumber dealers, including one from Bellême, several clog manufacturers, and four clog makers in addition to the Pinagots. Louis-François had indeed taken the trouble to visit the town hall. The mark he made in this book at this time is the only surviving trace of his handwriting, indeed the only palpable trace of his existence: it is a large, clumsy cross, and different from all the other crosses in the book, which proves that each of the illiterate signers of the petition made his own mark. The reader can well imagine my emotion when, after months of investigating Louis-François's life and living at close quarters with him, I at last discovered this mark and tried to imitate the gesture by which it had been inscribed. Here was a mark made by a seventy-four-year-old man who may on this occasion have been persuaded to take up a pen for the first time in his life.

Within the council, Louis-François Jr. and his friends Virlouvet and Sichou defended the forest project tooth and nail. They went so far as to guarantee a subsidy of six hundred francs if the project was approved. Obviously, the people who resided along the forest's edge were keen to be "opened up" to the rest of the world. The opposition submitted a petition that bore forty-one signatures and thirty crosses. The split between the two camps was obviously territorial rather than cultural.

On December 14, 1872, the prefect, probably responding to a request from the forest administration, asked the municipal council to examine the petition submitted by the proponents of the forest trail. The mayor opposed this challenge to the survey results. There was endless discussion of the number of households that would be "opened up" if the trail were improved. Finally, by a vote of seven to three, the municipal council stood by its original decision to oppose the improvement of the forest trail.

Soon, however, Pinagot, Virlouvet, and Sichou, now allied with César Buat, sought to exact revenge for their defeat. In 1873 they opposed the construction of a schoolhouse on land belonging to a widow by the name of Trottier, which the municipal council planned to expropriate. According to the four councilors, the proposed project was too costly. It would be better, they argued, to renovate the schoolroom currently in use, even if its ceiling was too low. On August 11, 1873, the proposal to expropriate Mme Trottier carried by a vote of five to four. On December 3, 1873, it was approved by six councilors, as was the construction of a schoolhouse. Virlouvet, Sichou, and Pinagot left the meeting. Although they were in the minority on the council, public opinion in the commune was on their side.[116] On June 17, 1874, the project was officially opened for comment at town hall, and groups of citizens were invited to express their views. Among those who did so, we again find a substantial number of illiterates. Of the fifty-three declarations on file, only ten favored the proposal to build a new schoolhouse. Thirty-eight people preferred purchasing the room currently in use.

The building plans were not finally approved until 1878, after the school inspector had filed a somber report on the state of the school in Origny-le-Butin.[117] The facilities consisted of "two filthy rooms, one of them located on an upper floor and accessible only by way of a miller's ladder." There is "no playground other than the adjacent streets." Since there were "no toilets, the children go wherever they can. Near the school is a large, unfenced pond, with nothing but a trail between it and the schoolhouse." During the summer, the stagnant water gave off a horrible stench. In short, the schoolhouse ought to be gutted completely. The debate of June 1874 revealed two different ways of looking at the school issue. In the light of Louis-François's entire existence, we can see why there was opposition to building a new school. For a time, Councilor Pinagot and his friends had the upper hand, but Louis-François Jr. was obviously ailing: for several months his handwriting had been deteriorating, as can be seen by looking at various samples of his signature.

A few weeks later, on August 19, Louis-François endured the loss of his son, no doubt his pride and joy. The father lived only two years longer than the boy. On January 31, 1876, he, too, died in the village of Basse-Frêne, in his tiny house with one door and one window, survived by various children and grandchildren who lived nearby. On that day the church of Origny tolled his death knell. As reconstructed here, the unfolding of his life seems misleadingly flat: the recording process itself smoothes things out. Thus we come to the end, not of a biography of Louis-François Pinagot, which has turned out to be impossible to write, but of an evocation of the life of a man who vanished almost without a trace on the day he died. May he forgive me for this fleeting resurrection, and for the various ways in which readers may, because of what I have written, imagine the man he was. What would he have thought of this book, which in any event he would not have been able to read?

The acronym ADO refers to Archives Départementale de l'Orne throughout.

Prelude

1. Scholars have, of course, tried to analyze the autobiographies of ordinary people, texts written by unknown individuals, usually for their descendants. Such writing is shaped, however, by the tendency of the authors to cast themselves in a heroic light: "I was a person of no significance, and I lived a worthy life," these writers want to say. As for novels about the lives of simple folk, it is no doubt belaboring the obvious to say that fiction is not history. But what about communal monographs? These come in two kinds. The first might be characterized as domestic ethnology. Studies of this sort are based on childhood memories and nostalgia. The second was pioneered by two American scholars, Lawrence Wylie and Patrice Higonnet. Their work revived the local monograph of the nineteenth century by adding an anthropological dimension. The focal point of their studies was the village, however, not the individual. Their work does not intersect ours, any more than do works in structural anthropology based on studies of marriage and kinship.

2. Michel Foucault, ed., *Moi, Pierre Rivière, ayant égorgé ma mère, ma soeur, et mon frère: Un cas de parricide au XIXe siècle* (Paris: Gallimard-Julliard, 1973). Carlo Ginzburg, *The Cheese and the Worms* (Baltimore: Johns Hopkins, 1980).

1. A Lifespace

1. See pages 74–76. To be sure, a brief stay outside the commune may have escaped our notice if it took place between censuses or between those events of Pinagot's public and private lives that are recorded in the archives.

2. For a view of another region, see Tina Jolas, "Bois communaux à Minot," *Revue forestière française*, special issue on "Société et forêts," (1980): 218–230.

3. Here I am borrowing a classic distinction first made by Marie-Claire Pingaud in regard to Minot in Châtillonais: see her *Paysans en Bourgogne: Les gens de Minot* (Paris: Flammarion, 1978).

4. A similar ambivalence is seen among the woodcutters in the Cher studied by Michel Pigenet, *Ouvriers, paysans nous sommes: Les bûcherons du centre de la France au tournant du siècle* (Paris: L'Harmattan, 1993).

5. See Marie-Claude Groshens, "Habitat et forêt," *Revue forestière française*, special issue on "Société et forêts," (1980): 263–273.

6. Such foraging seems to have been more common among tourists visiting the forest than among forest people, however.

7. *Bornage, fossés, confrontation et quantité de la forêt de Bellesme*, 1782. ADO M 2192*.

8. Arrêt du Conseil d'Etat du 24 juillet 1783, which approved the new improvement plan. ADO M 2192*.

9. This occurred in 1857. *Forêt de Bellesme, avant-projet d'aménagement*, 1858. ADO M 2194.

10. Ibid.

11. The only dispute I found concerned trees that grew on the embankment bordering the ditch in Origny-le-Butin, which the curé of La Fresnais (Sarthe) claimed to own. 1846–1854, ADO M 2178.

12. In this work I use the word "village" as it was used by locals. The term referred to what nineteenth-century poets and, later, geographers influenced by Vidal de la Blache would have called a "hamlet." It is not the same as a "commune," an administrative term that would be associated with "village" because of these influences.

13. At the end of the Ancien Régime, the forest of Bellême was the property of Monsieur, the king's brother. At that time forests were one of the nobility's favorite investments. See Denis Woronoff, *Révolution et espaces forestiers* (Paris: L'Harmattan, 1988), p. 6. The improvement plan mentioned in the text, approved by the Conseil d'Etat in 1783 (ADO M 2192*), illustrates the concern of nobles in this regard.

14. On the Chaptal survey, see Marie-Noëlle Bourguet, *Déchiffrer la France: La statistique départementale à l'époque napoléonienne* (Paris: Archives Contemporaines, 1988).

15. Dureau de la Malle, *Description du bocage percheron, des moeurs, et coutumes des habitants* (Paris: Imprimerie de Fain, 1823), p. 37. Paul Delasalle was similarly enthusiastic: *Une excursion dans le Perche* (Paris, 1839), p. 22.

16. Léon de la Sicotière, *Notice sur l'arrondissement de Mortagne* (Caen: Le Roy, 1837), p. 10.

17. It is part of a fairly extensive range of similar forests of roughly the same size: the forest of the Perche, the forest of Valledieu, the forest of Saint-Mard de Reno, and, nearby, the forests of Bourse and Perseigne. In addition, the forest of Bellême is bordered by the wood of Montimer and of Chêne-Galon, as well as by the heaths of Eperrais and Saint-Ouen. See ADO M 2194*.

18. See Roger Dupuy, "Forêt et contrerévolution," in Denis Wornoff, ed., *Révolution et espaces forestiers*, pp. 37–44.

19. On all these points, see *Bornages, fossés* (n. 7) and *Forêt de Bellesme* (n. 9).

20. Survey ordered in 1844 and published, insofar as it relates to the canton of Bellême, by Georges Courtois, clerk to a justice of the peace, in 1883: *Us et coutumes du canton de Bellême, recueillis jusqu'en 1882* (Bellême: Imprimerie Ginoux, 1883). Results were included in the 1846 *annuaire* of the *département*.

21. ADO M 2181. Permission confirmed by a ministerial order, dated September 19, 1893, for indigents of the commune.

22. Ibid. Permission was granted on an exceptional basis, for example, during the terrible drought of 1870.

23. See pages 95–105.

24. Here we touch on the debate around the impact of the Revolution on woodlands. See Woronoff, *Révolution et espaces forestiers*.

25. Report of 20 Frimaire, Year VI. AN F1 CIII Orne 8.

26. Honoré de Balzac, *Les Chouans* (Paris: Hetzel, 1845), p. 56.

27. As Rougier de la Bergerie noted in *Les Forêts de la France* (Paris: Arthus Bertrand, 1817), p. 356: "Seasons [in the Orne] have becomes so irregular that the fruit harvest can no longer be relied on."

28. As is apparent from the "progressive" bureaucratic language of the forest archives.

29. See the record for 1825. ADO M 2192*.

30. See *L'Atlas protatif* preserved in ADO M 2193.

31. More precisely: 1,748 hectares rather than 1,205; initially woodland covered 1,220 hectares.

32. See ADO M 2193 and M 2194.

33. ADO M 2193.

34. ADO M 2197.

35. The changes can be followed in detail thanks to the *Atlas portatif*, compiled in 1834.

36. Andrée Corvol, "La Forêt," in Pierre Nora, ed., *Les Lieux de mémoire*, vol. 3: *Les France*, part 1: *Conflits et partages* (Paris: Gallimard, 1992), pp. 672–738.

37. ADO M 2194, *Histoire de l'aménagement de la forêt de Bellême*, p. 52.

38. For industry, useful lengths ranged from 82 to 91 feet, which corresponded to trees about a hundred years old. The navy used trees two hundred years old or older.

39. Dr. Jousset, *Histoire de la forêt de Bellême* (Mamers: Fleury et Dangin, 1884), p. 25.

40. See Peter Sahlins, *Forest Rites: The War of the Demoiselles in Nineteenth-Century France* (Harvard: Harvard University Press, 1994).

41. ADO M 2194.

42. Jousset, *Histoire*, p. 14.

43. AM de Saint-Martin-du-Vieux-Bellême, ADO E dépôt 89/66.

44. ADO M 2181.

45. See Gilles Bry de la Clergerie, *Histoire des pays et comté du Perche et duché d'Alençon* (Paris: Le Mur, 1620); Delasalle, *Une excursion dans le Perche*, pp. 5–9; Louis Dubois, *Annuaire statistique de département de l'Orne*, 1809. According to Dubois, the fountain of La Herse was repaired and beautified in 1769 by the *grand maâtre des eaux et forêts* of the *circonscription* of Alençon. As early as 1717, the Latin inscription indicating that the spring was dedicated to Venus was discussed in a paper read to the Académie. In 1834 Joseph Odolant-Desnos produced a list of the spring's virtues and deplored the fact that no celebrated doctor had extolled them. See Joseph Odolant-Desnos, "Orne," in *La France, description géographique, statistique et topographique par M. Loriol* (Paris: Verdière, Mortagne, Imprimerie de Glaçon, 1834), pp. 10–11.

46. The whole history was typical of other hot springs of minor importance. See Roy Porter, *The Medical History of Waters and Spas* (London: Wellcome Institute for the History of Medicine, 1990). Chaudru's report is in AM de Saint-Martin-du-Vieux-Bellême, ADO E dépôt 89/149, "source d'eau minérale de la Herse."

47. Louis Charles Nicolas Delestang, *Chorographie du IVe arrondissement communal du département de l'Orne ou du district de la souspréfecture de Mortagne* (Argentan, 1803).

48. Dubois, *Annuaire statistique du département de l'Orne*, p. 170.

49. Jousset, *Histoire*, p. 39.

50. Delasalle, *Une excursion dans le Perche*, p. 9.

51. Abbé Louis-Joseph Fret, *Antiquités et chroniques percheronnes*, vol. 1 (Mortagne: Imprimerie de Glaçon, 1838–1840), p. 176.

52. Delasalle, *Une excursion dans le Perche op. cit.*, p. 6.

53. Jousset, *Histoire*, p. 40.

54. See Bernard Kalaora, *Le Musée vert ou le tourisme en forêt* (Paris: Anthropos, 1981).

55. Jousset, *Histoire*, p. 27.

56. Dr. Jousset, *La Croix de la Feue Reine, par abréviation Croix-Feue-Reine, Croix-Furène* (Mortagne: Imprimerie de Loncin et Daupeley, 1855), p. 2.

57. Jousset, *Histoire*, pp. 34–36.

58. *Forêt de Bellesme, avant-projet d'aménagement de la forêt*, 1858, ADO M 2194.

59. Jousset, *Histoire*, p. 39.

60. Fret, *Antiquités*, vol. 3, p. 524.

61. The following details are taken from census data. AM d'Origny-le-Butin, ADO E dépôt 88. Unfortunately, the sources do not help us get a handle on how many people worked on more than one job. In court documents we find innkeepers and artisans not included in the census lists.

62. ADO 13U583 and 13U585.

63. See pages 210–212.

64. Four years before his death, we find, in addition to the places mentioned in the text, two seamstresses, a carpenter, and a family of schoolteachers.

65. Delestang, *Chorographie*, p. 54.

66. See Dominique Margairaz, *Foires et marchés dans la France préindustrielle* (Paris: Ecole des Hautes Etudes en Sciences Sociales, 1988); Alain Corbin, *Le Village des cannibales* (Paris: Aubier, 1990), trans. by Arthur Goldhammer as *The Village of Cannibals* (Cambridge, Mass.: Harvard University Press, 1992).

67. See *Annuaires de l'Orne*, 1820.

68. By way of example, the reader may wish to consult the following studies of the construction of the image of Brittany: Catherine Bertho, "L'invention de la Bretagne: Genèse sociale d'un stéréotype," *Actes de la recherche en sciences sociales* 35 (November 1980); Denise Delouche, *La Découverte de la Bretagne* (Lille: Presses de l'Université de Lille III, 1977). For the Limousin, see Caroline Girard, "Les sociétés d'originaires et la réponse à l'image noire du Limousin à travers le *Limousin de Paris*," in Gilles Le Béguec and Philippe Vigier, eds., *Limousins de Paris: Les sociétés d'originaires du Limousin sous la IIIe République* (Limoges: Presses de l'Université de Limoges, 1990). In regard to the Orne as a whole, there is an important but late source devoted mainly to monuments of the past and the history of communes: *Le Département de l'Orne archéologique et pittoresque par MM: Léon de la Sicotière et Auguste Poulet-Malassis* (Laigle: Beuzelin, 1845).

69. On Chateaubriand and the Trappist site, see Alain Corbin, "Invitations à une histoire du silence," in *Foi, fidélité et amitié en Europe à la période moderne, Mélanges Robert Sauzet* (Tours: Publications de l'Université de Tours, 1995), p. 303. See also Edouard Herriot, *Dans la forêt normande* (Paris: Hachette, 1925).

70. Alain Corbin, "Paris-province," in Pierre Nora, ed., *Les Lieux de mémoire*, vol. 3: *Les France*, part 1 (Paris: Gallimard, 1992), pp. 776–824, translated by Arthur Goldhammer in *Realms of Memory*, vol. I (New York: Columbia University Press, 1996).

71. Delestang, *Chorographie*, p. 3.

72. Used by Louis Dubois in the series of articles he published in the *Annuaire de l'Orne*, starting in 1809.

73. Léon de la Sicotière, *Notice sur l'arrondissement de Mortagne* (Caen: Le Roy, 1837), p. 11.

74. See series of reports by the prefect of the Orne, 1834–1837. ADO M 268.

75. Joseph Odolant-Desnos, "Orne," p. 64.

76. Bourguet, *Déchiffrer la France*, passim.

77. On this point we are in full agreement with Claude Cailly, who wrote that the people who lived in the Perche were not clearly aware of its outlines. See Claude Cailly, *Mutations d'un espace protoindustriel. Le Perche aux XVIII–XIXe siècles* (Fédération des Amis du Perche, 1993), p. 22. According to Cailly, historians of the Perche, nostalgic for a bygone era, systematically created "a profound sociocultural reality" and "extended it to the political and ideological plane."

78. See the very detailed analysis in Odile Barubé-Parsis, *Les Représentations du Moyen Age au XIXe siècle dans les pays—bas français et leurs confins picards* (Paris: Université de Paris I, 1995).

79. P. Pitard, *Légendes et récits percherons* (Alençon: Imprimerie C. Thomas, 1875), p. 5.

80. We do not find any attempt to appropriate space analogous to that which has been seen in the construction of the legend of the forest of Brocéliande.

81. *Annuaire of the Orne*, pp. 109–111 and 114.

82. Dureau de la Malle, *Description du bocage percheron*, pp. 19–20. Joseph Odolant-Desnos, "Orne," pp. 64 ff., gives abundant details about the belief in these supernatural beings. Unlike Dureau de la Malle, he assures us that in the Orne ghosts maintained "an incredible hold" on people's minds. Especially feared were damned souls that came begging for the prayers of the living and emitted terrifying sounds. Chasse Artus, Hennequin, and Mère Harpine were a "supposed band of infernal spirits that traveled through the air led by the dreaded Mère Harpine and dropped shreds of corpses" on the unsuspecting. The werewolf was supposed to be a nameless criminal who had fallen into the devil's clutches for a period of seven years. By contrast, the goblin or *cheval Bayard* was a good demon that might on occasion get up to some mischief. On all these beliefs, common throughout the region, the reader will find a vast bibliography in the essential work by Léon de la Sicotière, *Bibliographie des usages et des traditions populaires du département de l'Orne* (Vannes: Lafolye, 1892).

83. Dureau de la Malle, *Description du bocage percheron*, pp. 5–6.

84. Paul Delasalle, *Une excursion dans le Perche*, pp. 1–2 and the quote that follows.

85. Dureau de la Malle, *Description du bocage percheron*, p. 9. My italics.

86. Ibid., p. 21.

2. *"The Low Multitudes"*

1. On this subject, see Philippe Boutry, "Le clocher," in Pierre Nora, ed., *Les Lieux de mémoire*, vol. 3: *Les France*, part 2: *Traditions* (Paris: Gallimard, 1992), pp. 56–89.

2. On the sonic environment of the nineteenth-century countryside, see Guy Thuillier, "Bruits," in *Pour une histoire du quotidien au XIXe siècle en Nivernais* (Paris-

The Hague: Mouton-EHESS, 1977), pp. 230–244; Alain Corbin, "Prélude à une histoire de l'espace et du paysage sonores," in *Le Jardin de l'esprit* (Geneva: Droz, 1995).

3. See Maurice Halbwachs, *Les Cadres sociaux de la mémoire* (Paris: Albin Michel, 1994).

4. Alain Corbin, *Les Cloches de la terre: paysage sonore et culture sensible dans les campagnes au XIXe siècle* (Paris: Albin Michel, 1994), pp. 43–47.

5. See the detailed inventories made in 1810 and 1850, ADO E dépôt 88/85.

6. Statements based on biographical dictionaries and the results of numerous departmental surveys.

7. See Daniel Fabre, "Une culture paysanne," in Adnré Burguière and Jacques Revel, eds., *Histoire de la France: Les formes de la culture* (Paris: Editions du Seuil, 1993), esp. pp. 193–200.

8. Jean-François Pitard, "Origny-le-Butin," *Fragments historiques sur le Perche: Statistique par commune* (Mortagne, 1806).

9. On this evolution in a lower-Norman *département*, see Gabriel Désert, *Les Paysans du Calvados, 1815–1895* (Lille: Presses de l'Université de Lille-III, 1975).

10. In 1852 wheat covered 2,329 hectares in the canton of Bellême and barley 2,034 hectares.

11. ADO M 1832.

12. Claude Cailly, *Mutations d'un espace protoindustriel: Le Perche aux XVIII-e-XIXe siècles* (Fédération des amis du Perche, 1993), pp. 155–168, insists that this evolution was slow. In 1837 Léon de la Sicotière stressed that the amount of fallow land in the Perche had not declined much. According to the results of the agricultural survey of 1840, artificial pasture covered only 8 percent of the surface of the Mortagne district, not including forests and timberland.

13. In addition to the results of the so-called decennial agricultural surveys, see Georges Courtois, *Us et coutumes du canton de Bellême, recuillis jusqu'en 1882* (Bellême, 1883), passim.

14. Léon de la Sicotière, *Louis de Frotté et les insurrections normandes*, vol. 1 (Paris: Plon, 1889), pp. 124–126.

15. The results of this survey should be treated with caution, however. See Gilbert Garrier, "Les enquêtes agricoles décennales du XIXe siècle: Essai d'analyse critique," in *Pour une histoire de la statistique*, vol. 1 (Paris: INSEE, 1975), pp. 271–279.

16. See the distribution of the population by type of dwelling in the commune of Origny-le-Butin at the beginning of the nineteenth century. ADO Z 390.

17. See page 115.

18. On the foregoing, see Courtois, *Us et coutumes*.

19. AM for Origny-le-Butin, ADO E dépôt 88/28.

20. For an example from a nearby region, see Arlette Schweitz, *La Maison tourangelle au quotidien: Façons de bâtir, manières de vivre* (1850–1930) (Paris: Publications de la Sorbonne, 1997).

21. ADO E dépôt 88/36. In 1879 it was estimated that it would be possible "to billet in houses, establishments, stables, shelters, and buildings of all kinds" 550 men in Basse-Frêne, 200 in Haute-Frêne, 22 in Basse-Croix, 150 in L'Hôtel-aux-Oiseaux, and 100 in Les Querrières.

22. See pages 114–115.

23. Marie-Rose Simoni-Aurembou, "L'alphabet du quotidien: Petite chronique du canton de Thiron au XIXe siècle (manuscrit d'Arsène Vincent [1831–1881])," in *Cahiers percherons*, nos. 69–70 (1982).

24. Emile Pelletier, *Visites agricoles dans l'arrondissement de Mortagne* (Caen: Hardel, 1862), pp. 106–108. The farm was located in the commune of Saint-Ouen-la-Cour.

25. Census of 1872. ADO E dépôt 88.

26. ADO M 1832.

27. ADO M 965.

28. I am thinking, of course, of Erving Goffman's *Presentation of Self in Everyday Life* (Endinburgh: University of Endinburgh, 1956).

29. For details, see ADO E dépôt 88, census lists from the AM of Origny-le-Butin.

30. Claude Cailly, *Mutations d'un espace protoindustriel*, pp. 553 ff, sees a modest growth in the population of the Perche from 1801 to 1851, then a sharp decline in the second half of the century. In the first few decades, the Perche was a region of emigration, which preceded the collapse of the natural movement. See also the *Atlas historique et statistique de la Normandie occidentale à l'époque contemporaine* (Caen: Editions du Lys, 1994).

31. With the exception, initially at least, of the family of Fidèle Armand de Bloteau. See pages 189–191.

32. Yves Lequin, *La Mosaïque France: Histoire des étrangers et de l'immigration* (Paris: Larousse, 1988).

33. Everyone of working age worked, except possibly for Sieur de Bloteau.

34. See pages 85–86.

35. Courtois, *Us et coutumes*, p. 38.

36. See Yvonne Creebow, "Dans les campagnes, silence quotidien et silence coutumier," in *Le Silence au XIXe siècle, 1848, Révolutions et Mutations au XIXe siècle*, no. 10. (1994).

37. In that year, eighteen women and girls were identified as beggars; all were also listed as spinners. Nine of them had never married, three were widows, and six were married. In other words, two-thirds lived alone. There were also four children and nine men listed as beggars, six of them laborers.

38. See chapter 9 and the maps in the thesis of Stéphane Muckensturm, "Indigence, assistance et répression dans le Bas-Rhin (1789–1870)" (thesis, Université des Sciences Humaines, Strasbourg, 1995).

39. See page 194.

40. In 1871 Pierre Renaud acquired a third house in the village.

3. Elective Affinities and Kinship Relations

1. See Martine Segalen, *Nuptialité et alliance: Le choix du conjoint dans une commune de l'Eure* (Paris: Maisonneuve et Larose, 1972).

2. On all these points, and on the family in Haute-Normandie, see Gemma Gagnon, "La Criminalité en France: Le phénomène homicide dans la famille en Seine-Inférieure de 1811 à 1900," (thesis, Ecole Pratique des Hautes Etudes en Sciences Sociales, 1996).

3. In Normandy kinship and neighborhood functioned in a manner quite different from that found by Yves Pourcher, Elisabeth Claverie, Pierre Lamaison, and Rolande Bonnain in the area south of the Massif Central or in the Aquitaine and Pyrenees, characterized by the importance of the authoritarian family.

4. For the following, I have relied on birth, marriage, and death records together with census lists for the communes of Origny-le-Butin and la Perrière. Dates of settlement in the commune were taken from documents in ADO E dépôt 88.

5. Did Louis-François have any real relationship with his half-sister and half-brother, who were, respectively, thirty-five and thirty-seven years younger than he? It seems highly unlikely. At the age of twelve, the half-sister, Jeanne-Françoise, was placed as a servant with a farmer from La Croiz, and at the age of seventeen she moved to another employer in Vieux-Hêtre.

6. Electoral list of July 24, 1848. Origny-le-Butin, ADO E dépôt 88/54.

7. ADO E dépôt 88/33.

8. See chapter 5.

9. The term *fille mère* for unwed mother was in common use in the region until the middle of the twentieth century.

10. See page 97.

11. See page 107.

12. ADO E dépôt 89/70. Register for the inscription of workmen's record books, 1855–1856.

13. *Mariage forcé* was the term commonly used in French.

14. ADO E dépôt 88/33. Conscription, name lists, class of 1839.

15. On all these points, ADO E dépôt 88, cadaster, folio 107.

16. ADO E dépôt 88/35 and 38.

17. ADO E dépôt 88/33. Lists of names, class of 1845.

18. Armand (1857), Elise-Mélie (1858), Marie Florine (1860), Emile Frédéric (1862), and Elise Léontine (1868).

19. ADO E dépôt 88/33.

20. In whose name the curé d'Ars performed miracles.

21. ADO E dépôt 88/33 ff.

22. On this point, see Gagnon, "La Criminalité en France," passim.

23. For the nineteenth century, the most comprehensive and detailed study of the logic of marital choice and the networks of witnesses is Alain Pauquet, "La Société et les relations sociales en Berry au milieu du XIXe siècle" (thesis, University of Paris I, 1993).

24. See pages 189–191. The study of spiritual kinship is based on the parish register, AP Origny-le-Butin.

25. The work of Claude Cailly allows us to situate the behavior of the residents of Origny-le-Butin in a broader context. The demographic transition began in *le Perche ornais* earlier than in nearby Beauce or in *le Perche Gouet*. At the beginning of the nineteenth century, the birth rate, which had been declining since the middle of the eighteenth century, was lower than the national average. It also declined more rapidly than in the rest of the country during the nineteenth century. This trend was not the result of a lower marriage rate. On the contrary, the average marriage age decreased under the July Monarchy. What changed was the fertility rate, hence the behavior of couples. Nevertheless, the agricultural cantons of the Mortagne district, including Bellême, had a higher fertility rate than their neighbors.

26. *Couple à la colle* was an expression used at the time to describe illicit relationships.

27. ADO E dépôt 88/33.

28. ADO E dépôt 88. Record of municipal deliberations, meeting of November 12, 1871.

29. See pages 177–178.

4. The Language of the Illiterate

1. ADO E dépôt 88/33. Names of conscripts, class of 1818.

2. Louis Charles Nicolas Delestang, *Notice statistique de la souspréfecture de Mortagne* (Mortagne, 1810), p. 6.

3. ADO R 673.

4. Also deplored by Jean-Marie Le Mouroux, "Les listes de tirage au sort, source d'histoire sociale: Exemple: l'arrondissement de Mortagne en 1818," *Revue d'histoire économique et sociale* 51 (1973): 183–212.

5. Inasmuch as his name does not appear on any prison records (ADO series Y).

6. See Jean-Paul Aron, Paul Dumont, and Emmanuel Le Roy Ladurie, *Anthropologie du conscrit français d'après les comptes numériques et sommaires du recrutement de l'armée* (1819–1826) (Paris-The Hague: Mouton, 1972).

7. Difficult but not impossible, since certain young people from the commune did know how to read and write.

8. ADO T 27. Situation of the schools in the canton of Bellême, 1819 (the next quotation is from the same source).

9. Note, moreover, that the teacher in Chemilly used the individual method of instruction, which was not the most efficient.

10. On the progress of literacy in the Orne, see Joseph Chollet, "Instruction, alphabétisation et société enseignante dans l'Orne au XIXe siècle" (doctoral thesis, University of Caen, 1977); and for an overview of the west of France in relation to the rest of the country, see Gabriel Désert, "Alphabétisation et scolarisation dans le grand Ouest au XIXe siècle," in Donald N. Baker and Patrick J. Harrigan eds., *The Making of Frenchmen: Current Directions in the History of Education in France, 1679–1979* (Waterloo: Historical Reflections Press, 1980), pp. 143–205.

11. ADO E dépôt 88, record of municipal deliberations, 10 Fructidor, Year XII.

12. ADO E dépôt 88, census of 1872.

13. Twenty-one boys and twenty-eight girls, aged six to twenty years, were able to read and write, while four boys and five girls knew "only how to read." Only seventeen boys and sixteen girls were still illiterate.

14. Forty-eight men and thirty women could read and write; fourteen men and twenty-eight women could "read only," and sixty-seven men and seventy women remained illiterate.

15. Alain Corbin, "Pour une étude sociologique de la croissance de l'alphabétisation au XIXe siècle: L'instruction des conscrits du Cher et de l'Eure-et-Loir (1833–1883)," *Revue d'histoire économique et sociale* 1 (1975): 99–120.

16. Chollet, "Instruction," passim.

17. It was not until 1869 that the municipal council contemplated providing housing for a schoolteacher.

18. To believe the school inspector, these volunteers were not very able.

19. See page 105ff.

20. ADO E dépôt 88, record of municipal deliberations, meeting of September 14, 1832 and August 10, 1833.

21. ADO M 43. Report of the prefect on the situation in the *département*, 1835.

22. ADO E dépôt 88, record of municipal deliberations, meeting of February 8, 1846.

23. Ibid.

24. But the commune refused to pay her sixty francs.

25. ADO T 425.

26. Attested by a series of memoranda in ADO T 425.

27. ADO E dépôt 88, record of municipal deliberations, meeting of May 16, 1854.

28. Ibid., meeting of February 14, 1854.

29. ADO T 425. Note on the situation of the primary schools in the canton of Bellême.

30. Ibid.

31. Ibid.

32. ADO E dépôt 88, record of municipal deliberations, meeting of December 1, 1869.

33. Ibid., meeting of February 26, 1870.

34. See Marie-Rose Simoni-Arembou, *Trésor du parler percheron* (Mortagne, Association des amis du Perche, 1979), pp. 16 ff. For an overview of these questions, see Philippe Vigier, "Diffusion d'une langue nationale et résistance des patois en France au XIXe siècle," *Romantisme* 25–26 (1979). For the Orne we used Louis Duval, "L'enquête philologique de 1812 dans les arrondissements d'Alençon et de Mortagne: Vocabulaires, grammaire et phonétique," *Actes de la société philologique*, vol. 18 (1888). For the Norman patois, see Julien Gilles Travers, *Glossaire du patois normand par M. Louis de Bois* (Caen: Hardel, 1856).

35. Duval, "L'enquête philologique de 1812," p. 103.

36. Obviously, what I have attempted here is not an ethnolinguistic study but merely a descriptive account intended to provide material for the imagination.

37. Duval, "L'enquête philologique de 1812," pp. 109 ff.

38. These words were still used by elderly people in the 1940s.

39. Abbé Louis-Joseph Fret, "Une veillée au Perche," *Le Diseur de Vérités*, 1842.

40. Here, we rely once again on the observations of Delestang.

41. Georges Courtois, *Use et coutumes du canton de Bellême, recueillis jusqu'en 1882* (Bellême, 1883), pp. 45 and 60–61.

42. Bernard Traimond, "Ethnologie historique des pratiques monétaires dans les Landes de Gascogne" (thesis, University of Paris I, 1992); Guy Thuillier, "La monnaie," *Aspects de l'économie nivernaise au XIXe siècle* (Paris: Armand Colin, 1961), pp. 113–131.

43. Many maps showing the extent of the area in which "patois" was spoken were derived from this survey.

44. All the preceding quotes are taken from a report by the primary school inspector for the Mortagne district, AN F17 9331.

45. Quoted in Charles Joret, *Des caractères et de l'extension du patois normand: Etude de phonétique et d'ethnographie* (Paris: Vieweg, 1883), p. 105.

46. Achille Genty, *Les Œuvres poétiques en patois percheron de Pierre Genty, maréchal ferrant. 1770–1821* (Paris: Aubry, 1865), pp. lvii and lxvi for all the following quotations.

47. Sicotière, *Notices littéraires*, p. 19, assures us that this poetry was by Achille Genty himself.

48. In 1883, seven years after Louis-François's death, Charles Joret argued that the "Corbonnais idiom" in use in the Haut-Perche was merely a transitional dialect between Norman and the "Le Mans idiom." In particular, it was characterized by the use of *io* rather than *é*. Delestang had noted this earlier: *morceau* was pronounced *morcio* rather than *morsé*, *couteau* was pronounced *coutio* rather than *couté* or *coutia*.

See Joret, *Des caractères et de l'extension du patois normand* (Paris: F. Vieweg, 1883), p. 111.

49. Which contradicts what I said earlier on page 24.

50. For what follows, Abbé Louis-Joseph Fret, "Un dîner de famille au Perche pendant les jours gras," *Le Diseur de Vérités: Almanach, spécial au Perche*, and in *Scènes de la vie percheronne*, revised by Abbé Gaulier (La Ferté Macé: Meynaerts, 1873), pp. 16–34.

51. Old people wore "hats done up in the old style," clothing "the color of chestnuts with many buttons, large, fake *boutonnieres*, thight-length scarlet jackets with big pockets, trousers with suspenders, nice white knee-high gaiters fastened at the calf with nice red wool ribbons, and round-tipped shoes with silver buckles." Young mothers wore their wedding gowns, of which they were very fond. "A simple and modest cornet was worn with a nice embroidered muslin scarf, a corset with long tails, short, wide sleeves, light blue tweed skirt, and an orange canvas apron . . . tucked up almost chin high." Ibid., p. 19.

52. "Une veillée au Perche," in *Le Diseur de Vérités*, 1842, and La Chapelle-Montligeon, 1896, p. 2.

53. See page 117.

54. See Jean Tulard, *Le Mythe de Napoléon* (Paris: Armand Colin, 1971), and *Napoléon ou le mythe du sauveur* (Paris: Fayard, 1977).

5. The Clog Makers, the Spinners, and the Glove Makers

1. ADO 12 U 380, September 6, 1836.

2. Georges Courtois, *Us et coutumes du canton de Bellême, recueillis jusqu'en 1882* (Bellême, 1883), p. 46.

3. ADO 12 U 374, audience of December 18, 1812 and March 27, 1813; ADO 12 U 375, audience of December 20, 1818.

4. See ADO M 981. Policy on hauling. Survey by the prefect of the Orne.

5. See my *Filles de noce: Misère sexuelle et prostitution, XIXe et XXe siècles* (Paris: Aubier, 1978) and *Les Cloches de la terre: Paysage sonore et culture sensible dans les campagnes au XIXe siècle* (Paris: Albin Michel, 1994).

6. ADO 12 U 374, 375, 378, and 380.

7. ADO 12 U 374; on December 30, 1809, Jacques Pinagot was caught in the act of taking a bundle of wood and maintained that it was a "piece of wood that he had found in the forest."

8. ADO 12 U 374.

9. See results of the survey on agricultural and industrial labor commissioned by the Constituent Assembly in 1848. The results for Bellême were published in the *Echo de l'arrondissement de Mortagne*, December 31, 1848, and January 7, June 17, June 24, and July 1, 1849.

10. The revival efforts that were so common between 1870 and 1920, and especially between 1890 and 1910, and which are quite apparent in postcards, made it all too easy to overestimate the importance of practices associated with anything that was picturesque.

11. ADO 13 U 584.

12. For example, Roger Verdier, *L'Art en sabots*, vol. 1 (Saint-Martin-de-la-Lieue, 1993), pp. 70 ff.

13. *Trésor de la langue française*, article "sabotier," and *Echo de l'arrondissement de Mortagne*, June 3, 1849.

14. ADO 12 U 975, March 14, 1819.

15. ADO 12 U 975, September 9, 1819.

16. ADO 12 U 975, October 31, 1825.

17. ADO 12 U 1009, affidavit of September 24, 1822.

18. Probably Mathurin Guillin, whom we shall meet again.

19. ADO 13 U 5/83, January 22, 1836.

20. ADO 12 U 974, February 2, 1824.

21. ADO 13 U 5/94, affidavit of October 31, 1854.

22. ADO M 1288.

23. ADO M 1923, report on the industrial situation, fourth trimester, 1867.

24. Here, I accept the view of the leading specialist on the subject, Claude Cailly, who writes that clog makers "worked and lived in dispersed workshops." See his *Mutations d'un espace protoindustriel: Le Perche aux XVIIIe–XIXe siècles* (Fédération des amis du Perche, 1993), p. 46.

25. Assertion by Lemay in the case cited above, 13 U 5/94.

26. See Raymond Humbert, *Métiers d'hier et d'aujourd'hui: Le sabotier* (Paris: Berger-Levrault, 1979).

27. As is clear from the many criminal cases that I will cite in the next chapter.

28. ADO 12 U 462, February 4, 1852.

29. Verdier, *L'Art*, vol. 1, pp. 59 ff.

30. ADO M 268, report of April 3, 1834.

31. ADO M 2194.

32. For details, see "Le sabotier," *Cahiers percherons* 59 (1978): 30 ff., on the Musée des Arts et Traditions Populaires of the priory of Sainte-Gauburge-de-la-Coudre. For what follows, I rely on the cassette tour offered by the Musée du Sabot in Neuchâtel-en-Saosnois and the catalog of the Musée du Sabotier in La Haye-de-Routot (Eure), written by Alain Joubert, as well as the works cited above by Raymond Humbert and Roger Verdier.

33. *Doloire* = adze.

34. Techniques varied from canton to canton, as can be seen by comparing the museum exhibits mentioned above.

35. *Cahiers percherons* 59(1978): 32.

36. Ibid.

37. See Jacques Léonard, *Archives du corps: La santé au XIXe siècle* (Rennes: Ouest-France, 1986), esp. pp 18–20 on "relaxed rhythms."

38. See Verdier, *L'Art*, vol. 1, p. 8.

39. See Humbert, *Métiers*, p. 41.

40. Alain Corbin, *Le Village des cannibales* (Paris: Aubier, 1990), p. 106.

41. Michel de Certeau, *L'Invention du quotidien: Arts de faire* (Paris: UGE, 1980), pp. 270–276.

42. Corbin, *Les Cloches*, p. 186, according to the master's thesis of Laurent Morin, "Les Incendies de 1830 en Basse-Normandie" (University of Paris I, 1992).

43. Humbert, *Métiers*, p. 78.

44. Verdier, *L'Art*, vol. 1, p. 19.

45. Ibid., p. 17, for the following observations.

46. Anne-Marie Sohn, *Du premier baiser à l'alcôve* (Paris: Aubier, 1996), passim, counsels caution in interpreting these matters: sexual behavior in this milieu was often more subtle than the superficial characterizations of some anthropologists might lead one to believe.

47. Cailly, *Mutations*, passim.

48. Louis Charles Nicolas Delestang, *Chorographie du IVe arrondissement communal du département de l'Orne ou du district de la souspréfecture de Mortagne* (Argentan, 1803), p. 110.

49. Humbert, *Métiers*, p. 24.

50. The term "worker" was sometimes applied to those who were not "master clog makers."

51. ADO 13 U 5 81, September 13, 1822.

52. ADO 13 U 5 82, August 1, 1827.

53. ADO 13 U 5 80, July 16, 1819.

54. Louis Dubois in *Annuaire statistique de département de l'Orne*, 1809, p. 159.

55. Joseph Odolant-Desnos, *La France: Description géographique, statistique, et topographique par M. Loriol* (Paris: Verdière), p. 90.

56. AM of Bellême, ADO E dépôt 495/107.

57. ADO M 1922. Claude Cailly believes this to be the most credible industrial survey. By contrast, he is quite critical of the reports for 1867 and subsequent years.

58. ADO M 1923. Report on the industrial situation, fourth trimester, 1867.

59. ADO M 2194.

60. As Claude Cailly convincingly argues in *Mutations*.

61. Ibid., p. 406.

62. See chapter 9.

63. In Saint-Martin, there were only 110 clog makers in Year VIII, not counting twelve dealers (see Cailly, *Mutations*, p. 67). The numbered had increased to 222 by 1841 and 280 by 1861. In 1855–1856, 345 clog makers were counted in Bellême and

Saint-Martin (AM for Bellême, ADO E dépôt 495/107). To be sure, the survey of 1862 found only 244 workers in the entire canton, distributed among twenty businesses (ADO M 1922). There were supposedly 22 in Origny-le-Butin at that time. In the survey of industry in the Mortagne district compiled by the prefecture in 1867, there were 598 male clog makers, 40 female clog makers, and 90 children employed in the industry (ADO M 1923). Employment remained at roughly this level until the war (see reports in ADO M 1923). Another series of documents puts the number of clog makers in Bellême and environs at around 700 in 1869; 798 in 1872; and 795 in 1874 (AN F12 4526).

64. Expression used by Claude Cailly.

65. AN F12 1626. On the spinners of the Bellêmois, see Cailly, *Mutations*, pp. 445 ff.

66. ADO M 268.

67. AN F12 1626.

68. Ibid.

69. ADO 13 U 5 81, September 25, 1823.

70. ADO 13 U 5 86, November 18, 1853.

71. AN F12 1326.

72. *Echo de l'arrondissement de Mortagne* (quoting industrial survey of 1848), issue of June 17, 1849.

73. AM of Bellême, ADO E dépôt 495/107.

74. The industrial survey for 1848 (see n. 72) indicates that there were 121 spinners and 398 glove makers in the canton of Bellême. This information does not agree with other available data.

75. According to Claude Cailly's calculations.

76. ADO M 1922.

77. ADO M 1923.

78. Cailly, *Mutations*, p. 407.

79. Alain Corbin, "Le grand siècle du linge," *Le Temps, le désir et l'horreur* (Paris: Aubier, 1991), pp. 23–52.

80. See Françoise Pytel, Christian Pytel, and Claude Cailly, *Le Filet dans le Perche. Histoire d'une industrie à domicile* (Meaucé, 1990).

81. ADO 13 U 5 94, January 12, 1855.

82. See Pytel, Pytel, and Cailly, *Le Filet*, p. 27, for this and subsequent quotes.

83. Sicotière, *Notes statistiques*, p. 67.

84. In 1848 a glove maker in the Bellême canton earned five centimes per hour, or .60 francs for a twelve-hour day (*Echo de l'arrondissement de Mortagne*, June 17, 1849). In 1852, in the same canton, earnings varied "according to skill, ability, speed, and type of lace" (ADO M 1832). Average wages were .90 francs per day. In documents pertaining to Bellême and Saint-Martin for 1855–1856, however, wages were down to .65 francs (ADO E dépôt 495/107). The author of a *départemental* survey

of 1862 was even more pessimistic. He put glove makers' wages at .45 to .60 francs per day "for diligent work" and indicates that young girls earned only .15 to .20 francs (ADO M 1922). By contrast, in a report on industry in the Orne for the fourth trimester of 1867, we read that glove makers earned .75 to 1.25 francs per day (ADO M 1923).

85. *Echo de l'arrondissement de Mortagne*, June 24, 1849.

86. ADO M 1923, subprefect for the Mortagne district, June 24, 1868.

6. The Pleasure of "Arrangements"

1. As defined by magistrates. Hence there is no reason to say that criminal behavior in the region was widespread.

2. Nowadays we are familiar with the gap between perceived and punished crime and actual crime. Crime statistics often reveal little more than differences in the visibility of crime, or random fluctuations in the severity.

3. Clearly, within the forest communal boundaries lost much of their significance. Several villages belonging to the commune of Saint-Martin-du-Vieux-Bellême were places that Louis-François visited on a daily basis.

4. ADO 12 U 374, affidavit of June 18, 1811.

5. ADO 12 U 376, affidavit of June 23, 1818.

6. ADO 12 U 974, affidavit of June 18, 1823.

7. ADO 12 U 462, affidavit of June 17, 1850.

8. ADO 12 U 462, affidavit of November 28, 1850.

9. ADO 12 U 385, affidavit of December 22, 1850.

10. ADO 12 U 462, affidavit of February 1, 1851.

11. ADO 12 U 374, affidavit of August 4, 1812.

12. ADO 12 U 378.

13. ADO 12 U 460, affidavit of November 6, 1844.

14. ADO 12 U 459, affidavit of January 29, 1842.

15. ADO 12 U 975, affidavit of October 27, 1819.

16. ADO 12 U 974, affidavit of June 13, 1823.

17. ADO 12 U 974, affidavit of March 21, 1823.

18. ADO 12 U 974, affidavit of March 1, 1823.

19. ADO 12 U 460, affidavit of February 18, 1844.

20. ADO 12 U 374, affidavit of March 18, 1812.

21. ADO 12 U 374, affidavit of April 28, 1812.

22. ADO 12 U 374, affidavit of November 24, 1812.

23. ADO 12 U 374, affidavit of December 29, 1812. A similar discovery was made the same year at Le Pissot at the home of Gueunet, a future in-law of Louis-François's.

24. Series of offenses: ADO 12 U 379, May 10, 1831; ADO 12 U 381, October 19, 1839; ADO 12 U 460, July 19, 1844.

25. ADO 12 U 376, affidavit of March 15, 1817.

26. ADO 12 U 378, affidavit of April 3, 1828.

27. ADO 12 U 378, affidavit of December 11, 1828.

28. ADO 12 U 381, affidavit of March 12, 1837 and September 8 and January 7, 1838.

29. ADO 12 U 381, affidavit of February 3, 1839.

30. ADO 12 U 380, affidavit of March 29, 1836.

31. ADO 12 U 381, affidavit of August 13, 1837.

32. See Carlo Ginzburg, *Mythes, emblèmes, traces: Morphologie et Histoire* (Paris: Flammarion, 1989), pp. 139–181; Jean-Marc Berlière, "L'Institution policière en France sous la IIIe République" (thesis, University of Dijon, 1991); Dominique Kalifa, *L'Encre et le sang: Récit de crimes et société à la Belle-Epoque* (Paris: Fayard, 1995), passim.

33. ADO 12 U 1009, affidavit of September 2, 1822.

34. See page 75.

35. ADO 12 U 380, affidavit of August 29, 1835.

36. ADO 12 U 459, affidavit of July 12, 1843.

37. ADO 12 U 462, affidavit of April 10, 1847.

38. See pages 174–178.

39. ADO 12 U 462, affidavit of April 29, 1847.

40. See Frédéric Chauvaud, "Tensions et conflits: Aspects de la vie rurale au XIXe siècle d'après les archives judiciaires: L'exemple de l'arrondissement de Rambouillet (1811–1871)" (thesis, University of Paris X, 1989), and *Passions villageoises au XIXe siècle: Les émotions rurales dans les pays de Beauce, du Hurepoix, et du Mantois* (Paris: Publiaud, 1995).

41. In October 1848 Jean-Louis Denin, former bailiff of Bellême, filed a complaint against Louis-Baptiste Lesueur, a clog maker of Origny-le-Butin. He claimed to have gone to that commune "to work on an arrangement with a Sieur Boulay." In connection with this, he visited several plots of land. Lesueur claimed that he had never commissioned any "job" and that if Denin made any trips, it was "for his personal pleasure." ADO 13 U5 84.

42. ADO 13 U5 83, 1836.

43. ADO 13 U5 82, December 12, 1828. (The references concern the dates of the hearings held by the justice of the peace.)

44. ADO 13 U5 84, February 9, 1849.

45. ADO 13 U5 83, June 23, 1837.

46. ADO 13 U5 83, November 9, 1838.

47. One has to distinguish between apple cider, usually referred to simply as *cidre*, and pear cider, often called *poiré*, which was rare in Origny-le-Butin but common in the western part of the département. ADO 13 U5 83, January 22, 1836.

48. ADO 13 U5 84, March 13, 1846.

49. ADO 13 U5 83, September 1, 1837.

50. I came across a series of cases in which a *pipe de cidre* was part of the terms of an arrangement.

51. ADO 13 U5 86, January 13, 1854.

52. ADO 13 U5 84, June 25, 1847.

53. ADO 13 U5 82, March 1826.

54. ADO 13 U5 83, no. 51, 1832.

55. ADO 13 U5 83, July 8, 1831.

56. Each plot of land had an identity, marked by a name.

57. ADO 13 U5 85, January 18, 1850.

58. Alain Corbin, *Archaïsme et modernité en Limousin au XIXe siècle* vol. 1 (Paris: Marcel Rivière, 1975), reprinted by Presses de l'Université de Limoges, 1998, pp. 163–172. See also Jean-François Soulet, *Les Pyrénées au XIXe siècle*, vol. 1 (Toulouse: Eché, 1986), pp. 82 ff.

59. A comparison should really be made with a study of changes of ownership due to death.

60. The phrase "village capitalist" was applied at the time to lenders of modest sums.

61. For these three cases, see ADO 13 U5 84, September 16, October 14, 1842 and March 20, 1846.

62. ADO 13 U5 81, March 1, 1822.

63. ADO 13 U5 82, August 19, 1825.

64. ADO 13 U5 80, October 5, 1821.

65. ADO 13 U5 80, May 19, 1820.

66. For example, on August 13, 1841 (ADO 13 U5 83) Marin Duc, a farmer from Origny-le-Butin, was sued for 41 francs by the widow Laporte, a dry-goods merchant from La Perrière. On March 20, 1846 (ADO 13 U5 84) Armand Pitou, a hardware dealer from Bellême, filed suit to recover 231 francs "for merchandise" from Tessier, formerly a blacksmith in Origny-le-Butin.

67. ADO 13 U5 80, July 9, 1820.

68. ADO 13 U5 83, February 28, 1834.

69. See above.

70. ADO 13 U5 86, July 15, 1853.

71. ADO 13 U5 80, February 5 and 12, 1819.

72. ADO 13 U5 82, August 1, 1827.

73. ADO 13 U5 84, September 25, 1846.

74. ADO 13 U5 84, January 22, 1847.

75. See above. Here, ADO 13 U5 84, hearing of June 8, 1849, crime of May 23. In all these cases, local memory played a part. On May 6, 1853 (ADO 13 U5 85), Jean Barré, a farmer from the town of Origny, was accused of clearing a path without permission. The judge relied on the memory of five witnesses to point out its location.

76. ADO 13 U5 81, December 24, 1824.

77. ADO 13 U5 82, May 19, 1826 (concerning events of May 10).

78. ADO 13 U5 83, May 25, 1838.

79. ADO 13 U5 82, August 19, 1825.

80. ADO 13 U5 82, 1829.

81. ADO 13 U5 84, March 16, 1849 (agreement of February 21).

82. ADO 13 U5 84, May 4, 1849.

83. ADO 13 U5 83, November 16, 1838.

84. ADO 13 U5 80, April 14, 1820.

85. See Gemma Gagnon, *La Criminalité en France: Le phénomène homicide dans la famille en Seine-Inférieure de 1811 à 1900*, passim.

86. See Sandra Gayol, "Sociabilité à Buenos Aires: Les rencontres dans les débits de boissons, 1860–1900" (thesis, Ecole Pratique des Hautes Etudes en Sciences Sociales, 1996, [concerning a very different society, in which challenges played an important role]).

87. On these two delinquents of the forest, see page 104.

88. ADO 13 U5 80, July 14, 1820.

89. ADO 13 U5 80, November 11, 1822.

90. ADO 13 U5 83, December 29, 1837.

91. ADO 13 U5 83, September 29, 1837.

92. ADO 13 U5 85, March 22, 1850.

93. See Alain Corbin, *Le Temps, le désir, et l'horreur* (Paris: Aubier, 1991), pp. 39–40.

94. ADO 13 U5 80, June 9, 1820.

95. ADO 13 U5 83, February 25, 1831.

96. ADO 13 U5 83, 1836.

97. For a fictional counterpart, see George Sand's *Maîtres sonneurs* (Brussels: Moline, 1853).

98. Unfortunately, the documents on arbitration in the Orne archives are unusable for our purposes.

99. See François Ploux, "Les Formes du conflit et leurs modes de résolution dans les campagnes du Lot (1810–1860)" (thesis, University of Paris I, 1994), and "L'arrangement dans les campagnes du Haut-Quercy, 1815–1850" *Histoire de la justice* 5(1992).

100. See Philippe Grandcoing, *La Bande à Burgout et la société rurale de la châtaigneraie limousine, 1830–1839* (Limoges: SELM, 1991).

101. See especially ADO E dépôt 88, "Nomination de maires et adjoints," for the period 5 Messidor, Year VIII, to May 31, 1828, and ADO Z 381 for the following decade.

102. See chapter 9.

103. Abbé Louis-Joseph Fret, *Le Diseur de vérités*, 1842.

104. On all these points, see ADO Z 370 and AN F19 347, "Affaires de culte: Orne." On regional resistance to the banning of holidays, see Alain Corbin, *Les Cloches de la terre: Paysage sonore et culture sensible dans les campagnes du XIXe siècle* (Paris: Albin Michel, 1994), pp. 119–122.

105. Ordinance of June 7, 1814.

106. ADO Z 370, letter of August 29, 1821.

107. Letter to mayor of Bellême and others, July 13, 1814, ADO Z 370.

108. Remember that this was solar time.

109. ADO 13 U5 83, March 31, 1843 (for events of March 19 and 20).

110. ADO 13 U5 83, April 4, 1845 (for events of March 29).

111. ADO 13 U5 94. "*Jugements de simple police.*" Events of November 13, 1851.

112. ADO 13 U5 94, 1852.

113. ADO 13 U5 94, June 17, 1855.

114. Ibid.

115. ADO 13 U5 83, January 22, 1836.

116. ADO 13 U5 94, 1852.

117. ADO 13 U5 83, July 1840.

118. ADO 13 U5 94, affidavit of November 26, 1852.

119. ADO Z 386, report of the mayor of La Chapelle-Montligeon, March 7, 1824.

120. ADO M 1298, prefect of the Orne to minister of the interior, 10 July 1835.

121. ADO M 1298, letter from the mayor of Tourouvre to the subprefect and inspection report of the conservator of forests, August 4, 1835.

122. Here they key was the notion of excess, determined by the threshold of tolerance, which was variable.

123. ADO 13 U5 84, February 21, 1845.

124. This and subsequent quotes are from the deputy mayor's affidavit of November 25, 1851.

125. See Corbin, *Les Cloches de la terre*, pp. 277–283.

126. See Alain Corbin, "Les aristocrates et la communauté villageoise: Les maires d'Essay," in Maurice Agulhon, ed., *Les Maires de France du Consulat à nos jours* (Paris: Publications de la Sorbonne, 1986), pp. 347–367.

127. AN, F 10 1649. "Eaux et forêts. Tolérance. Orne." There is a thick file on the forest of Bellême. See also AN, F 12 1262.

7. The Past Decomposed

1. Must we take a position as uncompromising as that of Oscar Lewis, who, in writing about Mexico, said that poor people find it impossible to imagine themselves in the future or to situate themselves in relation to the past? See Oscar Lewis, *The Children of Sanchez: Autobiography of a Mexican Family* (New York: Random House, 1963).

2. It was not until the nineteenth century that people began to count centuries in

numerical terms. It is unlikely that Louis-François would have been quick to assimilate this innovation.

3. For an excellent analysis, see Jean-Claude Martin's introduction to *Documents relatifs à la convocation des Etats généraux de 1789* (Alençon, 1988).

4. My earlier work on the Limousin convinced me of this. See Alain Corbin, "Prélude au Front populaire: Contribution à l'histoire de l'opinion publique dans le département de la Haute-Vienne (1934–1936)" (doctoral thesis, 1968), p. 98.

5. More precisely, some 15 *cahiers* out of 104.

6. Christine Peyrard, "Les Jacobins de l'Ouest: Formes de politisation dans l'Ouest intérieur pendant la Révolution française," 4 vols. (thesis, University of Paris, I, 1993), p. 559.

7. Gérard Bourdin, *Aspects de la Révolution dans l'Orne,* 1789–1799 (Saint-Paterne, 1991), p. 8.

8. See Léon de la Sicotière, *Louis de Frotté et les insurrections normandes,* 1793–1832 vol. 1 (Paris: Plon, 1889), pp. 299 ff. I have drawn on this learned work for various details in what follows.

9. Message of the Directory, 21 Fructidor, Year VII (September 7), to the Council of the Five Hundred, quoted in Sicotière, *Louis de Frotté,* vol. 2, p. 288.

10. Sylvie Denys-Blondeau, "Aspects de la vie politique de l'Ouest intérieur à l'époque de la transition directoriale: L'exemple ornais" (thesis, University of Rouen, 1995), p. 108.

11. Sicotière, *Louis de Frotté,* vol. 2, p. 435.

12. Ibid.

13. ADO M 1265. "Aid, damages done by chouans, letter from mayor of La Perrière to prefect, 12 Messidor, Year IX."

14. Report by Subprefect Delestang, undated, ADO M 1269.

15. Comment on report mentioned in note 14.

16. Ibid.

17. Louis Duval, *Le Département de l'Orne en 1799–1800* (Alençon: A. Manier, 1901), p. 242.

18. See the works cited by Léon de La Sicotière, Louis Duval, Paul Nicolle, Georges Lefebvre, Christine Peyrard, Sylvie Denys-Blondeau, Jean-Claude Martin, Pierre Flament, and Gérard Bourdin, as well as the compendium by Gabriel Désert, *La Révolution française en Normandie* (Toulouse: Privat, 1989), and the joint work, *A travers la Haute-Normandie en Révolution, 1789–1800* (Comité Régional d'Histoire de la Révolution Française, 1992). I drew on all of these works for the account that follows.

19. In particular, Christine Peyrard and Sylvie Denys-Blondeau.

20. See Bourdin, *Aspects,* pp. 19–20.

21. Dr. Jousset, *La Révolution au Perche,* part 4 (Mamers, 1878), esp. pp. 7–9.

22. Archives of the *maréchaussée* of Alençon, unnumbered bundle: "revolt of the populace of Bellême," used by Christine Peyrard.

23. Here, the term "populace" probably refers to forest workers in general.

24. Peyrard, "Les Jacobins," vol. 1, p. 5. See this work for a map of all these disturbances.

25. See Georges Lefebvre, *La Grande Peur de* 1789 (Paris: Armand Colin, 1988), esp. pp. 123 ff and 189 ff, and Bourdin, *Aspects*, p. 17.

26. See Peyrard, "Les Jacobins," vol. 1, p. 163, and ADO L 5165.

27. On these tools, see page 78.

28. Peyrard, "Les Jacobins," vol. 1, p. 163, and ADO L 5165.

29. Ibid.

30. See Paul Nicolle, "Le mouvement fédéraliste dans l'Orne," *Annales historiques de la Révolution française*, 1936, P. 498.

31. Georges Trolet, *Histoire du Perche* (Nogent-le-Rotrou, 1933), p. 199.

32. Peyrard, "Les Jacobins," p. 571.

33. Peyrard, "Les Jacobins," p. 560.

34. Ibid., p. 570.

35. Corbin, *Les Cloches*, passim.

36. Pierre Flament, *Deux milles prêtres normands face à la Révolution française, 1789–1801* (Paris: Perrin, 1989), preface by Pierre Chaunu, table in unpaginated appendix.

37. See the work of Gabriel Désert and Gérard Bourdin.

38. On the history of Norman charities, see Michel Bée, "La Croix et la bannière: Confréries, église, et société en Normandie du XVIIe au début du XXe siècle" (thesis, University of Paris IV, 1991). In this region, popular societies were seen as secularized, Jacobin, sansculotte substitutes for charities. It was through this network that Jacobin culture spread in rural aareas. "In the districts of Bellême and Mortagne, . . . 80 percent of the clubs were established that had charities before 1789." In November and December of 1792 there was a movement in the Perche to defend the charities (see Peyrard, "Les Jacobins," vol. 1, p. 171). So one interpretation of what happened is that a preexisting secular network of sociability served as a medium for the spread of Jacobin ideas. Opposed to this is the view that because the charities predated Jacobinism, they had developed a variety of views and convictions, hence it is misleading to suggest that the same Jacobin ideology prevailed everywhere. On this problem, see the debates from the colloquium on the politicization of the countryside held at the Ecole Française de Rome, February 20–23, 1997.

39. Jousset, *La Révolution*, part 4, pp. 45–46.

40. On these many incidents, see Louis Duval, *La Réouverture des églises en l'an III dans le district de Bellême* (Bellême: Imprimerie de Levayer, 1907), p. 9 (for Saint-Germain-de-la-Coudre).

41. Ibid., p. 10.

42. Ibid., p. 11.

43. Ibid., p. 12.

44. Ibid.

45. Since only one man was killed, the use of the term "massacre" is, strictly speaking, incorrect.

46. Pierre Caron, *Les Massacres de septembre* (Paris: La Maison du Livre Français, 1935).

47. Peyrard, "Les Jacobins," vol. 1, pp. 161 ff.

48. Corbin, *Le Village des cannibales*, pp. 192–193, with references to the works of Michel Bée, Denis Crouzet, Emmanuel Le Roy Ladurie, and Pieter Spierenburg.

49. Saint-Martin-du-Vieux-Bellême was then called Vieux-Bellême.

50. Peyrard, "Les Jacobins," vol. 1, p. 161.

51. Origny-le-Butin at that time was not part of the canton. It was attached to La Perrière.

52. See Paul Nicolle, "Les meurtres politiques d'août–septembre 1792 dans l'Orne," *Annales historiques de la Révolution française*, 1934, pp. 108 ff., and Pierre Flament, "Louis-François, Charles du Portail de la Bernardière assassiné à Bellême le 19 août 1792," *Cahiers percherons* 43no. 3 (1974): 21–48, and above all the documents in carton L 6317 of the ADO.

53. Jousset, *La Révolution*, vol. 4, p. 6. In fact, it was not until the final quarter of the century that scholars such as Léon de la Sicotière and Louis Duval produced quality works on the Revolution in the Orne. Dr. Jousset's works are relatively minor, but they interest us primarily because they concern the Bellêmois, and Saint-Martin in particular.

54. One may wish to compare with the Franche-Comté, which has been studied by Denis Saillard, "La Mémoire de la Révolution française en Franche-Comté (1815–1914)" (thesis, University of Paris I, 1995). It was not until 1876 that Abbé J. B. Blin published his history of the *Martyrs de la Révolution dans le diocèse de Séez*.

55. On the use and meaning of the term "cannibalistic," see Bronislaw Baczko, *Comment sortir de la Terreur, Thermidor, et la Révolution* (Paris: Gallimard, 1989). Abbé Louis-Joseph Fret used it in connection with the godson of Abbé du Portail in *Antiquités et chroniques percheronnes* (Mortagne: Imprimerie de Glaçon, 1838–1840), vol. 3, p. 309.

56. Fret, *Antiquités*, vol. 3, p. 309.

57. Ibid., p. 310.

58. Ibid., p. 309.

59. Ibid., p. 310.

60. Paolo Viola, *The Rites of Cannibalism and the French Revolution*, June 21–24, 1990, Milan Group, Fifth Biennial Symposium.

61. On all these episodes, see Jousset, *La Révolution*, passim.

62. ADO L 6317.

63. Peyrard, "Les Jacobins," vol. 1, p. 181, shows that not many peasants partici- pated and that poor peasants were not represented among the members of the few Jacobin clubs in *le Perche ornais* (see the composition of the Longny club). Never- theless, she argues that there was an early presence of Jacobin culture in the coun- tryside, based (p. 685) on a long history of local protest and on charitable confrater- nities: the "peasant revolution," she therefore claims, was "neither autonomous nor peasant" (p. 688). I do not wish to enter into this debate, because my purpose is only to reconstruct the local memory. In my view, however, Peyrard tends to overestimate the degree to which outside ideologies penetrated the rural Orne and took root, as well as the influence of the cultural mediators who supposedly made this possible.

64. See pages 186–187.

8. Invasions

1. By "youth," I mean the years between when Louis-François first went to work and when he married at the age of twenty.

2. In particular, André Armengaud, *L'Opinion publique en France et la crise nationale allemande de 1866* (Paris: Les Belles Lettres, 1962), and Claude Digeon, *La Crise allemande de la pensée française, 1870–1914* (Paris: Presses Universitaires de France, 1959).

3. Dr. Jousset, *Petite histoire d'une petite ville par un de ses citoyens* (Mamers: Fleury et Dangin, 1887), p. 56.

4. Georges Creste, "Souvenirs d'invasion," *Bulletin de la société percheronne d'his- toire, et d'archéologie* 6 (1907): 51–64. The quotations from Marin Rousseau are taken from letters reproduced in this article.

5. See Henri Tournouâr, *Les Prussiens dans l'Orne en 1815* (Alençon: Imprimerie Alençonnaise, 1921).

6. Ibid., p. 29.

7. Quoted in Tournouër, *Les Prussiens*, p. 23.

8. The Orne provided the Prussians with 715,939 meat rations and 513,503 bread rations, along with 8,107 quintals of wheat, 1,237 quintals of flour, and 24,762 kilo- grams of tobacco. To say nothing of 24,531 quintals of oats, 17,113 quintals of hay, and 5,892 quintals of straw for their animals. In addition, the *département* was obliged to provide full uniforms for 8,000 infantrymen and 2,000 cavalry. See ibid., p. 26. AN F7 9686, report of the prefect, July 31, 1815.

9. AN F7 9686, reports of the prefect (de Riccé), July 28 and 31, 1815.

10. There is a great deal of information in ADO series R. For instance, the pil- laging at Pervenchères: AN F7 9686, petition of residents of the commune, Septem- ber 3, 1815.

11. ADO R 94 and Tournouër, *Les Prussiens*, p. 21.

12. Quoted in Tournouër, *Les Prussiens*, p. 24.

13. See page 168.
14. Various incidents in ADO R 94.
15. ADO R 129, cited by Tournouër, *Les Prussiens*, p. 18.
16. Unlike the peasants of Hautefaye (Dordogne), who consequently had no memory in 1870. See Corbin, *Le Village des cannibales*, passim.
17. Sensitivity to the sensory messages and images of the other evolved between the two periods. For an example of olfactory sensibility, Dr. Jousset assures us that after the war was over, it took six months to air out the foul stench of the hospital: see his *Bellême*, p. 36. Even then, "the odor remained." In his mind, however, it was a matter of "the special perniciousness of war" and not of the Prussians in particular, whose courage inthe hospital he celebrated.
18. AN F1 CIII Orne 9. Report of the prefect, July 1, 1870.
19. Ibid., report of the prefect, August 1, 1870.
20. Ibid.
21. Ibid. for this and subsequent quotes.
22. See Stéphane Audoin-Rouzeau, 1870: *La France dans la guerre* (Paris: Armand Colin, 1989).
23. AN F1 CIII Orne 9. Report of August 1 for this and subsequent quotes.
24. ADO Z 495, 1870–1871. Mobilized national guard and franc-tireur companies. Louis Bergeron enlisted on October 11, 1870.
25. Ibid.
26. Ibid.
27. See Audoin-Rouzeau, 1870, passim.
28. The journal of Marie de Semallé, copied by family members, was given to me and then to M. Jousselin of the Bibliothèque du Centre de recherches en Histoire du XIXe Siècle at the Sorbonne. The date of each quote is indicated in the text.
29. Compare the rumors that circulated in the Dordogne at this time: see Corbin, *Le Village des cannibales*, pp. 62 ff.
30. At the beginning of his novel *Le Calvaire*.
31. See P. Pitard, *Garde mobile de l'Orne, 4e bataillon: Campagne 1870–1871* (Mortagne, 1872). This analysis by an eyewitness confirms that given by Stéphane Audoin-Rouzeau in 1870 and the description of Octave Mirbeau, whose fictional account is filled with images of livestock run amok, soldiers "driving through fields," the exodus, and the reactions of peasants as they shut themselves in their cottages. To be sure, these descriptions suited Mirbeau's literary purposes in *Le Calvaire*.
32. Pitard, *Garde mobile*, p. 20, and Brother Amédée Philippe, *Les Prussiens à Bellême pendant la guerre de 1870–1871* (Bellême: Levayer, 1903).
33. This obsession with fire was closely linked to the Prussian invasion. See Corbin, *Le Village des cannibales*, p. 62.
34. Jousset, *Bellême*, p. 23.

35. ADO E dépôt 88, record of deliberations of municipal council, Origny-le-Butin, December 20, 1870.

36. Here, perhaps, Marie de Semallé was only reporting a rumor.

37. Jousset, *Bellême*, pp. 37 ff.

38. Ibid., p. 38.

39. ADO R 158. Communal inventories related to the occupation.

40. Ibid.

41. Jousset, *Bellême*, p. 42.

42. ADO R 158, "List by order of needs, divided into five categories of individuals from the commune (Origny-le-Butin) who suffered under the Prussian invasion."

43. Jousset, *Bellême*, pp. 42–43.

44. Ibid., p. 43.

45. ADO E dépôt 88, record of deliberations of municipal council, March 1, 1871.

46. ADO R 158.

47. ADO O 1591.

48. ADO R 158. Calculations based on an analysis of lodging tickets.

49. Jousset, *Bellême*, p. 9. To ease the hostility, Jousset argued that the local population was of Germanic origin (p. 50): "In our province of the Perche, we are all children of Prussian race," as indicated, he maintained, by the frequency of Germanic place names.

9. *"The Audacity of the Poor"*

1. In 1967, while conducting an oral survey, I asked a poor Limousin peasant if he had lived through the Great Depression of the 1930s. He answered that he remembered good years, when his single calf lived, and bad ones, when the calf died. See Corbin, *Prélude*, p. 98.

2. See page 134ff.

3. Two theses have recently been written on bread riots: Denis Beliveau, "Les Révoltes frumentaires en France dans la première moitié du XIXe siècle" (thesis, Ecoles des Hautes Etudes en Sciences Sociales, 1992), and Nicolas Bourguinat, "Ordre naturel, ordre public, et hiérarchies sociales: L'Etat et les violences frumentaires dans la France de la première moitié du XIXe siècle" (thesis, University of Lyons II, 1997). On forests in particular, see Frédéric Chauvaud, "Le dépérissement des émotions paysannes dans les territoires boisés au XIXe siècle," *La Terre et la Cité, Mélanges offerts à Philippe Vigier* (Paris: Créaphis, 1994).

4. After a survey and a report by Léon de la Sicotière, *Conseil général de l'Orne, session de 1864, Rapport de M. Léon de la Sicotière sur l'assistance, et l'extinction de la mendicité* (Alençon: Imprimerie de C. Thomas, 1864).

5. AN F11 390. Subsistances. Orne. Year IV–1813. Report by Prefect La Magedelaine to the minister of the interior, 22 Floréal, Year X.

6. Ibid.

7. This obligation was maintained throughout the nineteenth century and could be quite onerous in case of an insurrection or revolt. See Pascal Plas, "De la responsabilité civil au cas de dommages causés par les barricades en France, XIXe siècle-début du XXe siècle," in Alain Corbin and Jean-Marie Mayeur, eds., *La Barricade* (Paris: Publications de la Sorbonne, 1997), pp. 283–296.

8. AN F11 390. Report of the prefect, 1 Prairial, Year X.

9. AN F11 715. Report of Prefect La Magdelaine, August 7, 1812.

10. AN F11 715. Report of prefect to minister of the interior, September 22, 1812.

11. Note the use of the word "fermentation," which suggests a relation between the political vocabulary and the theory of infection.

12. AN F11 715. Report of the prefect, September 22, 1812.

13. The decrees of May 4 and 8, 1811, reached the Orne on May 11 and 16 [respectively].

14. Quotes from a letter from the prefect, November 13, 1812, AN F11 715.

15. AN F11 715. Letter from the prefect of the Orne, November 11, 1812.

16. AN F11 715. Report from the prefect to the minister of the interior, September 22, 1812.

17. AN F11 715. Letter from the prefect, November 11, 1812.

18. Information sent by the prefect of the Orne to the ministor of the interior, July 1, 1812, AN F11 715.

19. AN F11 715. Prefect to the minister of the interior, December 24, 1812.

20. AN F11 715. Prefect to the minister of the interior, August 7, 1812.

21. Opinion of the mayor of Saint-Martin-du-Vieux-Bellême, ADO E dépôt 89/69.

22. All quotes from AN F11 731. Prefect to minister of the interior, December 18, 1816.

23. AN F11 731. Prefect to minister of the interior, May 23, 1817.

24. ADO M 1291, report of the subprefect of Mortagne to the prefect of the Orne, May 10, 1817.

25. Account of the Igé affair by the mayor, AN F11 731.

26. Emphasis in original. Report of the prefect of the Orne to the minister of the interior, May 9, 1817, AN F11 731 and F7 9686.

27. ADO M 1291, report of the subprefect of Mortagne to the prefect, May 10, 1817.

28. AN F11 731. Letter from the prefect to the minister of the interior, May 11, 1817.

29. AN F11 731. Decree of the prefect of the Orne, May 17, 1817.

30. Ibid., for this and subsequent quotes.

31. For a sample map of mendicancy, see ADO Z 531.

32. ADO Z 531. Letter from the prefect to the subprefect of Mortagne, January 12, 1818.

33. Mayor of Saint-Martin-du-Vieux-Bellême. ADO E dépôt 89/109. Although gleaning was always tolerated in the canton of Bellême, *râtelage*, or gathering with a rake, was not, nor was *chaumage*, the right to cut stubble. See Georges Courtois, *Us et coutumes du canton de Bellême, recueillis jusqu'en 1882* (Bellême, 1883), p. 33.

34. ADO Z 531. List of indigents of the communes of the canton of Bellême, January 18, 1818.

35. ADO Z 531. Letter from the mayor of Origny-le-Butin to the subprefect, January 2, 1818.

36. Ibid.

37. ADO Z 531. Letter from mayor of Bellême to subprefect, January 18, 1818.

38. ADO Z 531. Mayor of Saint-Martin-du-Vieux-Bellême, February 1, 1818.

39. AN F7 6771. Report of prefect, December 20, 1828.

40. AN BB18 1171. Prosecutor of Mortagne to minister of justice, May 8, 1829.

41. AN BB18 1171. Prosecutor of Mortagne to minister of justice, May 14, 1829.

42. AN BB18 1171. Prosecutor of Mortagne to minister of justice, April 27, 1829.

43. AN F2 I 1289. Prefect to minister of the interior, January 31, 1831.

44. AN F2 I 1289. Prefect to minister of the interior, January 25, 1832.

45. AN BB18 1171. Letter of April 27, 1829.

46. AN F2 I 1289. Memo from Prefect Clogenson, November 3, 1830.

47. Ibid.

48. See Catherine Freeman, *"Rébellion armée à Bellême"*: Examination of a Food Riot in Nineteenth-Century Normandy Through the Use of a Judicial Archive (Alençon, 1985). ADO J 364. Documents concerning the affair: ADO 4 U 216 and AN BB18 1379.

49. AN BB18 1379. Testimony of Subprefect Jean-Victor Bessin in report of the prosecuting magistrate dated September 27–28, 1839.

50. Ibid.

51. Prosecutor to minister of justice, September 24, 1839, AN BB18 1379.

52. AN BB18 1379. Prosecutor to minister of justice, October 27, 1839, and minister of justice to minister of the interior, November 2, 1839.

53. ADO 4 U 216.

54. ADO M 1299, letter from subprefect to prefect, October 22, 1846.

55. On the disturbances in Buzançais: Philippe Vigier, "Buzançais, le 13 janvier 1847," *La Vie quotidienne à Paris et en province pendant les journées de 1848* (Paris: Hachette, 1982), and Yves Bionnier, *Les Jacqueries de 1847 en Bas-Berry* (published by the author, 1979).

56. ADO M 1299.

57. Letter to the minister of the interior, ADO M 1299.

58. Report of the prefect, February 25, 1847, ADO M 1299.

59. ADO M 1299, "Means of helping the poor during the winter of 1846–1847," Origny-le-Butin.

60. ADO E dépôt 88, record of municipal deliberations, session of January 3, 1847.

61. ADO M 1299, comment in "Means of helping" (see note 59).

62. ADO E dépôt 88, deliberations of council of Origny-le-Butin, January 3, 1847.

63. ADO M 1299, "Means of helping."

64. ADO M 44, report of mayor of Bellême, March 29, 1848.

65. ADO E dépôt 88, record of municipal deliberations, Origny-le-Butin, session of August 15 and September 4, 1848.

66. ADO E dépôt 88, session of October 8, 1848.

67. ADO E dépôt 88, session of September 4, 1848.

68. AN F1 CIII Orne 9. Report of subprefect of Mortagne, October 29, 1853.

69. ADO E dépôt 88, Origny-le-Butin, deliberations of municipal council, sessions of January 14 and February 3, 1854.

70. AN F1 CIII Orne 9. Report of subprefect of Mortagne, December 25, 1853.

71. In July there were 5,385 "permanent indigents" and 6,460 "temporary indigents" listed on the rolls, for a total of 11,845 out of a population of 121,854: AN F1 CIII Orne 9, report of subprefect and results of statistical survey of begging in the district, July 15, 1854.

72. ADO E dépôt 88, session of February 3, 1855.

73. ADO M 965, report of cantonal police commissioner for Bellême, December 16 and 20, 1855.

74. AN F1 CIII Orne 14, February 1865.

10. The Parishioner, the Guardsman, and the Voter

1. See, for example, the work of Pierre Rosanvallon, Philippe Braud, Michel Offerlé, Yves Deloye, Olivier Ihl, Bernard Lacroix, and the many theses prepared under their supervision. In particular, Eric Phelippeau, "Le Baron de Mackau en politique: Contribution à l'étude de la professionnalisation politique" (thesis, University of Paris X, 1995), on the construction of political man and the mechanics of election campaigns in the *département* of the Orne.

2. Michel Pigenet, *Ouvriers, paysans, nous sommes: Les bûcherons du centre de la France au tournant du siècle* (Paris: L'Harmattan, 1993).

3. This is true of virtually all theses and works of regional political history from the past thirty years, which have been rather neglectful of private archives.

4. AN F7 6771, letter from Prefect Séguier to minister of the interior, June 12, 1828.

5. On what this phrase meant to administrators, see Alain Corbin and Nathalie Veiga, "Le monarque sous la pluie: Les voyages de Louis-Philippe Ier en province (1831–1833)," *La Terre et la cité*, pp. 217–229.

6. AN F7 6771, report of Prefect Séguier, October 22, 1828.

7. AN F7 6771, report of Prefect Séguier, December 20, 1828.

8. Ibid.

9. See Nicole Mozet, *La Ville du province dans l'oeuvre de Balzac* (Paris: CDU-SEDES, 1982).

10. AN F7 6771, report of Prefect Séguier, October 21, 1829.

11. In the prefect's office, synthesis was generally accomplished by cutting and pasting.

12. See pages 14–20.

13. The following quotes are therefore intended not as evidence but as examples.

14. ADO M 268. Report of subprefect for Mortagne district to prefect, September 30, 1834.

15. AN F1 CIII Orne 9, report of subprefect for Mortagne district, April 24, 1853.

16. A nice study of the logic, construction, and instrumentalization of regional temperament in the nineteenth century: Pierre-Yves Saunier, *L'Esprit lyonnais, XIXe–XXe siècle* (Paris: CNRS Editions, 1995).

17. AN F7 9686, report of subprefect d'Aubers to the prefect of the Orne, December 30, 1817. Note the emphasis on the links between anxiety and public opinion.

18. Ibid.

19. Ibid.

20. On this notion in the nineteenth century, see Alain Pessin, *Le Mythe du peuple et la société française du XIXe siècle* (Paris: Presses Universitaires de France, 1992).

21. ADO M 268. Report of subprefect for the Mortagne district to prefect, April 18, 1835.

22. On the logic of this competition, see Alain Corbin, *Le Temps, le désir et l'horreur* (Paris: Aubier, 1991), pp. 227–244.

23. ADO M 43. Report of the prefect of the Orne on the situation in his *département*, 1835.

24. As has been shown, most notably, by Jean Vidalenc.

25. AN F9 312, report of Prefect La Magdelaine to the minister of the interior, June 19, 1811.

26. On participation in elections in the Sarthe during the Hundred Days, see Jacques Hantraye, "Les Vautours de Bonaparte: L'état des esprits et la vie politique de la vallée du Loir (Sarthe) au début de la seconde Restauration (1815–1817)" (master's thesis, University of Paris I, 1992).

27. AN F1 CIII Orne 14, report of prefect, May 7, 1814 on the riots in Argentan and Laigle and on the Te Deum at Alençon on May 9, marking the change of regime.

28. AN F7 9686, report of prefect to minister of general police, June 27, 1815.

29. Ibid.

30. Ibid.

31. AN F7 9686, report of prefect of the Orne to minister, November 9, 1815. The "scheming" continued in February 1816 (report of February 28).

32. See pages 168–171.

33. ADO E dépôt 89/69.

34. AN F7 4111, tables submitted by the vicomte de Riccé in October, November, and December 1818.

35. AN F9 230, report of prefect of the Orne, July 15, 1819.

36. Ibid.

37. AN F9 230, report of prefect of the Orne, August 7, 1819.

38. Ibid., p. 83.

39. AN F7 CIII Orne 9, report of the prefect of the Orne, September 23, 1819. Other reports, dated 1824 and 1825, also point to a substantial number of deserters in the département of the Orne (AN F7 4111).

40. See Alain Corbin, "La Fête de souveraineté" and "L'impossible présence du roi" in Alain Corbin, Noëlle Gérôme, and Danielle Tartakowsky, *L'Usage politique des fêtes* (Paris: Publications de la Sorbonne, 1994), pp. 25 and 77. On the festivals of the Restoration, see Françoise Waquet, *Les Fêtes royales sous la Restauration ou l'Ancien Régime retrouvé* (Paris: Arts et Métiers Graphiques, 1981). On the commemoration of the "martyr king" in the countryside, see Bernadette Evenas, "Les Cérémonies expiatoires de la mort de Louis XVI sous la Restauration" (master's thesis, University of Paris I, 1992).

41. See ADO Z 370, files on the celebration of each of these holidays in the Mortagne district. On the death of Louis XVIII, see Pascal Simonette, "Mourir comme un Bourbon, Louis XVIII, 1824," *Revue d'histoire moderne et contemporaine* (January–March 1995): 91–106, and, more precisely, on news of the death, Catherine Beaucourt, "La Mort de Louis XVIII" (master's thesis, University of Paris I, 1996).

42. See ADO Z 370, Mayor of Origny-le-Roux, November 4, 1825. On the use of bells in festivals of sovereignty, see Corbin, *Les Cloches* (Paris: Albin Michel, 1994), pp. 248–264.

43. See pages 167–169.

44. For an example of semantic intensity in traditional practices in and on the edge of forests, see Peter Sahlins, *Forest Rites: The War of the Demoiselles in Nineteenth-Century France* (Cambridge, Mass.: Harvard University Press, 1994).

45. In the rural Orne there was no need to specify that "council" meant "municipal council."

46. ADO E dépôt 88, recofrd of municipal deliberations, Origny-le-Butin, "Assembly of October 5, 1824."

47. Fidèle de Bloteau is reminiscent of characters in Balzac's novels about the Alençonnais, *La Vieille fille*, and *Le Cabinet des antiques*.

48. AN F1 bII Orne 20, Origny-le-Butin. Letter from the prefect of the Orne, the vicomte de Riccé, to the minister, January 16, 1816.

49. AN F1 bII Orne 20, petition by M. de Bloteau, March 1, 1816.

50. AN F1 bII Orne 20, report of the prefect.

51. AN F1 bII Orne 20, petition in favor of M. de Bloteau, February 17, 1816, and letter from members of the Orne deputation, December 28, 1815.

52. M. de Bloteau, petition, see note 49.

53. ADO M 1295, affidavit of lieutenant of gendarmerie, September 15, 1819, for following quotes as well.

54. The government referred to was, of course, the one in which Duc Decazes held a prominent position.

55. See page 70.

56. ADO E dépôt 88, record of deliberations of municipal council of Origny-le-Butin, session of December 25, 1826. The details that follow are taken from the same minutes.

57. ADO E dépôt , record of municipal deliberations, 10 Fructidor, Year XII.

58. In fact, "Vaunoise had been eliminated and combined with Origny-le-Butin, but since that time special circumstances have dictated that Origny-le-Butin be assimilated to Vaunoise instead." Report on properties and income of the vestry. 25 Ventôse, Year XIII, ADO Z 525.

59. ADO E dépôt 88, 14 Thermidor, Year XIII.

60. AN F19 758, "Report on religious buildings in the branch parishes eliminated by combination, in compliance with order of September 30, 1807," diocese of Séez.

61. ADO E dépôt 88/85. Inventory of property in church crypt, 1810.

62. On these successive offers, see ADO E dépôt 88/2.

63. AN F19 758. Petition of residents of Origny-le-Butin, October 5, 1819.

64. Ibid., and ADO E dépôt 88, record of deliberations of municipal council, November 7, 1819.

65. This complicated story is told in file ADO 11 V 96. Vestry of Origny-le-Butin, Year XIII–1834.

66. AN F3 II 21, Origny-le-Butin, prefect of the Orne, October 31, 1823.

67. ADO 11 V 96.

68. ADO O 655. Description of presbytery acquired on February 6, 1824.

69. ADO 11 V 96.

70. Ibid.

71. Ibid.

72. ADO E dépôt 88, record of deliberations of municipal council, session of May 13, 1831.

73. ADO M 43, letter of subprefect for Mortagne district to prefect of the Orne,

August 9, 1830. On provincial support for the new regime, see Pamela Pilbeam, "Popular Violence in Provincial France after the 1830 Revlution," *English Historical Review* 91, no. 359 (1976): 278–297; " 'The Three Glorious Days': Revolution of the 1830 in Provincial France," *Historical Journal* 26, no. 4 (1983); and Roger Price, "Popular Disturbances in the Franch Provinces after the July Revolution of 1830," *European Studies Review* 1, no. 4 (1971): 323–350.

74. AN F9 616, report of prefect on the situation of the national guard in the Orne, October 1830. See also Louis Girard, *La Garde nationale (*1814–1870) (Paris: Plon, 1964).

75. ADO M 43, letter of subprefect, August 9, 1830.

76. However, in Bellavilliers, a commune on the northern edge of the forest of Bellême, the guard unit had enlisted 106 men, three of whom already wore uniforms.

77. See AN F9 616, letter of prefect of the Orne, November 7, 1830.

78. ADO Z 370, account of festival of the king in La Mesnière by the mayor, May 2, 1831.

79. AN F9 616, letter of prefect, November 7, 1830.

80. AN F9 616, letter of prefect, November 10, 1830.

81. See Girard, *La Garde nationale*, passim, and Bernard Ménager, *Les Napoléon du peuple* (Paris: Aubier, 1988).

82. AN F9 616, table of organization and strength of national guard, dated April 1, 1831.

83. AN F9 616.

84. See ADO E dépôt 88/41, sign-in sheet for national guard elections.

85. ADO E dépôt 88/42.

86. Unit strengths were roughly identical for the elections of 1837, 1840, and 1846. For details, see ADO E dépôt 88 (municipal archives), Origny-le-Butin, 40 (national guard, census), 41 and 42 (vote tally).

87. Corbin and Veiga, "Le monarque sous la pluie." Note, however, that the king did not come anywhere close to Origny-le-Butin when he traveled in Normandy.

88. AN F9 616, report of prefect on national guard reviews, June 21, 1831.

89. Corbin, "Les aristocrates."

90. AN F9 616, strength of cantonal national guard units, December 14, 1831.

91. ADO M 43, report of prefect of the Orne, 1835.

92. ADO M 268, report of prefect of the Orne, April 18, 1834.

93. ADO M 268, note on report of subprefect for Mortagne, fourth trimester 1834.

94. The most detailed study of these festivals in a regional setting is Rémy Dalisson, "De la Saint-Louis au cent-cinquantenaire de la Révolution: Fêtes et cérémonies publiques en Seine-et-Marne de 1815 à 1939" (thesis, University of Paris I, 1997).

95. ADO Z 370, letter of mayor of Origny-le-Roux, July 28, 1833.

96. ADO Z 370, letter of mayor of Bellavilliers, July 24, 1834.

97. ADO Z 370, letter of mayor of Damemarie, May 1, 1831.

98. On the importance of these municipal elections, see André-Jean Tudesq, "Institutions locales et histoire sociale: La loi municipale de 1831 et ses premières applications," *Annales de la faculté des lettres et sciences humaines de Nice* 3, (fourth trimester 1969); Philippe Vigier, "Elections municipales et prise de conscience politique sous la Monarchie de Juillet," *La France au XIXe siècle* (Paris: Publications de la Sorbonne, 1973); Rachel Gauducheau, "Le Déroulement des élections municipales sous la monarchie de Juillet en fonction de la loi du 21 mars 1831" (master's thesis, University of Paris I, 1992); and especially Christine Guionnet, "Elections et modernisation politique" (thesis, Ecoles des Hautes Etudes en Sciences Sociales, 1995), and *L'Apprentissage de la politique moderne: Les élections municipales sous la Monarchie de Juillet* (Paris: L'Harmattan 1997).

99. See summary table in *Annuaire du département de l'Orne*, 1841, "statistical information on municipal elections of 1834, 1837, and 1840."

100. For details, see ADO E dépôt 88/53, affidavits concerning municipal elections, and 88/54, voter lists.

101. As Yves Deloye and Oliver Ihl point out in "Le XIX siècle au miroir de la sociologie historique," *Revue d'histoire du XIXe siècle* 13 (1996): 54–55, historians have been too quick to identify learning electoral behavior with entering in the conceptual universe of ideological debate on which democratic representation is based. For bibliographic information on political activity in relation to socioeconomic status and education, see Guionnet, *L'Apprentissage*, p. 235.

102. ADO M 44, letter from an informant to the government commissioner, April 4, 1848.

103. ADO E dépôt 88/53 and 54 for details of what follows.

104. The list was checked and corrected to reflect the fact that some voters had left the commune.

105. ADO M 44, letter of subprefect for Mortagne to prefect, September 20, 1848.

106. ADO M 44, letter of subprefect for Mortagne, November 11, 1848.

107. Not counting nine men from the commune serving in the military.

108. See Ted Margadant, *French Peasants in Revolt: The Insurrection of* 1851 (Princeton: Princeton University Press, 1979).

109. ADO Z 385.

110. ADO E dépôt 88/53.

111. See sign-in sheets preserved in ADO E dépôt 88.

112. ADO E dépôt 88. See folio 43 of the commune's cadastral atlas, and ADO 3 Q 1817, record of names stricken from the list because of death, Louis-François Pinagot.

113. ADO E dépôt 88; record of "houses built or rebuilt," folio 107.

114. On the election of Louis-François Pinagot Jr., see ADO E dépôt 88/53.

115. The following account relies on the record of deliberations of the municipal council of Origny-le-Butin, ADO E dépôt 88. Quotes are also taken from this source.

116. On the debate over the schoolhouse, see file in ADO Z 425. Origny-le-Butin, 1873–1896.

117. ADO O 655

In this index, "P" refers to Louis-François Pinagot. The French participles "le," "la," "les," and "l' " are ignored in alphabetizing headings. Notes are indicated by the letter "n" after a page number, followed by the note number. Entries under "Pinagot, Louis-François" are divided into a general section as well as the following specific sections: as citizen, clog making, family, knowledge of history, life, social life, as voter.

charity kitchens, 167
charity workshops: application for
  work at, 170; increased reliance on,
  172; need for in 1846, 175; in
  Origny-le-Butin, 155, 176; popular-
  ity, 165
charivari, 124–125
Charles X, 188
Charron, Mlle, 58
Chartier, Louis-Jean, 106, 115
Chartier-Desrieux (subprefect), 182,
  204–205
Chasse Artus, 218n. 82
chateau La Gallardière, 147
chateau de la Grimonnière, 136
chateau La Pelleterie, 147
chateau ransackings, 136
chateau de Viantais, 147, 157
Chateaubriand, François Auguste, 14
Châtelier, 10
Chauvin, Marie, 99
Chavallier (farmer), 49
cheese, 27
Chemilly, 54
Chêne Saille (Ugly Oak), 10
Chevalier (woodcutter in Basse-
  Frêne), 33
Chevallier, Mme, 98
Chevallier, Pierre, 100
Chevauchée, Louise (P's mother-in-
  law), 40
children, 54, 176
children's clogs, 78
Choplain, Julien, 84
chores, 106
chouans (guerilla fighters), 4, 130, 131
Chrétien, Armand, 76, 83
Christianity, 16
churches, 12, 138, 139, 192–193. *See
  also* sacred objects

cider, 24
cider houses, 125
citizenship, 179, 195, 197
civil constitution of the clergy, 137, 141
civilians, aptitude for analyzing battle
  sounds, 156
class analysis, 183–184
class barriers, 154
classes, in parish census, 30
clay, 72
clear cutting, 6
clergy, 130, 143
Clinchamp, Jean, 113
clog makers, 73–88; biggest purchases,
  107; common delinquents, 99–100;
  cow ownership, 96; effects of
  industrial crisis on, 176; enjoyment
  at the tavern, 121, 122; as farmers,
  115; huts, 74–75, 76; income,
  85–86, 177; leaders of popular
  movements, 136; marriages with
  spinners, 41, 42; multiple residences, 75; need for good wood,
  77; numbers of, 227n. 63–228n. 63;
  offenses, 77; participation in voting, 203, 206–207; in Pinagot family, 42, 44, 45, 46, 47; places of
  work, 74, 76; in Pôté family, 44;
  ransacking of chateau de la Grimonnière, 136; in Renaud family,
  46; self-employed, 76; training, 79;
  work day, 73; working from home,
  76; working methods, 77. *See also*
  Bellanger, Louis; Jacques-Augustin
  Drouin; licensed master clog makers; master clog makers; Pinagot,
  Louis-François, clog making
clog makers' huts, 74–75, 76
clog making: coherent domestic system
  with glove making, 91; decline in

income, 86; communal identity, 192; conversations about Prussians, 153–154; distribution of bread to indigents, 170; enthusiasm of national guard unit, 198–199; geographical origin, 30–31; infantry of national guard, 197; mendicancy rate, 32; numbers of glove makers, 91; numbers of indigents, 170; numbers of voters, 201; outsiders' marriage partners, 40; population, 11–12, 28, 56; spinners' employers, 88–89; status, 29; teachers, 54; tradesmen, 25; youths' service in Franco-Prussian War, 150

Orne: archives of, xi; ban on mendicancy, 165; calmness during early years of Restoration, 186; center of industry during Second Empire, 87; construction of image of, 217n. 68; disaffection with national guard, 199; expectations of war with Prussia, 149; first elections, 135; forests of, 4; importation of grain, 166; lack of teachers, 57; number of electors, 201; popular agitation and protest in, 135–137; public opinion in, 181; survey of clog makers, 86; violence of summer of 1792, 140

other, 67
outsiders, 13–14, 16, 38, 40

Paris, 91
parish restoration movement, 21
paroir (clog-making tool), 79
past, representation of, 127–144
patois, 61, 64, 65
patriotism, 16
peasant attitudes, 205

peasants: clogs' importance in world of, 81; descriptions of speech, 61–62; differences from *va-nu-pieds*, 82; dislike of urban national guards, 133; Dureau de la Malle's views on, 19; language, 61, 62, 63; portrayals in playlets of Abbé Fret, 67; suspicion of nobles, 158; systems of representation, 205

people, anonymity, vii–viii
Le Perche ornais (Orne section of Perche), 14, 69, 133

Perche (region): assignment to three départments, 15; capital, 15; construction as scenic wonder, 17–18; construction of local identity, 15–16; Dureau de la Malle's views on, 19; family types, 37; as linguistic laboratory, 65; location, 3; outsider's impact on creation of local identities, 13–14, 16; population, 220n. 30; rudimentary structures in forests of, 75; as wilderness, 14

Percheron bocage, 139
Percheron idiom, 66
Percherons (horses), 26
Percherons (residents of Perche): contrast with Armoricans, 15; health, 14; local identity, 15; material attachments, 138; P's identification as, 13; stereotypic descriptions of, 183

La Perrière (town): capture by legion of the Perche, 130; Delasalle's homage to, 18; licensed master clog makers in, 82; occupation of, 133; P's attraction to, 12

La Perrière (triage area of Bellême forest), 5–6

personal honesty, 116

poor: actions during 1847 economic crisis, 175; avoidance of cash transactions, 108; desire for bread, 168; documents concerning, 164–165; indebtedness for food, 111; use of term in conversation, 67. *See also* beggars
popular movements, 131
popular songs, 81
popular unrest, 134
Portail, Louis François Charles du, de la Bénardière, massacre of, 139–143
Pôté, Anne-Louise (P's sister-in-law), 44, 89–90
Pôté, Anne (P's wife): death, 45, 175; early life, 44; geographical origins, 31; illiteracy, 54; occupation, 32; as outsider, 38; sexual relations with husband, 50; similarities with sister, 44; work as spinner, 88
Pôté, Jacques (P's brother-in-law), 44, 90, 101
Pôté, Jean (clog maker), 107
Pôté, Louis (P's father-in-law), 1; age at P's marriage, 40; at hearings for new presbytery, 194; importance, 189; income, 90; longevity, 1, 40; as new voter, 201; obligatory labor, 192; occupation, 40, 47; power of attorney for Maître de Villereau, 189; wealth, 40
Pôté, Marin (P's brother-in-law), 44, 101, 107, 195
Pôté family, 40, 90
poverty: in Basse-Frêne, 33–34; efforts to confine, 165; in Haut-Frêne, 33; levels of, 30; official policies dealing with, 164; unrest stemming from, 134. *See also* beggars; begging

poverty line, 93
power struggles, 120
price controls, 136
priests, attendance at deaths in Pinagot family, 60–61
Printemps, Louis-Tranquille, 49
professional competence, 116
professional endogamy, 47
properties, size, 29
property, 138
property damage, 115
protoindustrialization, 91
proverbs, 81, 82
provincial cities, 181–182
Prussians: behavior, 154; in Bellême, 146, 153, 154–155, 156; brutality, 148; dress, 153; gastronomic excesses, 148; hatred of, 149; imposition of demands, 146; ransacking of private homes, 147; spies, 152; stories of plunder and pillage by, 154; treatment of local nobles, 147–148; victims of, 154; withdrawal route, 148–149
public opinion, 180–181, 196
public records, 132–133
public relief policy, 164
Puisaye, marquis de, 187, 190

Les Querrières, 33

rabies, 27
reasoning class, 184
regional images, 13–20
regional speech, 61–63
regional stereotypes, 182
relatives (P's), influence on P's life, 37–52. *See also entries beginning with:* Pinagot, Drouin, Pôté
religious ceremonies, 200–201
religious services, 22, 121, 192

EUROPEAN PERSPECTIVES

A Series in Social Thought and Cultural Criticism

Lawrence D. Kritzman, Editor

Julia Kristeva   *Strangers to Ourselves*

Theodor W. Adorno   *Notes to Literature*, vols. 1 and 2

Richard Wolin, editor   *The Heidegger Controversy*

Antonio Gramsci   *Prison Notebooks*, vols. 1 and 2

Jacques LeGoff   *History and Memory*

Alain Finkielkraut   *Remembering in Vain: The Klaus Barbie Trial and Crimes Against Humanity*

Julia Kristeva   *Nations Without Nationalism*

Pierre Bourdieu   *The Field of Cultural Production*

Pierre Vidal-Naquet   *Assassins of Memory: Essays on the Denial of the Holocaust*

Hugo Ball   *Critique of the German Intelligentsia*

Gilles Deleuze and Félix Guattari   *What Is Philosophy?*

Karl Heinz Bohrer   *Suddenness: On the Moment of Aesthetic Appearance*

Julia Kristeva   *Time and Sense*

Alain Finkielkraut   *The Defeat of the Mind*

Julia Kristeva   *New Maladies of the Soul*

Elisabeth Badinter   *XY: On Masculine Identity*

Karl Löwith   *Martin Heidegger and European Nihilism*

Gilles Deleuze   *Negotiations, 1972–1990*

Pierre Vidal-Naquet   *The Jews: History, Memory, and the Present*

Norbert Elias   *The Germans*

Louis Althusser   *Writings on Psychoanalysis: Freud and Lacan*

Elisabeth Roudinesco   *Jacques Lacan: His Life and Work*

Ross Guberman   *Julia Kristeva Interviews*

Kelly Oliver   *The Portable Kristeva*

Pierra Nora   *Realms of Memory: The Construction of the French Past*
   vol. 1: *Conflicts and Divisions*
   vol. 2: *Traditions*
   vol. 3: *Symbols*

Claudine Fabre-Vassas   *The Singular Beast: Jews, Christians, and the Pig*

Paul Ricoeur   *Critique and Conviction: Conversations with Franáois Aҳouvi and Marc de Launay*

Theodor W. Adorno   *Critical Models: Interventions and Catchwords*

Alain Corbin   *Village Bells: Sound and Meaning in the Nineteenth-Century French Countryside*

Zygmunt Bauman   *Globalization: The Human Consequences*

Jean-Louis Flandrin and Massimo Montanari   *Food: A Culinary History*

Alain Finkielkraut   *In the Name of Humanity: Reflections on the Twentieth Century*

Julia Kristeva   *The Sense and Non-Sense of Revolt: The Powers and Limits of Psychoanalysis*

Régis Debray   *Transmitting Culture*

Sylviane Agacinski   *The Politics of the Sexes*